ELEMENTS OF
BUDDHIST ICONOGRAPHY

ANANDA K. COOMARASWAMY

ELEMENTS OF BUDDHIST ICONOGRAPHY

NEW EDITION
REVISED AND ENLARGED
IN ACCORDANCE WITH AUTHOR'S NOTES

Edited by
KRISHNA DEVA

INDIRA GANDHI NATIONAL CENTRE FOR THE ARTS
NEW DELHI

MANOHAR
2009

First published in 1935 by Harvard University Press
Second edition published by Manohar, 2009

ISBN 81-7304-432-5

Published by
Indira Gandhi National Centre for the Arts,
Janpath, New Delhi
in association with
Ajay Kumar Jain *for*
Manohar Publishers & Distributors
4753/23 Ansari Road, Daryaganj
New Delhi 110002

Printed at
Salasar Imaging Systems
Delhi 110035

CONTENTS

Preface 7

Introduction 9

Abbreviations 13

Foreword 17

Part I: Tree of Life, Earth-Lotus and Word-Wheel 19

Part II: The Place of the Lotus-Throne 55

Notes 79

Plates 113

PREFACE

By his holistic approach to art and religion, Ananda K. Coomaraswamy has inspired a whole generation of intellectuals, whereof the late Dr. V.S. Agrawala and Dr. Kapila Vatsyayan are among the leading lights. To Coomaraswamy the meanest craft and ritual forms an integral part of art and each element in the universe is in harmony with every other and participates in the total cosmic rhythm. This philosophy also inspired the activities of the Indira Gandhi National Centre for the Arts. Significantly enough the writings of Coomaraswamy are a constant reminder of his holistic philosophy and since the present work enunciates it in emphatic terms, the IGNCA has undertaken the republication of the book which had long been out of print. This new edition has been enriched by incorporating the additions made by the great savant in his own hand in his personal copy which has been made available for publication through the kind courtesy and cooperation of Dr. Rama P. Coomaraswamy, the savant's son. The new additions are now included as additional footnotes below each relevant page of the text and supplementary notes and descriptions which were appended to the earlier edition have now been incorporated at appropriate places.

I am glad to record here my profound gratitude to Dr. Kapila Vatsyayan, the moving spirit of the IGNCA and Shri M.C. Joshi and Dr. L.M. Gujraḷ for providing me the welcome opportunity and all facilities to undertake and complete the re-editing of this great work.

New Delhi
15 Aug. 2001

KRISHNA DEVA

INTRODUCTION

This is one of the seminal books by Ananda K. Coomaraswamy wherein he has ably demonstrated that the formula of Buddhist art and religion sprang from the fountain of Vedic and Upaniṣadic concepts. In fact Buddha was a direct heir to the Upaniṣadic lore and philosophical speculations which constituted a natural extension of the total Vedic Vision.

This book does not so much deal with iconography of Buddha as with the interpretation of a few basic symbols of Buddhist art, viz., the fiery pillar, the tree, the *triśūla* or *tri-ratna*, the lotus and the wheel. Pregnant with deep meaning, these symbols are often complementary and intertwined and allow an intimate peep into the secrets of Buddhist art and ontology.

Fiery Pillar: Buddha is comparable in many significant attributes with the Vedic god Agni, Indra, Varuṇa, Prajāpati and Āditya, etc., and even with the Upaniṣadic Brahman. Buddha's conception as a flaming pillar is strongly reminiscent of Agni and Śiva who are represented likewise. Numerous representations are known from Amarāvatī art of the Buddha as a fiery pillar, often with wheel-marked feet supported by lotus and with a *tri-ratna* head. In the *Ṛgveda* Agni is stated to be born of the Waters or from the Earth based on the Waters, hence from a lotus (*puṣkara*). The Buddhist fiery pillars also 'represent the survival of a purely Vedic formula in which Agni is represented as the axis of the Universe, extending as a pillar between Earth and Heaven' (p. 28).

Tree of Life: The tree symbol is the Tree of Life or the World-tree, signifying the Buddha. There is a unique representation of Buddha as *kalpa-vṛkṣa* on the Sāñcī gateway. Similar to the fiery pillar of Amarāvatī in the forms of the head and feet, its trunk is built up of superimposed palmettes bearing jewelled garlands as fruits. This jewel-tree corresponds to the Bodhi-tree of Amitāyu Tathāgata described in the Mahāyāna text *Mahāsukhāvatī-vyūha*. The World-tree is the procession of incessant life. Standing erect from earth to heaven and branching throughout space, the World-tree is verily turned into the Wisdom-tree 'whose roots strike deep into stability . . . whose flowers are moral acts. . . . Which bears Dharma as its fruit. . . . *Buddhacarita*, XIII 65' (p. 29).

Tri-ratna: The so-called *triśūla*-like 'Tri-ratna' symbol which is labelled in the Mauryan Brāhmī as *Nanidipaaṁ* (*Nandipadaṁ*) at the ancient monument on the Padana Hill has been aptly translated as hoof-mark or 'Taurine'. This symbol applies equally to Buddha, Śiva and Agni. In the *Ṛgveda* the metaphor is employed of tracing the lost Agni as a 'mighty bull' by his foot-prints. When doubled, this symbol forms a *vajra*, the special weapon of Indra of 'adamantine' quality. In Mahāyāna and Vajrayāna and particularly in Shingon Buddhism the metaphysical significance of the symbol *vajra* is specially emphasized.

Indra is known for his exploit of vanquishing Ahi-vṛtra by hurling *vajra* (thunderbolt). So also did Buddha sit in *vajrāsana* (adamantine pose) with a firm destination of attaining supreme Sambodhi (translated by Coomaraswamy as 'Awakening') after crushing Māra (*Māra-dharṣaṇa*) and is also known to have subjugated many Nāgas including the fire-spitting one in the hermitage of the Jaṭilas (Kāśyapa Brothers), leading to their conversion. Buddha also shares with Indra his miraculous birth from the right side of his mother (*tiraścīnajanma*).

Lotus: Lotus (*padma, puṣkara*) is the ground whereon and wherein existence is established. Buddha seated on *padmāsana* is comparable with Brahmā-Prajāpati, the creator, who sprang from lotus (*Kamala-yoni, Padmanābha*). Lotus has attributes of absolute purity and radiant beauty. Though born of mud (*paṅkaja*), lotus has faultless radiance and is free of all taints. So also the Tathāgata, though moving in the world, is free of all attachments and temptations. This analogy is also extended to the lotus leaf which though in water is untouched by it (*padma-patramivām-bhasā*).

We get sculptural representation of Buddha seated on lotus which is supported by a stem, flanked by nāgas. This is equivalent to the Brahma's manifestation on lotus which issues from the navel of Nārāyaṇa (Vedic Varuṇa), lying on the back of the waters. The concept of lotus-birth of the manifest deity of creation is coeval with Tree of Life, but there is a subtle distinction between the two. While Tree of Life denotes all existence, the lotus-birth is confined to that wherein the manifestation takes place. This navel of the creator is the firmament equivalent to *Hṛdākāśa* or *Antar-hṛdayākāśa* wherein Heaven and Earth are contained (p. 36). In the Upaniṣads, too, lotus represents the *Hṛdākāśa* wherein the Inner Self or Brahman resides.

Lotus is the principal attribute or cognizance of Śrī or Lakṣmī who is also born of and supported on lotus. The equivalents of Lakṣmī are Aditi, Prakṛti, Māyā and Apsarā (the Waters), all maternally personified. She is the same as Vasudhā, Vasudhārā and Vasundharā, as well as Gajalakṣmī, bathed by elephants with *soma*-bearing rains, besides a combined personification of the Earth-lotus and the Mother Earth.

Lotus has intimate association also with Sun-god (Vedic Āditya). The World-lotus blooms in response to the rising of the Sun, Earth as a reflection of the Heaven is stretched out in like measure. Hence the two lotuses in the hands of Sūrya represent the Upper and Nether Waters-source of all life.

The content of wheel symbolism is extraordinarily rich. Its dimensions are indefinite, its radius is the variable distance between an undimensioned centre and an immeasurable circumference. In the intermediate space between the centre and the felly are all the phenomena of the *saṁsāra-cakra*.

Dharma-cakra is identified in art with Buddha and comprises both Word-wheel and World-wheel. *Cakra* implies revolution of *Kāla* (Time) and is measured by solar movements of days, seasons and year, etc. Primarily the wheel is the Revolution of the year. In the sense that Time is the Sun, it represents the Sun or the movement of the Sun. In *Ṛgveda* the single wheel of the Sun's chariot is described as having twelve or five spokes (months or seasons) or 300 spokes (days), besides axle (*akṣa*) and triple nave (*nābhi*). More often the solar chariot is thought of as running on twin wheels connected by a common axle (*akṣa*). These twin wheels are heaven and earth, Puruṣa and Prakṛti, etc. In Buddhist religion the twin wheels are interpreted as principal *Dharma-cakra* and the phenomenal *saṁsāra-cakra*.

Dhramacakra-pravartana, marking the first preaching (*deśanā*) of Dharma by Buddha at the Deer Park constitutes the most significant event of Buddhist art and religion.

The concept of Buddha as *Cakravartī* has a direct reference to the *Dharmacakra-pravartana*. In early Buddhist art the Dharma-cakra is supported by a pillar with capital upon which are depicted four lions, symbolizing Buddha as *Śākya-siṁha*. The lions actually rest on lotus represented as a bulbous capital. This capital is the heavenly ground on which Dharma is manifested as *Dharma-cakra* while the earth or often the lotus on which the pillar stands is the terrestrial ground. The pillar is again reminiscent of the *axis mundi* linking Earth and Heaven.

Lotus Throne: In Gāndhāra and early Amarāvatī art Buddha is depicted seated on lotus throne while at Mathura he sits on the lion throne. In later art generally the lotus and lion thrones are combined.

The Chinese pilgrim Hsüan tsang quotes a tradition that the *Vajrāsana* (adamantine throne) on which Buddha sat at Bodhagaya is in the centre of the *Bodhimaṇḍa* (Wisdom Circle) and the *Bodhimaṇḍa* itself is at centre of the universe, extending axially down to the 'golden wheel'. Thus Buddha's seat is right on the navel of the World-wheel at the centre of the world axis.

However, the centre of Universe is not a spot fixed in space but a psychological centre, the focal point of consciousness (*antarbhūtasya*).

Buddha of the above quoted tradition is not the historical Buddha but is identical with *Dharma* (righteousness) and is *Svayambhū* (self-born), *Nitya* (eternal) and verily the *Lokapitā* (lord of the world) (*'padmāsanopaviṣṭaḥ piteva jagato bhaved-Buddhah'm'-Bṛhat Saṁhitā*). As elaborated in the *Saddharmapuṇḍarīka*, the Tathāgata keeps expounding *Dharma* at Vajrāsana (Bodhagaya) as well as on the Gṛdhrakūṭa Hill at Rājagṛha and is simultaneously present also in the *Sukhāvatī* paradise which is comparable with *Brahmaloka.*

Coomaraswamy often draws parallels between Buddhist and mediaeval Christian theological concepts, the latter discussed in the works of mystics like Michael Eckhart and Böhme. These similarities are so striking as to indicate that the language of mysticism is the same world over.

While explaining the ultimate goal of Buddhist spiritual realization, Coomaraswamy stresses on the distinction between *nirvāṇa* and *parinirvāṇa*. While *nirvāṇa* is *sopādiśeṣa*, i.e. having a residual ground of existence; *parinirvāṇa*, attained by Buddha, has no residual ground of existence.

Coomaraswamy has not treated Buddha as a historical figure but as a metaphysical presence that is best understood in terms of the symbols discussed in the book, which are Vedic or Upaniṣadic in origin but have acquired a special significance in Buddhist art and ontology. This is eruditely demonstrated by the stunning conceptual parallels and verbal correspondences cited between the Vedic lore and the Mahāyāna texts. The concepts have been aptly illustrated by beautiful art depictions.

This second edition of the book, first published in 1935, has been prepared from the author's copy (received through the kind courtesy of his son, Dr. Rama P. Coomaraswamy) wherein he had carried out in his own hand a few emendations, besides additions of numerous passages from old texts, largely as supplementary notes. While the emendations have been faithfully carried out in the text of the new edition, the additions are indicated as footnotes below each relevant page. These additions are independent of the footnotes, often quite lengthy, which appear after the text.

ABBREVIATIONS

A	Anguttara-Nikāya
AB	*Aitareya Brāhmaṇa*
Abhidh.	*Abhidharmakośa*
ASR	*Archaeological Survey Report*
AV	*Atharva Veda*
BD	*Baudāyana Dharmasūtra*
BÉFEO	*Bulletin de École Francaise d' Extréme-Orient*
BG	*Bhagavad Gītā*
Bull. Sch. Or Stud.	*Bulletin School of Oriental Studies*
CU	*Chāndogya Upaniṣad*
D	*Dialogues, Divyāvadāna*
Dh.	*Dhammapada*
Dh.A.	*Dhammapada Atthakathā*
HIIA	Coomaraswamy, *History of Indian and Indonesian Art*
HOS	Harvard Oriental Series
Ind. Ant.	*Indian Antiquary*
Ind. Hist. Qtly.	*Indian Historical Quarterly*
J	*Jātaka*
JAOS	*Journal of American Oriental Studies*
JASB	*Journal of Asiatic Society of Bengal*
JB	*Jaiminīya Brāhmaṇa*
JBORS	*Journal of Bihar and Orissa Research Society*
JRAS	*Journal Royal Asiatic Society*
JUB	*Jaiminīya Upaniṣad Brāhmaṇa*
KU	*Kumārasambhavam*
M	*Majjhima Nikāya*
Mem. ASI	*Memoirs of Archaeological Survey of India*
MU	*Maitrī Upaniṣad*
Muṇḍ	*Muṇḍaka Upaniṣad*
Mus	Paul Mus
NA	*New Antiquary*
NIA	*New Indian Antiquary*
OZ	*Ostasiatische Zeitung*
PTS	Pali Text Society
RV	*Ṛg Veda*

S	*Sūtrālaṅkāra, Saṁyutta Nikāya*
SB	*Śatapatha Brāhmaṇa*
SBB	Sacred Books of the Buddhists
SBE	Sacred Books of the East
Skr.	Sanskrit
SP	*Saddharma Puṇḍarīka*
Spt.	*Sutta Piṭaka*
Sum Th.	*The Summa Theologica of St. Thomas Aquinas*
Śvet	*Śvetāśvatara Upaniṣad*
TS	*Taittirīya Saṁhitā*
VIS	*Viśuddhimagga*
VS	*Vājasaneyī Saṁhitā*
ZDMG	*Zeitschrift der Deutschen Morgenländische Gesellschaft*

ELEMENTS OF BUDDHIST ICONOGRAPHY

BY

ANANDA K. COOMARASWAMY

CAMBRIDGE, MASSACHUSETTS

HARVARD UNIVERSITY PRESS

1935

"Symbols cannot be studied apart from the references which they symbolize."

Ogden and Richards, *The Meaning of Meaning*, p. 20

"To determine the import of names is the same as to determine the fundamental character of concepts."

Stcherbatsky, *Buddhist Logic*, I, p. 459

"I speak thus (in images) because of the frailty of the intelligence of the tender children of men." "But since thou takest they stand upon the principles (*dharmeṣu*), how is it that thou dost not enunciate the First Principle (*tattvam*) explicitly?" "Because, although I refer to the First Principle, there is not any 'thing' in Intellect corresponding to the reference 'First Principle'."

Laṅkāvatāra Sūtra, II, 112 and 114

"The picture is not in the colors . . . the Principle (*tattvam*) transcends the letter."

Laṅkāvatāra Sūtra, II, 118-19

Mirate la dottrina, che s'asconde, sotto il velame degli versi strani.

Dante, *Inferno*, IX, 61

FOREWORD

Coomarawamy's *A New Approach to the Vedas*, Luzac and Company, 1933, *The Transformation of Nature in Art*, Harvard University Press, 1934, and the present volume, which is published under the auspices of the Harvard-Yenching Institute, are based on the following convictions, which have gradually been developing in his mind.

In the first place, Buddhist art in India—and that is practically equivalent to saying art in India—begins about the second century before Christ with a well-developed set of symbols in its iconography. It does not seem possible to completely separate Buddhism as religion and as art from the main current of Indian religion and art, or to think that these symbols suddenly developed as a new creation. Therefore Coomaraswamy proceeded to study from a new point of view the symbolism which pervades the whole early Vedic literature of India, trying to discover whether concepts expressed symbolically in the literature of the aniconic Vedic period may not have found their first iconographic expression in early Buddhist art.

In the second place, he noted many surprising similarities between passages in the mediaeval Christian theologians and mystics, such as St Thomas, Meister Eckhart, Ruysbroeck, and Böhme, and passages in the Vedic literature—similarities so striking that many sentences from the Christian writers might be taken as almost literal translations of Sanskrit sentences, or vice versa. The conviction developed in him that mystical theology the world over is the same, and that mediaeval Christian theology might be used as a tool to the better understanding of ancient Indian theology. This theory he proceeded to apply even to the *Rig Veda*, assuming, contrary to the general opinion, no complete break in thought between the *Rig Veda* and the Brahmanas and Upanishads. In many obscure and so-called "mystical" stanzas of the *Rig Veda* and *Atharva Veda* he finds the same concepts vaguely hinted at which are employed in a more developed form in Brahmanism and Buddhism.

The present study of the Tree of Life, the Earth-Lotus, the Word-Wheel, the Lotus-Throne, and the Fiery Pillar tries to show that these symbols can be traced back beyond their first representation in Buddhist iconography through the aniconic period of the Brahmanical Vedas, even into the Rig Vedic period itself, and that they represent a universal Indian symbolism and set of theological concepts.

Objective linguistics is apparently near the end of its resources in dealing with the many remaining obscurities of Rig Vedic phraseology. This new metaphysical approach is welcome even though to the matter-of-fact linguist it may seem that ideas are not being built-up on the basis of words but that words are being made to fit ideas.

Harvard University WALTER EUGENE CLARK
June 27, 1934

PART I

TREE OF LIFE, EARTH-LOTUS, AND WORD-WHEEL

TREE OF LIFE, EARTH-LOTUS, AND WORD-WHEEL

> "Die Menschheit . . . versucht sie, in die greifbare oder sonstwie wahrnehmbare Form zu bringen, wir könnten sage zu materialisen, was ungreifbar, inchtwahrnehmbar ist. Sie schafft Symbol, Schriftzeichen, Kultbild aus irdischen Stoff und schaut in ihnen und hinter ihnen das sonst unschaubare, unvorstellbare geistige und göttliche Geschehen." —Walter Andrae, *Die ionische Säule, Bauform oder Symbol?* 1933, p. 65.

The iconography (*rūpa-bheda*) of Indian and Far Eastern art has been discussed hitherto almost exclusively with respect to the identification of the various hypostases as represented "anthropomorphically" in the later art. Here it is proposed to treat those fundamental elements of Buddhist symbolism which predominate in the earlier aniconic art, and are never dispensed with in the later imagery, though they are there subordinated to the "human" icon. In neither case is the symbol designed as though to function biologically: as symbol (*pratīka*) it expresses an idea, and is not the likeness of anything presented to the eye's intrinsic faculty.[1] Nor is the aniconic image less or more the likeness of Him, First Principle, who is nothing, but whose image it is, than is the "human" form. To conceive of Him as a living Tree, or as a Lamb or Dove, is no less sound theology than top conceive of Him as Man, who is not merely *mānuṣya-laukika* but *sarva-laukika*, not merely *mānuṣa-raupya* but *viśva-raupya*, not human merely but of Universal Form.[2] Any purely anthropomorphic theology is to that extent specifically limited; but He takes on vegetative, theriomorphic, and geometrical forms and sounds just as much and just as little as he dons flesh.[3][a] So the Bodhisattva vows that he will not be Utterly Extinguished until the last blade of grass shall have reached its goal.

What has been said above is to dispel the notion that in discussing symbolism we are leaving life behind us; on the contrary, it is precisely by means of symbols that *ars imitatur naturam in sua operatione*, all other "imitation" being idolatry. Before proceeding, it only remains to be said that if any particular stress seems to be laid on Buddhism, this is strictly speaking an accident. Buddhism in India represents a heterodox development, all that is metaphysically "correct" (*pramiti*) in its ontology and

[a] Dionysius, *Theoi* III, "For it is not more true to affirm that God is life and goodness than that He is air or stone."

symbolism being derived from the primordial tradition; with the slight necessary transpositions, indeed, the greater part of what is said could be directly applied to the understanding of Christian art. In the following discussion, no ideas or opinions of my own are expressed, everything being taken directly, and often verbally, from Vedic or Buddhist sources.

It has often been remarked that in Pali texts there is no express tradition prohibiting the making of anthropomorphic images of the Tathāgata, originally "So-come" or "So-gone," later "Who has entered into the Suchness," which might account for the designation of the Buddha only by aniconic symbols in the early art.[4] And this is essentially true; the representation by aniconic symbols is not in kind a Buddhist invention, but represents the survival of an older tradition,[5] the anthropomorphic image becoming a psychological necessity only in *bhakti-vāda* offices. However, the *Kāliṅga-bodhi Jātaka* (*J.*, IV, 228), in the Introduction, enunciates what amounts to such a prohibition, and may well have been the point of view current in Buddhist circles at a much earlier date than can be positively asserted for the Jātaka text. Here Ānanda desires to set up in the Jetavana a substitute for the Buddha, so that people may be able to make their offerings of wreaths and garlands at the door of the Gandhakuṭi,[a] as *pūjanīyaṭṭhāna*, not only when the Buddha is in residence, but also when he is away preaching the Dharma elsewhere. The Buddha asks how many kinds of hallow (*cetiya*)[6] there are. "Three," says Ānanda, with implied reference to contemporary non-Buddhist usage, "viz., those of the body (*sārīraka*), those of association (*pāribhogaka*),[7] and those indicative (*uddesika*)." The Buddha rejects the use of bodily relics on the obvious ground that such relics can only be venerated after the Parinibbāṇa. He rejects the "indicative" symbols also because such are "groundless and merely fanciful" (*avathukaṁ manamattakaṁ*),[b] that is to say only artificially

[a] *faux mienst*, really intended to be given to Buddha, but left at the door because he is absent.

[b] *Manamattakam* is predicated of the anthropomorphic *cetiya* in a pejorative sense because the worshipper may fancy that the Buddha really subsisted or subsists in such a manner, that the Buddha is in some sense "like" the icon. The same danger inheres in the use of verbal symbols; the hearer goes far astray if he thinks that the words depict the principle, on the contrary they merely point to it, the principle itself is not a thing in any likeness. This is developed at length in the *Laṅkāvatāra Sūtra*, text pp. 194-6, cf. Ch. II, 114 and 118-19, and Ch. III, 74. *Saṁyutta Nikāya*, text I, p. 11, is also very pertinent: "Those who take their stand on what is literally expressed, without comprehending *what* was expressed, fall into the bondage of mortality; those who understand what was really indicated form no vain concepts of (*na maññati*) him who makes the indication."

and by convention referable to the absent being for whom a substitute is desired; the terms as employed here in a derogatory sense can only mean "arbitrary". So "Only a Mahābodhi-rukkha, Great-Wisdom-tree, that has been associated with a Buddha is fit to be a *cetiya*, whether the Buddha be still living, or Absolutely Extinguished." This occurs also in the *Mahābodhivaṁsa*, PTS. ed. p. 59.[a]

In the absence of specific definition, it may be assumed that the class of "associated" symbols included also such other aniconic representations as the wheel (*cakra*), feet (*pāduka*), *triśūla* (trident, called '*nandi-pada*' in Buddhist art), and/or other geometrical, vegetative, or even theriomorphic forms actually met with in early Buddhist art. It is true that, like the tree, these symbols had older than Buddhist application, and one could imagine objections made accordingly—had not Sujātā indeed mistaken the Bodhisattva for a *rukkha-devatā*? But where no objection had been made to the tree, none could have been logically raised in connection with the other symbols. These in fact came into use in conncetion with the setting up of local *cetiyas* as objects of reverence, as substitutes for pilgrimage to the original sites, the different symbols serving, as is well known, to differentiate between the several Events. The wheel, for example, had special reference to the first preaching in Benares. At the same time, the use of such symbols, with their inherent metaphysical implications, must have contributed to the early definition of the mythical Buddhology. It is perhaps because the *Jātaka* passages do not yet take account of Four Events, but only of the most important, the Great Awakening—a recent event from the Hīnayāna point of view—that the Buddha is made to say that a Buddha can *only* be represented rightly by a Great-Wisdom-tree.

By *uddesika* "indicative" corresponding to *vyakta*, "manifest," in the Brahmanical classifications of icons, we should expect that anthropomorphic images were indicated, and this confirmed in the *Khuddakapāṭha-Atthakathā* (PTS. ed., 1915, p. 222), where *uddissaka-cetiyaṁ* is explained by *buddha-paṭimā*, "an image of the Buddha."[b] Notwithstanding that a use

[a] (*Divyavadāna*) iii. 144 (*lakkhaṇa*) Buddha "has the rounded symmetry of a banyan tree" (*nigrodha parimaṇḍala hoti*): a definite "similitude".

cf. *JUB*. IV 18.6 "where Brahman is *not* that which one thinks by the mind (*yaṁ manasā na manute*), but by which the mind is thought of, they say (*yenāhur manomataṁ*) only that knew as Brahman, not what they worship (*upāsate*) here": similarly "iconoclastic" and *via remotionis* cf. various texts including "concept" form highest knowledge.

[b] See de la Vallée Poussin: *Staupikam* in *JHAS*, II. 276 ff. *uddissaka*-"indicative" of

of anthropomorphic images of any kind must have been rare in the Buddha's lifetime, it is clear that the Commentators understood that the Buddha's own position was definitely iconoclastic. It is true that the Buddha image, with its non-human *lakkhaṇas*, can no more than other Indian images be thought of as the likeness of a man, nevertheless the objection made must have depended on the generally human appearance of such images, this appearance being inappropriate to him who was "not a man." We ought perhaps rather to say that it was in this way that the ancient custom of using predominantly aniconic imagery was thus explained and justified. The attitude of those who actually made use of anthropomorphic images is defined in the *Divyāvadāna*, Ch. XXVI, where it is explained that those who look at earthen images (*mṛnmaya-pratikṛti*) *Harṣacaritam*, 163.12 *mṛṇmaya-patimā śālabhañjikā vā* "do not honor the clay as such, but without regard thereof, honor the deathless principles referred to (*amara-saṁjñā*) in the earthen images."

The Buddha is represented as dealing again with the same problem in later life, and now (*Mahāparinibbāṇa Sutta*, V, 8 and 12 = *Dīgha Nikāya* II, 140-3), in view of his approaching death, he declares that after the Total Extinction there are four places proper to be visited by the community, and these "places which should stir deep feeling" (*saṁvejanīyāni ṭhānāni*, cf. *pūjanīyaṭṭhāna* cited above) are those at which the four crises of the Buddha's life had been passed. With respect to the edification resulting from such visits, we are told that at the sight of the *thūpa* of the Rāja Cakkavatti "the hearts of many shall be made calm and glad."

Later traditions represent the Buddha himself as having not merely sanctioned but actually instituted the use of anthropomorphic images. Thus, according to the *Divyāvadāna*, p. 547, Rudrāyaṇa (sc. Udāyana) desires as means of making offerings to the Buddha when he is absent; the Blessed One said "Have an image of the Tathāgata drawn on canvas, and make your offering thereto" (*tathāgata-pratimām paṭe likhāpayaitvā*, etc.). Rudrāyaṇa calls his painters (*cittakarā*). They say that they cannot grasp the Blessed One's exemplum (*na śaknuvanti bhagavato nimittam udgrahītum*). The Blessed One says that is because they are affected by lassitude (*kheda*,[a] equivalent to *śithilasamādhi* in *Mālavikāgnimitra*, II, 2), but "bring me a piece of canvas" (*api tu paṭakam ānaya*). Then the Blessed One

---

the Tathāgata, i.e. indirect or allusive. Yogaśāstra (cited *ibid.*, p. 281) *yad bodhisattvastathāgataṁ uddiśya stūpaṁ vā gahaṁ va kūṭaṁ vā purāṇacaityaṁ vā abhinavacaityaṁ pūjayati.*

[a]Cf. *yāvan na khedo jāyate bhāvayet* in *Sādhanamālā* texts.

projected his similitude upon it (*tatra . . . chāyā utsṛṣṭā*), and said "complete it with colors" (*raṅgaiḥ pūrayata*), adding that certain texts are to be written (*likhitavyāni*) below. And so "everything was by them depicted according to prescription" (*yathāsaṁdiṣṭaṁ sarvam abhilikhitam*).

According to the version of this legend preserved by Hsüan-tsang (Beal, *Life*, p. 91) it was an image of sandal-wood rather than a painting that was made for Udāyana; a skilled imager was transported to the Trayastriṁśas heaven by Maudgalyāyana, and after contemplating there the appearance and features of the Buddha, who was preaching the Law to his mother, the artist was brought back to earth and carved the figure in his likeness. This image, which Hsüan-tsang identified with one that he saw at Kauśambī, was nevertheless as he mentions elsewhere (*Si-yu-ki*, Beal, *Records . . .*, II, p. 322) borne through the air (we may interpret, "transferred as a mental image in the mind of a sculptor") to Khotān, and there became the archetype of innumerable later copies, which are regarded as possessing a similitude of univocation, so that we find at Long Men a statue called "Udāyana's" (Chavannes, *Mission archéologique . . .*, pp. 391-2). There is also the tradition of still another image, made in gold after the Buddha's final departure, and it is with reference to an image in this "succession" that an inscription of about 665 at Long Men (Chavannes, *loc. cit.*, p. 362), remarks "Si l'influence et le modèle ne disparurent pas, c'est grace à celà" where the thought expressed is tantamount to this, that the image is still his whose image it is. With respect to such traditional representations it is also said in an inscription of 641 (Chavannes, *loc. cit.*, pp. 340-1) "Le K'i-chö est devant nos yeux; Na-kie peut être représentée," that is, "when we look at these statues, it is just as if we saw the Buddha himself on Vulture Peak, or his likeness in the cave at Nāgarahāra" (where he left his "shadow", cf. *chāyā utsṛṣṭā* in the *Divyāvadāna* passage cited above). As the Long Men inscription of 543 (Chavannes, p. 593, Mus, 1928, pp. 244, 248) reminds us, "they cut the stone of price in imitation of his supernatural person." In the absence of the past manifestation in a human body (as Śākya-muni) and before the future manifestation (of Maitreya) the Wayfarer resorts to a means of access to the transcendental principles from which all manifestations proceed. The image merely as such is of no value; all depends on what he does who looks at it; what is expected of him is an act of contemplation such that when he sees before him the characteristic lineaments, it is for him as though the whole person of the Buddha were present; he journeys in the spirit to the transcendent gathering on Vulture Peak (*Saddharma Puṇḍarīka*, Ch. XV). Aesthetic and religious experience are here indivisible; rising to the level of reference intended, "his heart is broadened with a mighty understanding" (inscription of 641, Chavannes, p. 340). Cf. Mus, *Le Buddha paré . . .*, *BÉFEO*, 1928, pp. 248-9 and *Barabudur* II.1. The experience of those who beheld the likeness of Buddha is further described at length in the *Divyāvadāna*, Ch. XXVI, in connection with Māra's exhibition of the Buddha's similitude.

Our present concern is, however, primarily with the aniconic representations, and first of all with the symbolic representation by means of the Tree. That the ancient symbol of the Tree of Life, *vṛkṣa* (= *rukkha*), *vanaspati*, *akṣaya-vaṭa*, or *eka aśvattha* of the Vedas and Upaniṣads, should thus have been chosen to represent the Buddha is highly significant; for as we have already indicated, every traditional symbol necessarily carries with it its original values, even when used or intended to be used in a more restricted sense. In order to appreciate the full content of Buddhist symbolism we must accordingly take into account the fundamental implications of the symbols employed; in fact only a knowledge of the symbols in their total significance will suffice for an understanding of their values as they are employed in connection with the developed Buddhology. To sum up, then the pre-Buddhist and some possibly later references:[8] the Tree of Life, synonymous with all existence, all the worlds, all life, springs up, out, or down into space[9] from its root in the navel center of the Supreme Being, Varuṇa, Mahāyakṣa, Asura, Brahman, as he lies extended on the back of the Waters, the possibilities of existence and the source of his abundance. That Tree is his procession (*utkrama*, *prasaraṇa*, *pravṛtti*) in a likeness (*mūrta*), the emanation of his fiery-energy (*tejas*) as light, the spiration of this breath (*prāṇa*); he is its wise, indestructible mover (*rerivā*).[10]

The "Lord of the Forest" (*vanaspati*) is already in the Vedas a familiar symbol of the supreme deity in his manifested aspect. There may be cited, for example, *Ṛg Veda*, I, 24, 7, "King Varuṇa as pure act lifted up in the Unground the summit (*stūpam*) of the Tree"; I, 164, 20-1, "Two Fairwings (*suparṇāḥ*, birds, angels) in conjoint amity rest in the one same Tree; one eats the tasty fig (*pippalam*), the other looketh on and does not eat . . . there those Fairwings sing incessantly their part of lasting-life"; Varuṇa, Prajāpati, or Brahman manifesting as the moving spirit in the cosmic Tree is called a Yakṣa, cf. *Atharva Veda*, X, 7, 38, "A great Yakṣa proceeding in a seething on the back of the waters, in whom abide whatever Angels be, as branches of the Tree that are round about its trunk," and *Kena Up.*, 15-26, "What Yakṣa is this? . . . Brahman."

The description of the World-tree in the *Maitri Up.*, VI, 1-4, VII, 11, and VI, 35, may be quoted at length:

"There are verily two forms of Brahman, with and without likeness (*mūrta, amūrta*). Now the That which is in a likeness is contingent (*asatya*); the That which is imageless is essential (*satya*) Brahman, light. That Light is the light of the Supernal-Sun. He verily becomes with OṀ as Self. He assumed a Trinity, for the OṀ has three factors, and it is by these that 'the whole world is woven, warp and woof, on Him.' As it has been said, 'beholding that the Supernal-Sun is OṀ, unify therewith thyself.' . . . The threefold Brahman has his root above, His branches are space, air, fire, water, earth, and the rest. This is called the Single Fig-tree (*eka aśvattha*); and therein inheres the fiery-energy (*tejas*) that is the Supernal-Sun . . . the One Awakener (*eka sambodhayitṛ*[a]). This, verily, is the intrinsic form of space in the vacuity of the inward man (*antarbhūtasya khe*); that is the supreme fiery-energy (*tejas*), determined as the Trinity of Fire, Supernal-Sun, and Spirit . . . the Imperishable-Word, OṀ. And by that Imperishable-Word, the fiery-energy awakens (*udbudhnyati*), spring up, and expands; that is verily an everlasting basis (*ālamba*) for the vision of Brahman. In the spiration it has its place in the dark-heat that emaṇates light, proceeding upwards as is the way of smoke when the wind blows *samīraṇe*, as a branching forth in the firmament, stem after stem . . . all-pervading as contemplative vision. . . . He who is yonder, yonder Person in the Supernal-Sun, I my-Self am He."

Here the World-tree becomes a "Burning Bush," in an imagery closely related to that by which in several Vedic texts Agni is spoken of as a cosmic pillar, supporting all existences. Almost all of this is valid Buddhology, if only we substitute "Buddha" for "Brahman", remember the large part played by the concept of the Fiery-Energy (*tejas*) even in canonical texts, and take account of the early iconography as well as of the literature. Especially noteworthy is the designation of the "Single Fig-tree" as the World-form of the "One Awakener" (*eka sambodhayitṛ*)[b] and "enduring basis of the vision of Brahman" (*brahma-dhīyālamba*); for just

[a] *tejas . . . udayati . . . utkramya skandhāt skandhaṁ anusarati.*

J.VI. 330 *rājāṅgaṇe catusu kaṇṇesu majjhe upanna aggikhandho.*

[b]Irenaeus, *Adv. Haer.* 1.27.I "The tree which is itself also called gnosis."

E.S. Drowa, *Mandaeaus*, p. 11, "Thou art the great tree which is all *mandia* (pl.) generally rendered by "gnosis."

1.161.13 *śvānaṁ basto bodhayitāraṁ abravīt* "The goat (or antelope) declares that the roarer is the awakener" Sāyaṇa *śvānaṁ-antarikṣe śvasantam vāyum.* cf. *samīraṇe* above.

so also is the Buddha's Fig-tree (*aśvattha*) constantly spoken of as the "Great Awakening" (*mahā-sambodhi*)[a]; being the chosen symbol of the Buddha's unseen essence, it is an enduring basis for the vision of Buddha; it might have been called in Pali *Tathāgata-jhānālamba*, cf. the terms *ārambaṇa, āvaraṇa, upadarśana*, used of the Tathāgata's various manifestations, *Saddharma Puṇḍarīka*, text, p. 318, and *ālamba* = *viṣaya-grahaṇa*, Vasubandhu, *Abhidharmakośa*, I, 34, and II, 34, b-d. The *Mahā Sukhāvatī-Vyūha*, 32, in fact, merely paraphrases the words of the *Maitri Up.* cited above, when it is said that "All those beings that are constant in never turning away from the vision of that Bodhi-tree are by the same token constant in never losing sight of the supreme and perfect Awakening" (*tasya bodhi-vṛkṣasya . . . yad uta anuttarāyāḥ saṁyak-sambodheḥ*). In the *Maitri Up.* text the expression *udbudhnyati*, "awakens from its ground," applied to the Tree, is significant, and like the designation *uṣarbudh*, "awakened at dawn," which in the *Ṛg Veda* is commonly applied to Agni, recalls him who is typically *buddha*, the "Wake."[11] As for the Fiery-Energy (*tejas*), this is the element of fire present as an unseen energy in all existences, but preëminently manifested by Arhats or the Buddha, e.g. in the case of the "Double Miracle," the "Conversion of Kassapa," or when (*Saṁyutta Nikāya*, I, 144) the Buddha takes his seat in the firmament immediately above Brahmā. In *Theragāthā*, 1095, where *arahatta* is clearly synonymous with Buddhahood, the *uggetejo*, "sharp fiery-energy," is the flaming sword of Understanding (*paññā* = *prajñā*) whereby Māra is defeated. In *Dhammapada*, 387, the Buddha "glows with fiery-energy," *tapati tejasā*.[12]

Amongst the late Āndhra reliefs from Amarāvatı may be seen numerous remarkable representations of the Buddha as a fiery pillar, with wheel-marked feet, supported by a lotus, and with a *triśūla* "head" (Figs. 4-10);[13] these have been almost completely ignored by students of Buddhist iconography.[14] Remembering, however, (1) that Agni is born of the Waters, or more directly from the Earth as it rests upon the Waters, hence specifically from a lotus (*puṣkara*), *Ṛg Veda*, VI, 16, 13, and (2) is frequently spoken of as the pillar that supports all existences, e.g. *Ṛg Veda*, I, 59, 1-2, and IV, 13, 5, it is clear that the Buddhist fiery pillars represent the survival of a purely Vedic formula in which Agni is represented as the axis of the Universe, extending as a pillar between Earth and Heaven.[15]

No less remarkable than the fiery pillars of Amarāvatī is the unique representation of a Buddha in the form of a *kalpa-vṛkṣa* or "wishing-tree"

[a] D.11.4 *sammā-sambuddho assathassa mūle abhisambuddho.*

at Sāñcī (Fig. 1).[16] This tree of Life is like the fiery pillars at Amarāvatī as to its head and wheel-marked feet, but its trunk is built up of superimposed lotus palmettes,[17] and bears laterally by way of fruits pearl garlands and other jewels suspended from pegs such as are elsewhere spoken of as *nāgadanta*. It may be remarked that only perhaps a century later (*Mahā Sukhāvatī-vyūha*, 16 and again, *Saddharma Puṇḍarīka*, V, 29-33) the seekers after Buddhahood are compared to small and great herbs, and small and great trees, and that Sukhāvatī is said to be crowded with jewelled trees made of precious metals and gems, presumably representing various degrees of enlightenment. The jewel-tree of Sāñcī corresponds directly to the Bodhi-tree of Amitāyus, Tathāgata, described in the *Mahā Sukhāvatī-vyūha*, 32: "A thousand *yojanas* in height . . . it is always in leaf, always in flower, always in fruit, of a thousand hues and various foliage, flower, and fruit . . . it is hung with golden strings, adorned with hundreds of golden chains . . . strings of rose pearls and strings of black pearls . . . adorned with symbols of the *makara*, *svastika*, *nandyāvarta*, and moon . . . according to the desires of living beings, whatever their desire may be."[a] Such a symbol as this, though assuredly of Buddhist import, is not of Buddhist origin; even the words "fulfilling the desires of living beings, whatever they may be" ring strangely in the ambient of early Buddhist monasticism. All this implies in relatively early Buddhism already existing Mahāyānist tendencies, which are really a prolongation of Vedic tradition. Amitāyus, "Immeasurable Life," corresponds to innumerable Vedic designations of Agni, often also invoked as Vanaspati, "Lord of the Forest," or "King of Trees," as Viśvāyus, "Life Universal," or Ekāyus, "The One Life"; Amitābha to Vedic notions of the all-seeing Sun, or Agni whose beams dispel all darknesses, cf. I, 65, 5 *dūrebhā*, "shining from afar," and VI, 10, 4, *paprau . . . urvī dūredṛśā bhāsā*, "filled heaven and earth with a far-seen light." It is certainly not impossible that the notions "Amitāyus" and "Amitābha" had received a Buddhist interpretation in or before the first century B.C.: this need not have prevented a connection of the jewelled tree with Śākya-muni, who is in fact the earthly counterpart of Amitābha.

The World-tree then, equally in and apart from its Buddhist application, is the procession of incessant life. Standing erect and midmost in the garden of life, extending from Earth to Heaven, branching throughout Space (we shall see later that "space" is "within you"), that is the one Wishing-tree

[a] *yathā āśaya sattva vijñapti-samalaṅkṛta* cf. *MU* VI.30.

(*kappa-rukkha, kalpa-vṛkṣa*) that yields the fruits of life, all that every creature calls "good." Buddhism interprets this, as it interprets the corresponding symbol of the Dharmacakra, from an edifying point of view: that Wisdom-tree (*jñāna-druma*) "whose roots strike deep into stability . . . whose flowers are moral acts . . . which bears righteousness (*dharma*) as its fruit . . . ought not to be felled," *Buddhacarita*, XIII, 65. But amongst the accidents of being, the fruits of life, are also the wages of desire, that is our mortality, *jarā-maraṇa*, all that every existence, each embodies will to life, calls "evil." So the World-tree, as an exteriorization of the Will to Life, *kāma*, and corresponding Craving, *taṇha, tṛṣṇa*, from the point of view of all those who would be naughted is a tree to be felled at the root: in Buddhism, a "vine of coveting (*taṇhā-latā*), who shall cut (*chind*) it off?" (*Theragāthā*, 761 and 1094). For in a modeless mode there is a Principle "higher and other than the World-tree . . . the Bringer of Truth (*dharma*) and Remover of Evil (*pāpa*)," *Śvetāśvatara Up.*, VI, 6; note the "Buddhist" ring of these Aupaniṣada expressions. He who Understands, or who is become a Comprehensor, *ya evaṁ vidvān*, a Buddha, who beholds the tree with seeing and undesirous eyes, sees in it the One Awakener, *eka saṃbodhayitṛ*, the Great Awakening, *mahāsambodhi*. By that very Understanding, *paññā, prajñā*, he fells it at the root, *aśvattham . . . chittvā*, *Bhagavad Gītā*, XV, 3, he is quit of Brahmā, quit of Māra at one stroke;[18] for him the Garden of Life, *prāṇārāma*, becomes the Circle of Wisdom, Bodhimaṇḍa(-la); for him the world is voided of any personal content, of any self or Self, and as *anātmya, anatta*, he is emancipated from mortality, Totally Extinguished, *parinirvāta*. But he who desires and eats the fruits or shoots (*viṣaya-pravālāḥ, Bhagavad Gītā*, XV, 2), be he man or angel, and thereby comes into operation or existence, thereby also perishes at last, for, as is repeatedly enunciated in the Pali Buddhist canon, "Whatsoever has an origin, in that is inherent the necessity of dissolution." He only whose desires are all liberated (*pramucyante*), who does not desire, becomes immortal (*amṛta*), being very Brahman goes to Brahman (*Bṛhadāraṇyaka Up.*, IV, 4, 6, and 7): that is, in Buddhist terms is *parinibbuta, parinirvāta*, in Christian terms is dead and buried in the Godhead, having died to God and all his works.[19] Inasmuch as works of any kind are necessarily purposeful, being undertaken with an end in view, it is a perfectly correct theology which represents Brahmā, Buddha, or God, *qua* Creator or *qua* Saviour, as a mortal being, uttering a Word which as it is in itself cannot be thought or spoken. *Dharmacakra-pravartana*, then, has an essential content wider than that of merely "Preaching the

Gospel"; it implies the creation of the world, and in this capacity as Lokapitā, and equivalent to Brahmā, the Buddha can only be thought of as *prajā-kāmya*, philoprogenitive; even in early Buddhism, that the Buddha teaches (and at first he hesitates to do so) is because he is moved by compassion. "Philoprogenitive" and "compassionate" are to be understood, of course, in a metaphysical, not in a sentimental, sense.

The distinction between Nirvāṇa and Parinirvāṇa is no less fundamental and necessary than that of God from Godhead in Christianity.[20] Those who maintain the "rationalism" of early Buddhism may deny the value of its theological development, yet the fact remains that without this development and such distinctions Buddhist and Christian iconography would be devoid of intelligible meaning; the only Buddhist or Christian art which could have existed must have been an art of realistic portraiture, "in memory" of the Founders and their Saints. For example, the representation of the Parinirvāṇa by the *stūpa*, essentially a tomb, or alternatively by the actual scene of death, is altogether appropriate, whether we regard the Great Decease from a human or a transcendental point of view. In the same way the *Bṛhadāraṇyaka Up*., I, 2, speaks of That which is logically antecedent to the Self, and whereto the Self returns un-Selfed, as "Death" and "Privation." Again the double negative, privation being here privation of a limiting affirmation.[21]

To think of these as "pessimistic" expressions is to confuse Existence with Being and Non-being, destiny with liberty. Beside the Buddha's deathbed only Brahmā and those Arhats who were "the same" in singleness and wisdom shed no tears; Angels such as Indra wept and wailed, being still attached to their and to his existent Personality. At the same time, it was taken for granted that the possibilities of existence amply provided for those who clung to individual immortalities throughout immeasurable aeons; this would be in familiar Christian terms until the "Last Judgment"; the individual could not be liberated from limiting conditions, from himself, unless by his own effort, much less against his will. A majority of Buddhists, like the majority of Christians, looked forward to a resurrection in "Heaven," Sukhāvatī, beholding God or Buddha face to face. The Buddha by no means denied such possibilities; but he taught a Way leading to an End beyond Heaven, though he would not, because he could not, God himself could not, explain or define that End in any language, save only on terms of negation.

Although their history and significance can hardly yet be fully explained, some consideration of the symbolic forms representing the head and feet of the jewelled Tree of Life at Sāñcī and the Fiery Pillars at Amarāvatī is necessary. The *triśūla*, in Buddhism (Figs. 1, 4, 23, etc.), commonly understood to denote the jewel-trinity (*ratna-traya*) of Buddha, Dharma, and Saṅgha, is certainly not exclusively of Buddhist nor even wholly of Buddhist and Jaina (Fig. 17) significance; Buddhism, as usual, is adapting an older symbolism to its immediate purposes. Sénart (*La légende du Bouddha*, p. 484) already regarded the Buddhist *triśūla* as a Fire symbol; we could think of it as naturally representing either the three aspects of Agni Vaiśvānara, or the primordial Agni as the triunity of the Several Angels. This would not in any way conflict with the Śaiva association suggested by Marshall, *Mohenjodaro*, p. 55, cf. our Figs. 21, 22, and indicated also by the use of the symbol in connection with Śiva at a later time, e.g. on the Śaiva coins of Kadphises II and on the Śaiva seal from Sirkap, A.S.I., A.R., 1914-15, p. 51 and Pl. XXIV.[22] That the form corresponds to that of Śiva's trident in the later iconography is indeed evident enough. It has not been so much observed that if the symbol is doubled, so as to consist of two addorsed tridents connected by a common stem, there is obtained the usual form of the *vajra*, or if quadrupled that of the fourfold *vajra*. In our representations (Figs. 1, 4, 6, etc.), the *triśūla* forms the termination of a stem or trunk which we have been able to identify with the pillar (*skambha*) that supports-apart Heaven and Earth, and with the axle-tree (*akṣa*) of the Solar chariot, i.e. with the axis of the Universe.[23] Recalling now the kenning *akṣa-ja* = *vajra*, it is not implausible to assume that our *triśūla* may also be thought of as a "single *vajra*."

What we know of the form of the Vedic *vajra* suggests in fact that it was of the single type; *Ṛg Veda*, I, 52, 15, tells us that it was pronged (*bhṛṣṭimat*), I, 121, 4, that it was three-pointed (*trikakubh*).[24] In *Ṛg Veda*, IV, 22, 2, the *vajra* is said to be a four-angled rain-producer (*vṛśaṁdhiṁ caturaśrim*), and in *Aitareya Brāhmaṇa*, X,1, to be eight-angled. In *Ṛg Veda*, VIII, 7, 22, the Maruts are said to have "put it together joint by joint" (*parvaśo saṁ dadhuḥ*); in I, 80, 6, and VI, 17, 10, it is spoken of as hundred-jointed (*śataparvan*), and in the latter text also as thousand-pointed (for joints or nodes cf. Figs. 2, 3, 41, 42). It may be noted that in *Ṛg Veda*, VI, 22, 6, Indra's weapon is called *parvata*; Sāyaṇa is probably right in saying that this refers not to the "mountain," but to the many-jointed *vajra* (*bahuparvaṇā vajreṇa*). In the *Ṛg Veda* generally the *vajra* is said to have been made by the Divine Craftsman, Trvaṣṭṛ, who is "most skilled in handiworks" (*apasām apastamaḥ*, X, 53, 9), and hence the *vajra* itself is called "most well-made" (*svapastaman*, I, 61, 6, where also it is said to be "of the nature of light," *svaryam*, as in V, 31, 4, where it is "glittering," *dyumantam*). The *vajra* is wielded typically by Indra, who represents the temporal power (*kṣatra*) in relation to Agni as spiritual power (*brahma*); and after the weapon, Indra is styled *vajrin*, *vajra-bāhu*, etc. With the *vajra* he slays the dragon, Vṛtra, Śuṣṇa, or Ahi, and thus brings about the whole cosmic manifestation. In the Buddha legend, the Vedic defeat of Ahi-Vṛtra is represented (1) in the Māra-dharṣaṇa, and (2) in the Buddha's defeat of the serpent on the occasion of the conversion of the Jaṭilas.[a] It may be observed that in the Māra-dharṣaṇa, Māra makes use of the characteristic weapons of Vṛtra (cf. *Ṛg Veda*, I, 32, 13), and that the affrighted Angles desert the Bodhisattva, as they do Indra in the battle with Vṛtra (*Ṛg Veda*, IV, 8, 11; VIII, 93, 14-15; VIII, 96, 7; *Aitareya Brāhmaṇa*, VI, 5); while in the Conversion of the Jaṭilas, the serpent is referred to as *ahi-nāga* (*Mahāvagga*, I, 15, 7). In northern Buddhism Māra is sometimes identified with Namuci.[b]

Further as to the shape of the *vajra, Aitareya Brāhmaṇa*, II, 35, tells us that it was narrow at the beginning, and divided above like a club or axe, comparison being made with the bifurcation of human legs (cf. Foucher, *Beginnings of Buddhist Art*, Pl. I, Fig. 6); this, indeed, implies a two-pronged rather than a three-pronged termination, and it may be remarked that in actual iconography (cf. Foucher, *ibid*., Fig. 7) the two lateral tines are often much more conspicuous than the central tine, which is in fact a prolongation of the stem. Types with from one to eight tines are found in Shingon usage. In Śaiva usage, the three-pronged *triśūla* is borne by the Father (Śiva), the one-pronged *śūla* by the Son (Kārttikeya, Kumāra). In the *Kauṣītaki Brāhmaṇa*, VI, 9, "Vajra" is one of the eight names of Śiva.

The question of terminology offers still another problem. In European Literature, the term *nandi-pada* (lit. "Nandi-foot" or "-trace") has been applied to the *triśūla* symbol in Buddhist or presumed Buddhist usage, this name deriving from the form *nandi-paaṁ* inscribed beside the symbol as found on the Padaṇa hill near Bombay,[25] where hoofmarks are clearly indicated (Fig. A). I have argued against the general applicability of this term,[26] and it is far from clear that the label applies to the symbol, and not exclusively to the hoofmarks. Yet in fact the designation "Nandi's track" and the actual representation of hoofprints at Padaṇa accord well enough with the Śaiva associations, the notion of hoofprints equally well

[a] *Mahāvagga* 1.15.2 and 6 *Nāgarājā iddhimē āsīviso ghoraviso* 1.15.7 *ahinagaṃ*.
[b] *S*.1.106 Māra assumes form of a *sapparāja*: detailed description.
S.1.67 Māra called Namuci by Buddha.

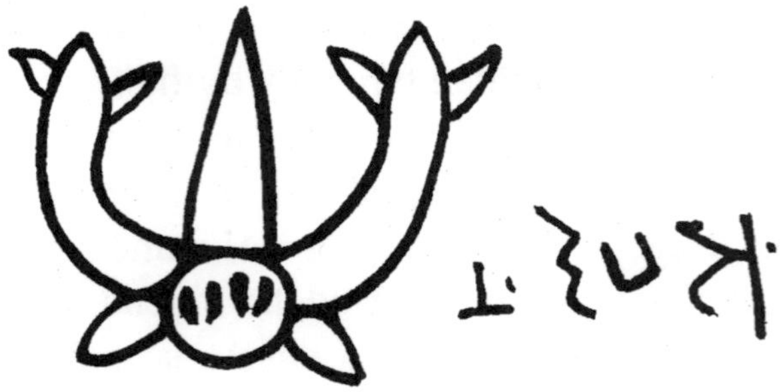

Fig. A. *Nandi-paaṁ*: from Padaṇa.

also with an original connection with Agni; that Śiva and Agni can be assimilated and in certain aspects identified needs no demonstration here. The designation "taurine," employed by some authors, is probably the best available for our symbol, being appropriate equally to Agni, Śiva, or Buddha. In *Ṛg Veda*, I, 65, 1 (*padaiḥ*), and IV, 5, 3 (where Agni is a "mighty bull," and the Sāman chant "naught other than the hidden track of an ox," *padaṁ na gor apagūḷhaṁ*), the metaphor is employed of tracing the lost Agni by his footprints; cf. X, 71, 3, where the tracks (*padavīya*) of Wisdom (*vāc*) are followed by means of the ritual sacrifice, and *ibid.*, III, 39, 6, where Indra finds "by foot and hoof" (*patvat . . . śaphavat*) the wine of life and makes himself master of all the possibilities of existence "hidden" or "hoarded" in the Waters; cf. again *Bṛhadāraṇyaka Up.*, IV, 4, 23, "He should be a knower of the tracks of Brahman" (*tasyaiva syāt padavittaṁ*), and *ibid.*, I, 4, 7, "As though by a footprint (*pada*), indeed, one should find the Angel"—his trace or footprint "set down in the secret place" (*guhā, guhā nihitam, passim*) being found "by the Sacrifice in the Seers" (*Ṛg Veda*, X, 71, 3), "in the heart" (*ibid.*, X, 177, 1), "in the Sea, the Heart, in living things" (*antaḥ samudra hṛdy antar āyuṣi*, *ibid.*, IV, 58, 11). "Footprint"[a] or "track" is thus tantamount to "vestige" as understood in Scholastic phraseology: *Dhammapada* should perhaps be translated in this sense as "Vestige of the Law," *dharma-padāni* as "traces of the Law," cf. *Ṛg Veda*, X, 71, 3 *vācaḥ padavīyam . . . ṛṣiṣu praviṣṭām*, "footprint of the Word vested in the Seers," and *pada* as "statement," "dictum," in *Laṅkāvatāra Sūtra* II, 98 (see Suzuki's discussion in his tanslation, p. 31, note 2). One can hardly doubt that a reminiscense of these ideas underlies the Ch'an Zen allegory of searching for the lost ox, cf. Suzuki, *Essays in Zen Buddhism*, pp. 357 ff.

The "tracks" by which He is to be found are primarily the symbolic expressions of the ritual sacrifice and hymns, "seen" and "warded" by the

[a] See also note 146, below.

poetic genius (*Ṛg Veda*, IX, 73, 9, X, 71, 3, etc.); and in just the same way any symbol such as our *triśūla*, or any other "motif" of a canonical iconography, constitutes a "track" by means of which He may be "followed after," the symbol (*pratīka*) being employed, not for its own sake, but as a call to action. It is evident enough that "tracks" of this kind neither are nor need be represented literally in the form of a spoor, the indication of actual hoofprints at Padaṇa being quite exceptional. If, on the other hand, the notion be interpreted more literally and in connection with a more anthropomorphic concept, then all the passages cited above can be quoted in sanction and explanation of the cult of the "feet of the Lord" (*pādukā*, Buddha-pada, Viṣṇu-pada, etc.) in Buddhist, Jaina, and Vaiṣṇava practice alike. And if the Tree and Fiery Pillar are supported by such feet,[a] it is because He is firmly established (*pratiṣṭha*) on solid ground (*pṛthivī*, represented by a lotus in the case of the Fiery Pillars), in the Waters, in the Depths, existent (*sthita*) in the world, that is in the last analysis "within you," in the lotus of the heart.

From the Tree of Life we turn to consider the Earth-Lotus. In Vedic formulation, the Tree of Life rises into Space from the navel-centre of deity recumbent on the back of the Waters, its trunk representing the axis of the Universe, its branches all extension and differentiation on whatever plane of being. By the time that Nārāyaṇa takes the place of Varuṇa reclining on the Waters at the dawn of a creative cycle, it is not a forest tree (*vanaspati*, often also a designation of Agni) that rise thus from the navel-centre of immortality, but a lotus. This lotus bears on its expanded flower the Father of the World, Lokapitā, Brahmā-Prajāpati, whose epithets are "navel-born" (*nābhija*), "lotus-born" (*abjaja*, *abja-yoni*), and "lotus-seated" (*kamalāsana, padmāsana*), while the recumbent Nārāyaṇa is "lotus-navelled" (*padmanābha, puṣkaranābha*) (Fig. B.). Corresponding descriptions of this "Birth of Brahmā" appear only in "late" books of the Epic, and corresponding representations in art not before the fifth or sixth century A.D.,[27] the archaeological data thus indicating a formulation not much before the Gupta period, though, as will presently appear, the motif is really Vedic. In some remarkable Burmese representations (Fig. 17), the one stem rising from the navel of the recumbent Nārāyaṇa bears on three flowers the Trinity of Brahmā, Viṣṇu, and Śiva.[28] It would seem at first sight as though the tree of the earlier texts had later been interpreted or misinterpreted to be a lotus. The concept of the Lotus-birth of manifested creative deity is, however, coeval with that of the Tree of Life: and

[a] Cf. Figs. 13-15.

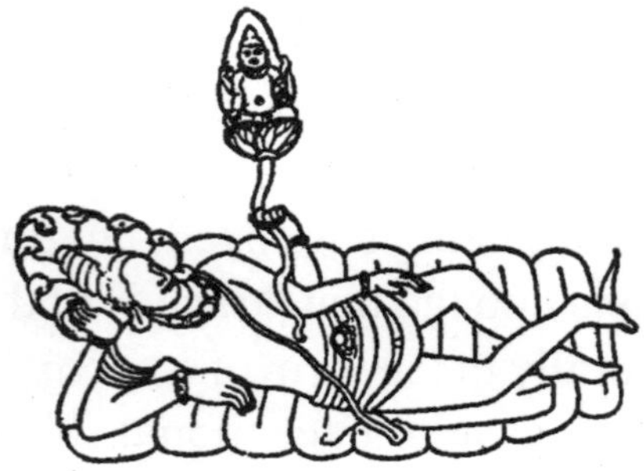

Fig. B. Birth of Brahmā; Elūrā

furthermore, a clear distinction of significance is made as between the Tree and the Lotus, the former being, as we have seen, "all existences," viz. "that which" is manifest, the latter "that wherein" or "that whereon" there is and can be manifestation. For "this lotus (of the heart, *hṛt-puṣkara*) is verily the same as Space (*ākāśa*); these four quarters and four inter-quarters are its constituent petals (*dalasaṁsthāḥ*),"[29] *Maitri Up.*, VI, 2, cf. *Chāndogya Up.*, VIII, 1-3; and it rises appropriately from the navel-centre since "the navel (*nābhi*) of Prajāpati's world-form is the Firmament," *Maitri Up.*, VI, 6. Again the Lotus is explained to be the Earth, any one plane of being, that whereon and whereby existence is supported, *Taittirīya Saṁhitā*, IV, 1, 3, and IV, 2, 8, and *Śatapatha Brāhmaṇa*, VII, 4, 1, 8. Or considered as a receptacle as implied in the expressions *padma-garbha*, *padma-kośa*, then "in this Space (*ākāśa*), coextensive (*yāvān* . . . *tāvān*) with Space-in-the-Heart (*antarhṛdayākāśa*), are contained both Heaven and Earth . . . all is contained therein," *Chāndogya Up.*, VIII, 1, 3.

Before proceeding to a discussion of the subjectivity of Space, and therefore of Existence, implied in the expression "Lotus of the Heart," the primary connotation of the lotus symbolism must be further clarified. The earliest references to a lotus-birth, seat, or support occur in *śruti* in connection with Vasiṣṭha and Agni, in their capacity as the positive existence of all things.[30] In *Ṛg Veda*, VII, 33, 11, we have "O Vasiṣṭha, thou art the son of Mitra-Varuṇa, Brahman, born of (the Apsaras) Urvaśī and of Intellect (*manas*), thou the drop (*drapsa* = *retas*, "seed") that fell by angelic efflux (*daivyena brahmaṇā*); the Several Angels waited upon thee (*ādadantam* = *sarvataḥ ādhārayan*) in the Lotus (*puṣkare*)." That is, Mitra-Varuṇa in Intellect (*manas*) beheld and were beguiled by the Fascination (Apsaras) of the possibilities-of-existence (Waters), their seed fell into the Waters, and thence arose the lotus-ground supporting Vasiṣṭha, surrounded by the Several Angels.[31] In *Ṛg Veda*, VI, 16, 13, Agni is similarly born of or (re-)produced (*niramanthata*, lit. "rubbed" or "churned," cf. "*samudra-manthana*") from a lotus, *puṣkarāt*, cf. *Taittirīya Saṁhitā*, IV, 1, 3g, and *Kauṣītaki Brāhmaṇa*, VIII, 1, "Thee, O Agni, from the Lotus"; and that he is thus mothered by the Lotus flower (or leaf, as in *Taittirīya Saṁhitā*, V, 1, 3) merely enunciates in other terms the epithets constantly applied to him as "born from the lap or navel of the Earth" and "kinsman of the Waters."[32] All birth, all coming into existence, is in fact a "being established in the Waters," and to be "established" is to stand on any ground (*pṛthivī*) or platform of existence; he who stands or sits upon the Lotus "lives."[33] The Vedic passages cited above are thus valid prototypes of the "late" Epic legend of the Birth of Brahmā; the birth of Vasiṣṭha or of Agni is virtually the birth of Brahmā-Prajāpati or of Buddha.[34]

Other ritual and exegetical texts can be cited in which the meaning of the Lotus is explained in the sense already deduced. *Nirukta*, V, 14, explains the Lotus (*puṣkara*) as Firmament or Middle Space (*antarikṣa*), which maintains (*poṣati*) existences (*bhūtāni*), cf. *Maitri Up.*, VI, 2, cited above. *Taittirīya Saṁhitā*, IV, 1, 3c, and 1V, 2, 8c, = *Vājasaneyi Saṁhitā*, XIII, 2, identifies the Lotus (*puṣkara*) with the Earth, extended on the back of the Waters, as the birthplace (*yoni*) of Agni. Sāyaṇa, commenting on *Ṛg Veda*, VI, 16, 13, *puṣkarāt*, substitutes for *puṣkara*, *puṣkaraparṇa*, "lotus-leaf," but explains in the traditional manner that "the property of the lotus-leaf is that of upholding all the worlds," *puṣkara-parṇasya sarvajagad-dhārakatva*.[35] In *Śatapatha Brāhmaṇa*, VII, 3, 2, 14 Prajāpati finds the lost Agni on a lotus-leaf (*adbhya upodasṛptam puṣkaraparṇe*) cf. *AB* VI. 1 'where *arbuda upodasarpat*'. In the construction of the Fire Altar (*Śatapatha Brāhmaṇa*, VII, 4, 1, 7-13; VIII, 3, 1, 11, and X, 5, 2, 8 and 12) a lotus-leaf is laid down centrally (that is in the centre of the Universe, as represented by the whole altar) as the "birthplace of Agni" (*agni-yonitvam*), the "symbol of his womb" (*yoni-rūpatvam*), and as a chthonic basis (*pratiṣṭhā . . . pṛthivyām*): "the lotus means the Waters, and this earth is a leaf thereof . . . and this same earth is Agni's womb." On the lotus-leaf is laid a round gold disk representing the Sun; and thus the lotus-leaf becomes in effect the Sun-boat, though this is not specifically mentioned. Over the Sun-disk is laid the figure of a golden man (*puruṣa*), representing Agni-Prajāpati, the Person in the Sun; the golden Puruṣa and the Sun-disk, lying back to back, form a Janus-type, as explained *ibid.*, VII, 4, 1, 18.

Thus it is abundantly clear that the lotus, flower or leaf (see the alternative representations, Figs. C, F), but in actual iconography usually "flower,"[36] arising from or resting on the Waters, represents the ground (*pṛthivī*) or substance of existence, both that whereon and that wherein

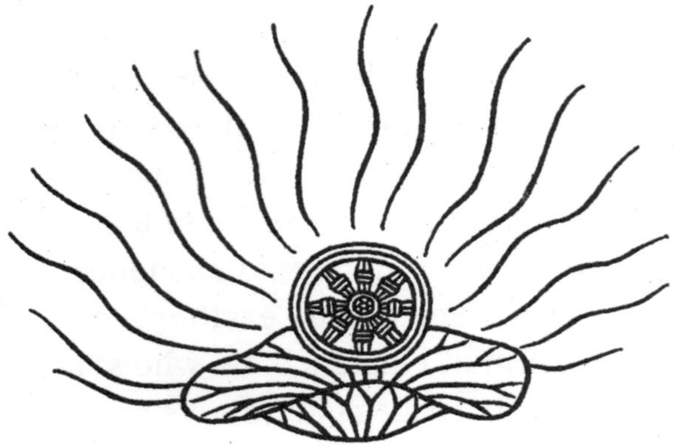

Fig. C. Rimbō (Dharmacakra) supported by a lotus leaf. After Ōmura Seigai, *Sanbon Ryōbu Mandara*. Cf. Fig. F.

existence is established firmly amidst the sea of possibility. And just as it is said of the Cosmic Horse (Varuṇa) that he whose birthplace is the Waters (*samudre yoniḥ*), stands firm in the Waters,[a] and that he who understands himself stands firm wherever he may be, so we may say that he who realizes the meaning of the Lotus stands firm wherever he may be.[37]

The world-lotus naturally blooms in response to the rising of the Sun "in the beginning"; in answer to and as a reflection of the Light of Heaven mirrored on the surface of the Waters. Earth as a reflection of Heaven is stretched out in like measure (*Taittirīya Saṁhitā*, IV, 1, 3, and IV, 2, 8), this world is the counterpart (*anurūpam*) of yonder world (*Aitareya Brāhmaṇa*, VIII, 2); hence, no doubt, the two lotuses held by the Sun in iconography, corresponding to Upper and Nether Waters, *para* and *apara* Prakṛti.[38] However, the light of Heaven may be thought of not merely as the Sun, but collectively as the Lights of Heaven, and so we find in *Pañcaviṁśa Brāhmaṇa*, XVIII, 8, 6, and *Maitrāyanī Saṁhitā*, IV, 4, 7, and 58, 16, a more general statement as follows: "Through the down-shining (*avakāśe*) of the Lights of Heavan (*nakṣatrāṇām*)[39] the Lotus (*puṇḍarīka*) is brought to birth (*jāyate*)," the text further making it clear that the Lotus implies Earth, the lights Heaven. It is further explained, *Pañcaviṁśa Br.*, XVIII, 8, 2, and 9, 6, that the wreath of lotuses put on by the Brahman officiating in the Rājasūya ceremony represents sensible operation, virility, and temporal power (*indriyam, vīryam, kṣatram*).[b]

[a] *TS* V. 6.4.2-3 *āpo vā idam agre salilam āsīt sa prajāpatiḥ puṣkaraparṇe vāto bhūto' lelayat, saḥ pratiṣṭhāṁ nāvindat sa etad apāṁ kulāyam apaśyat tasmin agniṁ achinuta tad iyam abhavat, tato sa pratyatiṣṭhat.*

JB III. 272 *samudre pratiṣṭhām avindat.*

[b] Cf. *SB*, IV, 1.5.16 (Aśvins).

Some more familiar, but less essential, aspects of the lotus symbolism may be alluded to in passing. Amongst these is the lotus as a metaphor of purity: growing in the mud, it betrays no trace of its origin, nor is the flower or leaf wetted by the water it rests upon, and such also is the truly wise man, who lives in the world, but is not of it. For example, *Saṁyutta Nikāya*, III, 140, "Just as, Brethren, a lotus, born in the water, full-grown in the water, rises to the surface and is not wetted by the water, even so, Brethren, the Tathāgata, born in the world, full-grown in the world, surpasses the world, and is unaffected by the World"; or the metaphor may be reversed, as in *Chāndogya Up.*, IV, 14, 3, and *Maitri Up.*, III, 2, where the Self, Ātman, is compared to the drop of water that rests on a lotus leaf, but does not cling to it. It may be inferred from what was previously explained, on the other hand, that when the image of a supreme deity is represented with a lotus in hand as *līlā-kamala*, "lotus of play," it stands for the Universe, his toy, just as an actual lotus, *līlā-kamala* or *līlābja*, held by a human being, is actually his, or more often her, toy. But when the lotus is offered by the worshipper to a deity, that would imply a rendering up of one's own existence to its source, a resignation of one's own nature and ground of separate existence; cf. *Nirukta*, V, 14, where a hermeneutic derivation of *puṣkara* from *pūj* + *kar*, with the sense "to perform an office," is proposed.[40] Furthermore the lotus is a thing loved and admired by all, and is used as a means of adornment, or lends itself to laudatory similes, as when we speak of lotus-eyes or lotus-feet.

In actually surviving works of art we do not find representations of the Buddha supported by a lotus-throne before the second centry A.D., viz., in the art of Gandhāra, and in late Āndhra works from Amarāvatī, nor, as we have already seen, of Brahmā *kamalāsana* before the Gupta period. A second century Kuṣāna example from Mathurā is reproduced by Foucher, *L'art gréco-bouddhique du Gandhāra*, Fig. 552. Long before this, however, at the very beginning of artistic history so far as it is recorded in permanent materials, we meet with the lotus-flower employed as a support in various ways, nor is it at all likely that these examples had not been preceded by others in evanescent material, or painted. The lotus is most conspicuously connected in this way with Śrī-Lakṣmī, viz., in representations dating from the second century B.C. onwards; I have shown elsewhere[a] that these compositions are comprehensible only with reference to Vedic notions,

[a] Cf. Fig. 23.

and that early Indian art is essentially the continuation of a mainly aniconic "Vedic" style.[41] [a]

Śrī-Lakṣmī is essentially Aditi, Prakṛti, Māyā, Apsaras, Urvaśī, the Waters, all the possibilities of existence substantially and maternally personified. The Lotus is preëminently hers, because she *is* the Lotus and the Earth, at once the source and support of all existences, Vasudhā or Vasudharā; that is, with respect to their substance, as the Supernal-Sun is with respect to their form. So she is represented either aniconically by the Lotus, as Padmā, springing from the brimming vessel (*pūrṇa-ghaṭa*) of the Waters (Fig. 23), or in human form upon the Lotus, as Padma-vāsinī, and then typically as receiving a lustral bath of *soma*-bearing rains downpoured from the skies by the elephants of the Quarters (Fig. 23). These early representations occur for the most part in a Buddhist association, though this need not be assumed for all the coins and terracottas.[42] It has been argued by some scholars, Foucher particularly,[43] that the representations in a Buddhist environment, as at Bhārhut, Bodhgayā, and Sāñcī, are actually of Buddha nativities, a theme which would otherwise be lacking in the series of Four Great Events, so far as the early art is concerned. Others, myself included, have opposed this view, and not without justification inasmuch as the formula is certainly of pre-Buddhist origin,

[a] [this fn. relates to notes 41-48] In a monograph *On the Iconography of the Buddha's Nativity,* Mem. Arch. Surv. India, No. 46, received as the present volume goes to press, M. Foucher reasserts the view that the Śrī-Lakṣmī representations at Bharhut and Sāñcī are Buddha nativities, and expresses the hope that I may agree with him. He will find that I do so to the extent that I admit the fact and propriety of a Buddhist application in this sense. At the same time I am very far from agreeing that Buddhism originated the formula; in my view there is nothing specifically or originally Buddhist in early Buddhist imagery, whether visual or verbal. The present case is very much to the point; for to postulate a Buddhist invention or development of the lotus-seated Mother Śrī type would be possible only by assigning a considerably post-Buddhist date to the *Śrīsūkta*, in which the lotus-seated (*padme-sthitām . . . śrīyam . . . puṣkariṇīm . . . lakṣmīm*) Śrī-Lakṣmī is invoked as the mother of Agni-Jātavedas and darling of Viṣṇu (cf. Aditi as the "lady of Viṣṇu" in *Taittirīya Saṁhitā*, IV, 4, 12 and VIII, 5, 14, and *Vājasaneyī Saṁhitā*, XXIX, 60) and described as "bathed by royal elephants with golden jars" (*gajendrair . . .snāpitā hema-kumbhair*). But "the *khila* texts . . . are by no means a modern product, they belong rather to the Vedic age. . . . Only a few of them can be assigned to a late Brāhmaṇa period. . . . The *Śrīsūkta* is connected with the cult of Śrī and Lakṣmī which came into prominence in the Yajurveda period" (Scheftelowitz, *Die Apokryphen des Ṛgveda*, 1906, pp. 2-4). It may be added that Śrī and Lakṣā are mentioned as *brahmavādinī* in the *Bṛhad Devatā*, II, 84.

See Mus in *BÉFEÓ*, 1935, pp. 401-4, The Yakṣī is the wood of which the child is born, cf. *RV* V. 78; cf. F.O. Schrader in *ZDMG*, 1934, p. 188 note (Gaja-Lakṣmī not mother of Buddha).

and because what is represented is certainly not the birth of Siddhārtha, but rather Śrī-Lakṣmī herself, at once Earth-Lotus and Mother-Earth personified, Universal Mother, Mother Nature, Aditi, Māyā,[44] the magical ground or substance of existence, fertilized by heavenly showers.[45] It must not be overlooked, too, that *Jātaka*, I, p. 53, affirms that when the Bodhisattva was born, "two streams of water came down from the sky (*ākāsato dve udakadhārā nikkhamitvā*) and refreshed the bodies of the Bodhisattva and his mother;"[46] in this sense it may be legitimate to say that these are *virtually* Buddha nativities, inasmuch as they represent Her who is the Mother of all Existence, and so preëminently of the Buddha, when he is considered not as the man Siddhārtha, but as Universal Man, in whom all things are lively imaged, Ādityabandhu and Sūryavaṁśin, "Kinsman of the Supernal-Sun" and "Of the Solar Race," and as Māyā-maya, "magically-natured."[47a] It can scarcely have been an accident that Siddhārtha's mortal mother's name was Māyā-devī, Lady Māyā."[48] Siddhārtha's birth from his mother's side is anticipated in *Ṛg Veda*, IV, 18, 1-2, where in connection with Indra's birth from Aditi we find . . . *tiraścatā pārśvān nir gamāṇi*, "I will go forth traversely, from the side"; a lateral procession is mentioned in several other passages, e.g. VI, 10, 4, X, 129, 5, and *Jaiminīya Upaniṣad Brāhmaṇa*, I, 29, where the life-ray (*raśmi asumaya*) is *tiryaṅ pratiṣṭhitaḥ*.[49] Siddhārtha's visibility while yet unborn (*Jātaka*, I, 52, *antokucchigataṁ . . . passati*) may be compared to *Ṛg Veda*, VI, 16, 35, with reference to Agni, *garbhe mātuḥ . . . akṣare vididyutānaḥ*, "shining in the Mother's eternal womb." If we suppose that Śuddhodana means "cloud" (as stated in the *Nighaṇṭu*, rather than "pure rice" as generally assumed), we have a striking parallel in the *Dīpaṅkara Jātaka*, where the Bodhisattva's name is Megha,[50] "Cloud," and his wife's either Bhadrā, "Abundance," or Prakṛti, "Nature"; but as designating the Father, it more likely corresponds to *pakvam odanam* and *kṣīrapākam odanam* in *Ṛg Veda*, VIII, 77, 6 and 10, *odanam pacyamānam* in VIII, 69, 14 *pacatam* in I, 61, 7, the cooking of rice with milk being thought of as an essential element of the Interior Operation; in *Jātaka*, I, 66, the Bodhisattva is represented as remembering the good food that was served in his father's house, where food and drink abounded ("fleshpots of Egypt"). The Bodhisattva's three palaces[51] may be regarded as the three seasons of the Year, Prajāpati; it is noteworthy that until the Bodhisattva leaves his palaces he knows nothing of old age, decline, or death. The Buddha himself is

[a] *RV* VI.7.4 "*Tvāṁ viśve amṛta jāyamānaṁ śiśuṁ na devā abhi saṁnavante*" applies equally to Agni, Buddha and Christ.

Āditya-bandhu, and Śūryavaṁśin, Mahāpurisa and *amanussa*, recalling Agni as the *amānava puruṣa* who leads the Comprehensor through the gateway of the worlds, *Chāndogya Upaniṣad*, V, 10, 2; that the Buddha is an Aṅgirasa, "a descendant of the messengers," is equally significant, Agni in the *Ṛg Veda* being a son of Aṅgiras and himself *aṅgirastama*, "the best of messengers." The Buddha's given name Siddhārtha, denoting the "attainment of the goal," corresponds to *artha*, the "end" or "goal" envisaged by Agni, *Ṛg Veda*, X, 51, 4.

It is clear then that the genealogy of the Buddha, as we have it, is mythical, and it may be that he had been thought of very early in, or before, the rise of "Buddhism," as "a descent of the Sun"[a] or aspect of Agni. If the representations of Māyā-Lakṣmī with the elephants were really regarded as Buddha-Conceptions, that too implies a Buddhology far advanced in centuries B.C. The later Nativity type, in which the Buddha comes to birth from the side of Māyā-devī as she stands like a Yakṣī beneath a tree, has equally mythical implications, though more anthropomorphic in expression, and corresponds in this respect to the coming in of the "anthropomorphic" image. It would seem indeed as if the Buddha had not so much been "deified" in later times, as humanized; assuming that there had been a veridically historical figure, it would seem that this figure had been clothed with a mantle of Fire almost from the beginning, and that, just as in the case of Jesus, the Great Events of the life must be thought of as "stages crowded together as though to present, in a single lifetime, the whole Epic of Transcending of Mortal Destiny."[52] In the development of a crowned and regal Buddha image and in the doctrinal development represented by the *Saddharma Puṇḍarīka* we seem to sense a renewed stressing of the Buddha's divinity, in conscious opposition to the rationalistic interpretations.[53]

That a very advanced Buddhology already existed in the Pali texts, if not from the beginning of "Buddhism," is also very apparent from the terminology and epithets made use of. When the Buddha is represented as saying, "I shall not become either Deva, Gandhabba, Yakkha, nor Man," *Anguttara Nikāya*, II, 38, it is evidently to be understood that what he *is* is a principle, *the* Principle, Dharma, Logos, Word, cf. *Dīgha Nikāya*, III, 84, and *Saṁyutta Nikāya*, III, 120, cited below, p. 51. Amongst his epithets, mostly of Vedic or Aupaniṣada origin, or taken from these sources with only very slight modification, are Mahāpurisa, "Great Person," Appati-

[a]He is a 'reincarnation' of the Bodhisattva Mahāsudassana – Sun of *D*. III.

puggala, "Ineffable Man" (*aprati-pudgala* in *SP*, III, 33), Ādicca-bandhu, "Kinsman of the Supernal-Sun," Rājā cakkavattī, "Sovereign Mover of the Wheel," Devātideva, "Angel of the Angels" (cf. Agni, *devo devānām*, *Ṛg Veda*, I, 94, 13). As Mahāpurisa he is endowed with all the lineaments (*lakkhaṇa*) proper to the Superman. The conception of the Buddhas as "the Eye in the World" (*cakkhuṁ loke*, *Dīgha Nikāya*, II, 158, and *Sutta Nipāta*, III, 9, 6) corresponds to Vedic notions of Mitra ("Agni when enkindled," *Ṛg Veda*, V, 3, 1), who "seeth with unclosing eyes," *animiṣā abhicaṣṭe*, *ibid.*, III, 59, 1, or of the Sun, who "sees all things," *viśvam abhicaṣṭe*, *ibid.*, I, 164, 44, and is the "Eye of Varuṇa," *passim*. With "Lion of the Śākyas" cf. Agni as "lion," *Ṛg Veda*, I, 90, 5 and III, 2, 11, cf. I, 115, 5. The so-called deification of the Buddha, the recognition of the universality of his essence and operation, cannot be denied to the Hīnayāna.[a]

We must now consider the representation of the Buddhas as Dharmacakra, Word-wheel (and World-wheel), or Wheel of the Law or Norm, of which early Buddhist art affords so many examples, amongst which the most famous is that wheel which was set up by Aśoka in the Deer Park at Benares on the site of the *prathamadeśanā*, "First Preaching," which was also the *dharmacakra pravartana*, "First turning of the Wheel of the Word."[54] The pre- and non-Buddhist meanings of the symbol must be studied. What the Wheel stands for in Indian symbolism is primarily the Revolution of the Year, as Father Time (Prajāpati, Kāla), the flowing tide of all begotten things (*Aitareya Brāhmaṇa*, II, 17), dependent on the Sun (*Maitri Up.*, VI, 14-16). In *Ṛg Veda*, I, 164, 2, 11, 13, 14, and 48, the one wheel of the Sun's chariot has twelve or five spokes (months or seasons), or 360 spokes (days), axle (*akṣa*), and triple nave (*nābhi*); it is a revolving wheel of life (*amṛta*) undecaying (*ajara*), therein insist (*tasthuḥ*) the several worlds (*viśvā bhuvanāni*): *ibid.*, I, 155, 6, "He (Viṣṇu) by the names of the four (seasons) has set in motion the rounded wheel that is furnished with ninety steeds" (the ninety days in each quarter of the solar Year); similarly, *Atharva Veda*, X, 8, 4-7, and *Śvetāśvatara Up.*, I, 4 (*brahma-cakra* in I, 6, and VI, 1); in the *Kauṣītaki Brāhmaṇa*, XX, 1, "the Year (elsewhere identified with Prajāpati) is a revolving Wheel of the Angels, that is undying; therein is the sixfold proper food (i.e. means of existence) . . . thereon the Angels move round all the worlds."[55] In the sense that Time is the Sun, a circle is its centre, the Wheel represents the Sun, but more exactly the movement of the Sun, in his heavenly car, with

[a] cf. *BG* 11.50. *CU* VIII-VI-5 "He reaches the Sun as quickly as the flame of the mind".

one or two correlated wheels. The Sun or Solar Wheel is constantly spoken of as "revolving" or as being revolved, with use of root *vṛt* as in the Buddhist *pavattana, pravartana*: e.g. I, 35, 2, where Savitṛ is *vartamānaḥ*; I, 155, 6, *cakram . . . avīvipat*; II, 11, 20, *avartayat sūryo na cakram*; V, 30, 8, *aśmānaṁ cit svaryaṁ vartamānam*; VII, 63, 2, *samānaṁ cakraṁ pary āvivṛtsan.*

Actually to represent all possible states of being, the Wheel would have to be conceived in the manner of a gyroscope, revolving simultaneously in an indefinite number of planes, though still with a motionless centre: just as the Cross must be thought of from this point of view as constituted of three arms, mutually at right angles, intersecting at the one common point which is also the centre of the sphere in which the Cross stands. Actually, however, this would be to introduce a needless complication, and in fact the symbol as employed is essentially an ordinary chariot-wheel,[56] just as also in common usage the two-armed cross stands for a cross extended in three directions. Although, then, the Wheel, as the "round of the world" and "earth plain," strictly speaking corresponds only to a given ensemble of conditions, it represents analogically the indefinite totality of all possible conditions, the entire *saṁsāra*. As thus representing the Universe in its entirety, the Wheel symbol remains in use unchanged from *Ṛg Veda*, I, 164, through *Śvetāśvatara Up*., I, 4, and *Anugītā*, XXX, to Kabīr and the present day.[57]

The content of the wheel symbolism is extraordinarily rich, and can only be outlined here. Its dimensions are indefinite, its radius the variable distance between an undimensioned (*amātra*) point and an immeasurable (*asaṅkhya*) circumference; there in the "middle space" (*antarikṣa, ākāśa*), between the "I" and the "not-I," essence and nature, lie procession and recession (*pravṛtti, nivṛtti*), there are good and evil (*dharmādharmau*), joy and sorrow (*sukha, duḥkha*), light and shade (*chāyātapa*), birth and death (*janma maraṇa*), all local movement and affection; and that motion and possibility are greater the greater the distance from the centre. Beyond the felly lies only the inexistence of the irrational, an impossibility of existence, as of square circles or the horns of a hare; within the nave, the non-existence of the supra-rational.[58]

The cycle of ego-consciousness implies an outward movement from the nave to the ever-receding felly, and a return from the however distant felly to the unchanging centre. A progressive enlightenment (*krama-mukti*) can then be expressed as a gradual contraction of the radius, bringing the circumference ever closer to the centre, until that which seemed to enclose the point is seen to be contained within it, knowledge being thus concentrated into a single form, which is the form of very different things.[59] That is *Nirvāṇa*, unitary being, "with residual existential elements," and by a vanishment of the point becomes also Parinirvāṇa without residuum of existence.

He whose seat is on the lotiform nave or navel of the wheel,[60] and himself unmoving sets and keeps it spinning, is the ruler of the world, of all that is natured and extended in the middle region, between the essential nave and the natural felly; "On whom the parts stand fast, as it were spokes on the nave of the wheel, Him I deem the Person to be known," *Praśna Up.*, VII, 6. In Pali Buddhist and later Sanskrit texts this Royal Person is designated Cakkavattī, Cakravartin, "He who turns the Wheel," and the same designation is applied analogically to any terrestrial "Universal Ruler" or Emperor (Figs. 19, 20). As we have seen, the term Cakravartin, as an essential name of the Buddha, and the corresponding expression Dharmacakra-pravartana denoting the setting in motion of the Word or Law, are constantly met with in early and later Buddhism. These terms do not occur as such in Vedic texts, where *cakri*, "doer," and other forms of the verb *kṛ*, to "do," "make," "cause," "instigate," etc.,[61] must be distinguished etymologically from *cakra*, "wheel"; it may be surmised, however, that the "popular" etymology of Indian hermeneutists might have seen a significance in the assonance of *cakri* and *cakra*. And if the word *cakravartin* is absent in the Vedas, the meaning is nevertheless to be found there; the notion of a supreme Power, Lord of *ṛta* = *dharma*, whose sovereignty (*kṣatra*) is over all the world (*viśvā bhuvanāni*) and is also the axial mover of the twin world wheel of the car of Time and Life is so constantly presented that we can hardly speak of the notion of the King of the World as something new in Buddhist times. Varuṇa alone or with Mitra is often called *samrāj*, mention is often made of the Premier Angel's autonomy (*svarājya*), and in III, 55.4, Agni is universal King, *samāno rājā*.[62] In X, 5, 3 and 4, the notions *viśvasya nābhiṁ carato dhruvasya*, "navel of all that is proceeding or concrete," and *ṛtasya vartanayaḥ*, "propulsions of the Law"; in X, 168, 2, and 174, 1, and 5, the notions *viśvasya bhvanasya rāja*, "King of the Universe," *abhīvartaḥ*, "victorious," and *asapatnaḥ*, "without a rival," imply a sovereign power. In X, 51, 6, *rathī'va adhvānam anvāvarīvuḥ*, "as one who drives a car upon its way," tantamount to "Cosmic Charioteer,"[63] [a] X, 92, 1, *yajñasya vo rathyam viśpatim*, "your charioteer of the sacrifice and lord of the folk," and I, 143, 7, *dhūrṣadam*

[a] *RV* VI. 48.9 *(agni) asya rāyas tvaṁ agane rathirasi.*

aganim mitram na, "Agni as Mitra seated on the pole," i.e. as driver, necessarily imply the setting in motion of the principal Wheel or Wheels.[a] No distinction of meaning can be drawn as between the driver of the solar chariot and him who makes the solar wheel revolve. "Seven treasures" (*sapta ratna*), apparently the same as those of a Cakravartin[b] (cf. figs. 19, 20) are mentioned in *Ṛg Veda*, V, 1, 5, and VI, 74, 1.[c]

We considered above mainly the case in which the cosmic wheel is thought of as single. Perhaps more often the chariot of the Sun is thought of as running on twin wheels connected by a common axle-tree (*akṣa*), and this involves a consideration of the world from two distinct but inseparable points of view (cf. *Aitareya Brāhmaṇa*, VIII, 2, cited above, p. 38). As the Sun shines equally for angels and for men (*Ṛg Veda*, I, 50, 5, etc.), so of the twin wheels of his chariot one touches Heaven, the other Earth (*Ṛg Veda*, I, 30, 19, and X, 85, 18); and their common axle-tree is identified with the axis of the universe that holds apart (*vitaram, viṣvak*) Heaven and Earth (*Ṛg Veda*, V, 29, 4, and X, 89, 4).[d] Or again, when the chariot of the sun is thought of as three-wheeled (*tricakra*), *Ṛg Veda*, X, 85, 14 two of the wheels are identified as aforesaid with Heaven and Earth ("one looks down upon the several worlds, the other ordains the seasons and is born again," cf. I, 164, 44 and 32), and these "proceed by magic," *māyayā caranti*; but the third is hidden (*guhā* = *guhāyāṁ nihitam*, sc. "in the heart"), and only the adepts (*addhātayaḥ*) are Comprehensors (*viduḥ*) thereof.[e] This third wheel evidently corresponds to the "secret name," *nāma guhyam*, of X, 55, 1, and the "third light" of X, 56, 1. These doctrines of three wheels, three lights, etc., are tantamount to the *trikāya* doctrine in Buddhism.[64]

The axle-tree of the twin wheels (which axle must be thought of analogically also as penetrating the third wheel) is the primary source of moving power (as noted incidentally in *Ṛg Veda*, I, 166, 9): not itself revolving, it is the unmoved mover in relation to the wheels. But to complete our understanding of the *pratīka* it must be realized that the revolution of

[a] *Pracodayitr*, *MU*, 11.4.

[b] See K.A.N. Sastri, "Cakravartin" in *NIA* III, 307.

[c] In *BD*. V. 123 called the 7 treasures "of a Cakravartin" (+2 text Interpreted by *BD* as those "of every Cakravartin")

AV 1.29 *abhīvarta-maṇi* amulet made of the rim of a chariot wheel, "for measure unto dominion".

[d] *JUB*.1.20.3 Wheels like heaven and earth separated by axle.

1.30.19 one wheel runs on earth, the other in heaven.

[e] *J*.IV. 61 . . . of Deva as Sun, the other Moon.

RV.X.85.18 one wheel Sun, the other Moon.

the wheel requires the operation of an opposing force operative at the felly, where in actual experience contact with the ground supplies a fulcrum. In other words, revolution depends on the interaction of conjoint principles, which may be called Heaven and Earth, Puruṣa and Prakṛti, *sattva* and *tamas*, I and not-I, subject and object, etc. This is recognized in several passages in which the infixation of the axle, or the movement of the wheels, is effected by the deity by means of his abilities (*śacībhiḥ*, *Ṛg Veda*, I, 30, 15, and X, 89, 4), powers (*śaktibhiḥ*, X, 88, 10), or magic (*māyayā*, X, 85, 18), *śaci*, *śakti*, and *māyā* being synonymous feminine designations of his "means whereby," the "ground" of manifestation, coöperating with his "essence," who is Śacīpati, Māyin, etc.

The axle-tree is also the axis of the universe, as most clearly stated in *Ṛg Veda*, X, 89, 4, *yo akṣeṇeva cakriyā śacībhiḥ viṣvak tastambha pṛthivīm uta dyām*, "by the axle of his wheeled-car indeed, by his abilities, he pillars-apart Heaven and Earth," cf. V, 29, 4, *rodasī vitaraṁ viṣkabhāyat*, and other passage cited above, p. 28, notes 15 and 139.

In *Ṛg Veda*, X, 85, 12, "the chariot is in the mode of Intellect (*ano manasmayam*), the separating Breath (*vyāna*) was the axle (*akṣa*) fastened there." It will be understood that the axle-point (*āṇi*) that penetrates the hollow (*kha*) in the nave (*nābhi*) is central in each wheel X.156.3 *aṅgdhi khaṁ vartayā paṇim*;[65] so in *Ṛg Veda*, I, 35, 6, the Undying Angels (sc. The Several Angels, *viśve devāḥ*, Ādtiyas) are said to depend upon Savitṛ (the Supernal-Sun as prime mover) "as on the chariot's axle-point (*āṇi*)," and in *Aitareya Āraṇyaka*, II, 7, the Self (*ātman*) is compared to the "twin axle-points (*āṇi*)" of the Veda. We have thus dwelt at some length on the Vedic implications of the wheel or wheels, because it is important to realize the wider content and consequent power of this symbol which was so extensively employed in Buddhism, though with a more restricted application.[a]

The continuity of the ideology is often very striking; compare for example *Ṛg Veda*, I, 164, 13, "its axle is never heated (*na tapyate*), its heavy-laden nave (*nābhi*) is never worn away," with the edifying application

[a] Cakra: "von Rade der Sonne . . . . gewöhnlich mit *pravṛt* verbunden," Grassmann
RV I.130.9 *śūraś cakraṁ pravṛhat*
V.29.10 *pra cakraṁ . . . avṛhat*
I.155.6 Viṣṇu: *cakraṁ na vṛttaṁ*
VII.63.2 Sun: *samānaṁ cakraṁ paryāvivṛtsan*
I.56.1 Indra: *hiraṇyayaṁ rathaṁ āvṛtya*
II.11.20 Indra: *avartayat sūryo na cakraṁ*
VI.75.6 *susārathi* cf. *sārathi* also in Buddhism.

of the same notion in *Saṁyutta Nikāya*, I, 33 (I, 5, 7), where the chariot which with its twin Word-wheels (*dhamma-cakkehi saṁyutto*) conducts the rider to *nibbāṇa* is by name "Frictionless" (akūjana).[a]

In actual Buddhism, the Wheel, like the Tree, is regarded from two points of view, cf. *Brahma-vṛkṣa* and *Saṁsāra-vṛkṣa*, that is to say as a pair of wheels, principal (Dharmacakra) and phenomenal (Saṁsāracakra, Bhavacakra); hence from the standpoint of the Wayfarer, broken on the wheel, as either to be turned or stayed,[66] but from that of the Omniscient Comprehensor as one and the same uninterrupted Form, his own intrinsic form. For, from any point of view within it, the movement of a wheel can be regarded as having two directions,[b] as it were right and left; or again, the movement being continuous, any point on the circumference may be regarded either as beginning or as end. It can be understood from either point of view that when Buddha "hesitates" to set going the Principal Wheel, which is also the Existential Wheel, the Angels are in despair, that Brahmā exclaims, "Alas, the world is altogether lost," *vinassati bata bho loko*, and prays that the Word may be spoken, *desatu bhante bhagavā dhammaṁ*, *J.*, I, 81. Taking *dharmacakra-pravartana* and *prathama-deśanā* in their universal sense. That is with respect to the creation of the world, the Angels are naturally dismayed at the "hesitation," for their very existence depends on the operation of the Wheel, the revolution of the Year; as in *Ṛg Veda*, X, 51, where Agni has "fled in fear from the high priestly office (*hotrāt*) lest the Angels should thus engage (*yunajan*) me . . . which as my goal (*artha*) I foresaw," the Angels answering "Come forth, for man is fain to serve us, he waits prepared . . . make easy paths, create the Angelic Way (*devayāna*, cf. *hīnayāna*, *mahāyāna*, *brahmayāna*, *dhammayāna*, etc.) . . . let the Four Quarters bow (*namantām*) before thee."[67] Or taking the words in their specifically Buddhist application, with respect not to the procession of life, but its recession, and as the preaching of a Gospel to that end, the Angels must be thought of as equally despaired at the "hesitation," for all things moving seek their rest.[68] *RV* VI. 7.4. *tvām viśve amṛta . . . devā abhi saṁnavante.*

[a]*S* IV.299 *ekāro ratho* (of the Buddhists) -āro : skr arin, 'spoked' i.e. "wheel" hence "one-wheeled chariot".

[b]cf. *J.*IV. 61 *deva* speaks of the *cakkayuga*, viz. Sun and Moon, by which his golden chariot shines (the chariot body in which he was born, *uppanno rathapañjaro mama* lacks wheels, hence his death).

JUB. I.20.3 heaven and earth two wheels separated by *akṣa*

X 85.16.18 two wheels Sun and Moon.

cf. *J.*VI. 252 with *KU* III.3f.

In monastic Buddhism and from an edifying point of view, stress is naturally laid upon the Dharmacakra only as a Word-wheel to be set in motion to the end that men may find their Way (*magga*, *mārga*), and here the cosmic significance of the Dharmacakra as an embodiment of the Year, "Eniautos Daimon," is thus obscured; it is only gradually brought out again that the revolution of the Principial and Existential Wheels is interdependent and indivisible, in the last analysis one and the same revolution.[69] That is developed in the *Saddharma Puṇḍarīka*, III, 33, where he who preached the Word at Sārnāth *and* on Mt Gṛdhrakūṭa is addressed as having "set in motion the Principal Wheel which is the origin *and* passing away of the factors of existence," *dharmacakraṁ pravartesi . . . skandhānām udayaṁ vyayam*.[70] That identity of Word-wheel and World-wheel—Vajra-dhātu and Garbha-kośa-dhātu in Shingon formulation—is equally implied in the well-known formula, *Yaḥ kleśaḥ so bodhi, yaḥ saṁsāras tan nirvāṇam*, "Error and Awakening, World-flux and Extinction, are the Same," cf. Maitreya-Asaṅga, *Sūtrālaṁkāra*, XIII, 12 (Commentary), *avidyā ca bodhiś-caikam*, "Experience and gnosis are one,"[71] and in the doctrine that Omniscience, *sine qua non* of Nirvāṇa, is the realization of the sameness of all principles, *SPt*, p. 133—the same, *sama*, but differently seen by the eye of flesh (*māṁsa-cakṣus*, viz. the eye's intrinsic faculty in the sensible world), the angelic eye (*divya-cakṣus*, viz. the mind's eye in the intelligible world), and the eye of wisdom (*prajñā-*, *dhamma-*, *ananta*, or *buddha-cakṣus*, viz. the Comprehensor's eye in the world of gnosis).

In another way the correspondence of manifested and transcendental being, here viewed as a correspondence of the twin Wheels and their dependence on a common axis, is developed in Shingon Buddhism as the identity of (1) the "Germ-calyx-plane" or "Germ-womb-plane" (*taizō-kai* = *garbha-kośa-dhātu* or *garbha-kukṣi-dhātu*) and (2) the "Adamantine plane" (*kongo-kai* = *vajra-dhātu*).[72] Here the premier powers or principles of the two rationally but not really distinguished planes are represented respectively by the "seed-words" A and VAṀ (OṀ), according to the significance attached to these sounds in the Upaniṣads. In the Shingon *mandaras* these sounds are represented by diagrams or letters supported by lotus thrones (Fig. D, 32, 33, 40).

In any case, the Dharmacakra as Buddha symbol implies a conception of the Buddha as Dharmakāya, "Embodiment of the Word"; he is at once the Sovereign Mover of the Wheel, *rājā cakkavattī*, cf. the Buddha's "three fields" *Vis.* II.414. Cakravartin *Farvardin yast*, XXIV (89) SBE XXIII, p. 201, and the Wheel itself, the Word as set in motion, *pravartita*. From

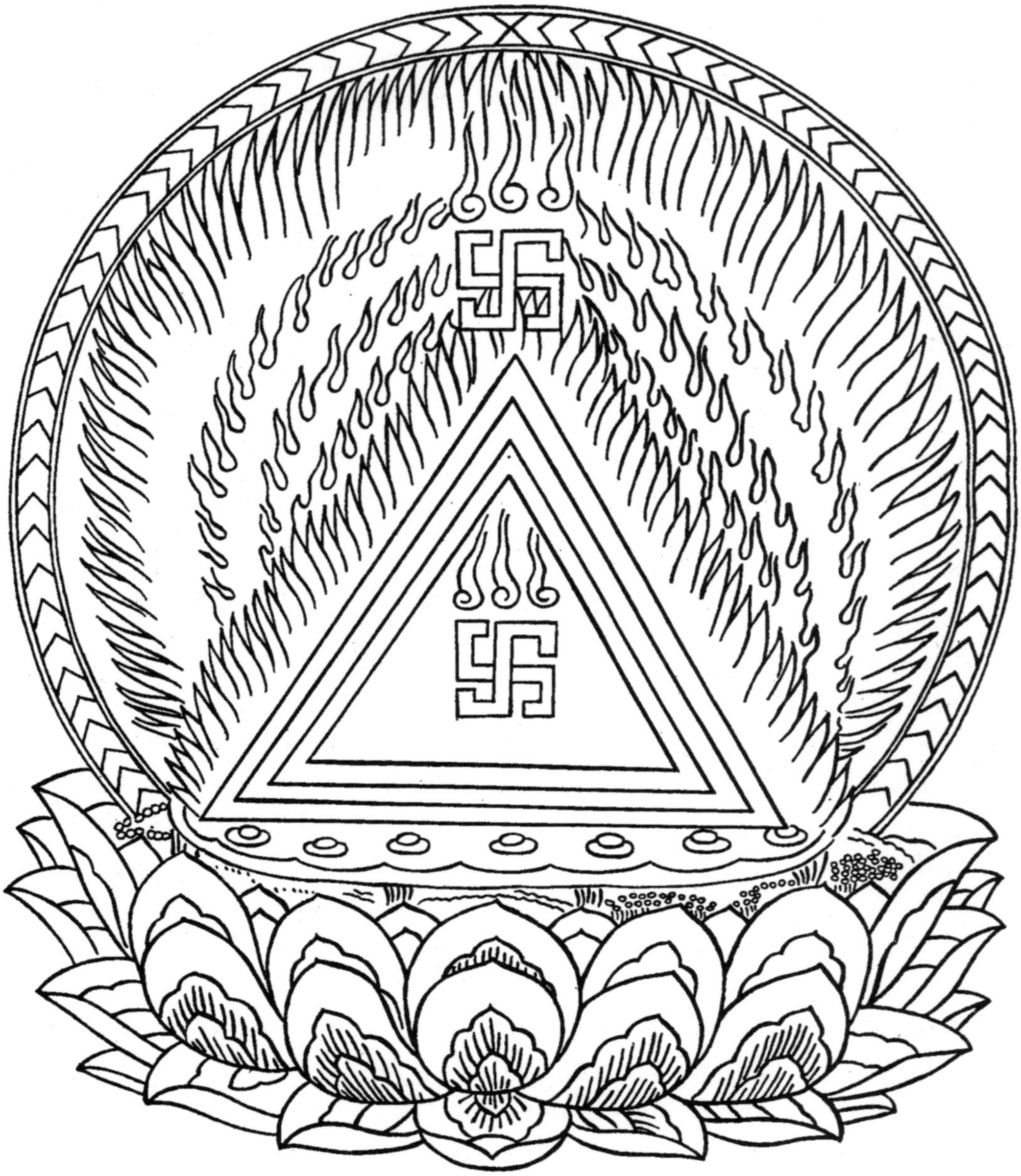

Fig. D. Issai Nyoraichi-in, "Signature of the Possible Intellect of all the Buddhas." Detail from a Shingon Garbhakośa-dhātu maṇḍala[a], see description of Fig. 31. After Ōmura Seigai, *Sanbon Ryōbu Mandara.*

[a] (12 gods at Toji), Fire god carries flaming △ (9th-10th century).

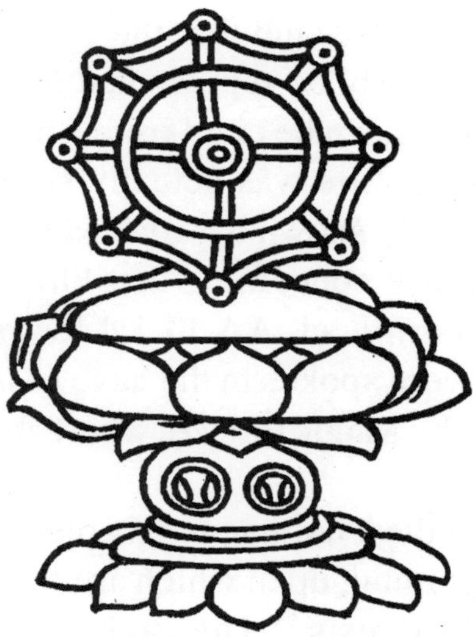

Fig. E. Dharmacakra, detail from a banner, from Tun Huang.
After Stein, *Serindia*, Pl. LXXV.

the fact that the words Sambhogakāya and Nirmāṇakāya do not occur in canonical Pali texts it may be inferred that the Trikāya doctrine was not originally developed; nevertheless, the Pali texts already reveal a very conscious Buddhology, as already observed above, pp. 41. Here we need only indicate that the Dharmakāya concept of the Buddha is certainly presented, e.g. *Dīgha Nikāya*, III, 84[a], "The Tathāgata may be spoken of as Dhammakāya, or Brahmakāya,"[73] and *Saṁyutta Nikāya*, III, 120, "Who sees the Dhamma sees Me, who sees Me sees the Dhamma." So then, in the abundant early Dharmacakra representations, the Buddha is already ideally iconified as a Principal Wheel supported by a universal ground; the Word is embodied (*-kāya*).

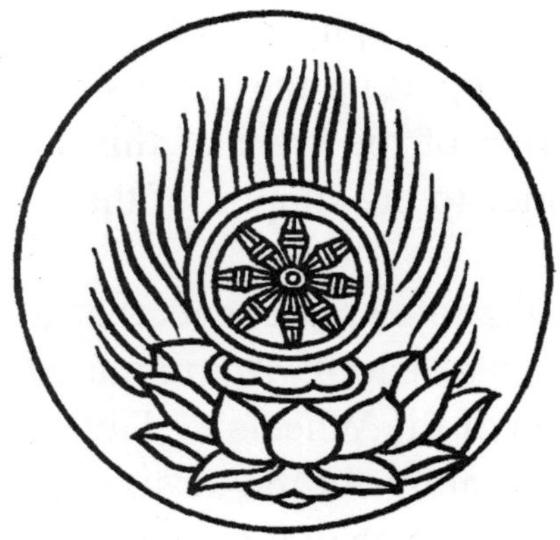

Fig. F. *Rimbō* (Dharmacakra) supported by the lotus,
After Ōmura Seigai, *Sanban Ryōbu Mandara*. Cf. Fig. C.

[a] *DN* III, 84 *tathāgatassa ti evaṁ adhivacanaṁ dharmakāyo iti pi brahmakāyo iti pi dharmabhūto iti pi brahmabhūto iti pi ti*

This prepares us to understand that the Dharmacakra, like any other Buddha symbol, can properly be represented as supported by a lotus, of which very clear examples can be cited from Shingon *mandaras* (Figs. C, E, F).[74] That the Wheel of Life was actually so thought of in a certainly pre-Buddhist time is clearly shown by *Atharva Veda*, X, 8, 34, a prayer for fullness of life, "I ask thee concerning that Flower of the Waters (*apām puṣpa*) wherein insist (*śritāḥ*, cf. AA 11.1.4 for *śritāḥ prāṇāḥ . . . śirasi*) Angels and Men, as it were spokes in the nave (*nābhi*) (of a wheel), which was there infixed (*hita*) by Magic (*māyā*), where the "flower of the waters" is" (of course the lotus.)?[a]

In early Buddhist art the Dharmacakra is respresented as supported by a pillar with a bulbous capital, upon which are four lions, on which in turn the Dharmacakra directly rests.[75] The capital and lions I take to be the lotus and lion thrones which are so often combined in the later anthropomorphic iconography. I have discussed elsewhere[76] the morphology of the lotus capital, and now take it for granted that the pillar itself corresponds to the stem, cable moulding to stamens, and abacus to pericarp. The capital, then, represents the heavenly ground on which the Word is manifested, while the actual earth in which the pillar stands is that terrestrial ground on which the Word is actually preached; the pillar extends from Earth to Heaven, it is the Axis of the Universe; the whole represents the Universe.

Allusion may also be made to one other way in which the Word may be shown as explicitly supported by a lotus; that is when the Word is embodied in a given text, any given *sūtra* or "alternative formulation," *dharma-paryāya*. Inasmuch as "he who makes a manuscript of the *dharma-paryāya* and cherishes it, thereby cherishes the Tathāgata" (*SPt*, p. 338), it is a perfectly correct iconography which represents Prajñāpāramitā or Mañjuśrī (cf. Fig. 39) supporting the "Lotus of Transcendent Wisdom" upon a lotus, the holding of the stem of this lotus being a formulation equivalent in significance to the support of the pillar of the Dharmacakra by its ground.

We have seen that the lotus represents that wherein existence comes to be and passes away, the seat of *pravṛtti* and *nivṛtti*, of Him who starts and stays the revolution of the Wheels of Time, but have alluded only in passing to what is ultimately the most significant aspect of the lotus symbolism, i.e. the identification of the lotus with the "heart" or "mind" of

[a] *TS* V 4.4.2 "the reed is the flower of the water" *etat puṣpaṁ yad vetaso'pām.*
AV X.7.41 Vetasa = skambha = brahma etc.,
(= sun = pillar) so *apāṁ puṣpa hoti* = "the one lotus of the sky".

man. Again and again in the Upaniṣads that elemental Space (*ākāśa, kha, nabha, antarikṣa*, etc.[77]) in which the Principal Being is manifested as all the forms of natured being is located in the cave or secret chamber (*guhā*), dwelling (*veśma*), hollow (*kha*),[78] temple (*āyatana*), abode (*ālaya*), coffer or calyx (*kośa*), or nesting-place (*nīḍa*)[79] in the Lotus of the Heart (*hṛt-puṣkara*) or inward man (*antar-bhūta*), i.e. "in the innermost." There in a universal mode abides the Self (*ātman*), the Lord (*īśa*), Person (*puruṣa*), indefinitely dimensioned, "smaller than an atom and surpassing magnitude," *aṇor aṇīyān mahato mahīyān, Śvetāśvatara Up.*, III, 20 etc. "This space-within-the-heart (*antarhṛdaya ākāśa*), therein is the Person (*puruṣa*) in the mode of Intellect (*mano-maya*) . . . there he becomes as Brahman in a spatial embodiment, as very Selt, as the playground of the Spirit (*prāṇārāma*), as Intellect and Bliss, Peace uttermost and everlasting," *Taittirīya Up.*, I, 6, 1, "who is the Logos (*dharma*)," *Bṛhadāraṇyaka Up.*, II, 5, 11. Are we not reminded that "The Kingdom of Heaven is within you"? Or again, "That golden Person in the Supernal-Sun who from that golden station looks down upon this earth, it is even He that dwells in the Lotus of the Heart and functions there. He who dwells in the Lotus of the Heart is that same numinous solar Fire that is spoken of as Time, unseen and all-devouring," *Maitri Up.*, VI, 1-2, cf. *Jainminīya Upaniṣad Brāhmaṇa*, I, 27. So "what is within that should be searched out, that assuredly is what one should desire to understand . . . (for) everything is contained therein, both what is ours (now) and what is not (yet) ours," *Chāndogya Up.*, VIII, 1-3, i.e. not merely those possibilities that can be realized within the circle of a particular ensemble of conditions such as "ours," but all that can be realized in the indefinite totality of all states of being, all that God can "be." Thus Time and Space, manifested Deity in other words, are not external facts, but all contained at the core of our own being; there lies that "nothing" out of which the world was made; there can be realized the Kingdom of Heaven, in a degree proportionate to the measure of our Understanding.[80]

These considerations carry us far beyond the iconography of Brahmanical or Buddhist art to its ultimate content. This content is no less essential in the visual than in the literary art; to use only the eye in looking at a sculpture is no better than to use the ear alone in listening to the recitation of a text or the chanting of a hymn, however "artistic" these performances may be. The visual and literary formulations have precisely the same "uses," their references are the same; for some purposes the one, for others the other, may be more efficacious; cf. Kōbō Daishi, speaking with reference to the propagation of the doctrine. "The reverend Divine informed me that the secrets of the Shingon sect could not be conveyed without the aid of pictorial representations" (cf. Figs. C, D, E, 32, 33, 40).[81] In any case, it is the content that gives rise to the iconography, whether this be visual or verbal, just as the soul is said to be the form of the body ("form" is the principle that determines a thing in its species). To regard only the symbols, and not their form, is nothing but sensationalism, if not fetishism:[82] *Docti rationem artis intelligent, indocti etiam voluptatem*, where *ratio* is *raison d'être*. The humane point of view, that the symbols are merely indications or stimuli, not to be judged as ends in themselves, but as means or supports of realization, has been strongly emphasized in the East, nowhere more explicitly than in the *Laṅkāvatāra Sūtra*, ed. Nanjio, p. 48: "As a master painter seated before some picture applies his colors for the purpose of making a picture, so do I preach (*deśayāmi*); the (real) picture is not in the color nor in the surface nor in the environment (*bhājana*), (but in the mind of the painter). The picture is devised in colors as a means of attracting living beings; and (just as the picture may be defective, so) the preaching may err, but the principle (*tattvaṁ*, cf. *tattvārtha* in *Bṛhad Devatā*, VII, 110; Dante's "*vera sentenzia*") transcends the letter"[a] (*akṣara-varjitam*). As Dante expresses it, "Behold the teaching, that escapes beneath the veil of its strange verses."[83] The vocabulary of art, sensible in itself, is necessarily built up from the elements of sensible experience, the source of all rational knowledge; but what is thus constructed is not intended to resemble any natural species, and cannot be judged by verisimilitude or by the ear's or eye's sensation alone; it is intended to convey an intelligible meaning, and beyond that to point the way to the realization in consciousness of a condition of being transcending even the images of thought, and only a self-identification with the content of the work, achieved by the spectator's own effort, can be regarded as perfect experience, without distinction of "religious" and "aesthetic," logic and feeling.

[a] Cf. in the *Tilakamañjarī* of Dhanapāla, *Kāvyamālā* No. 85, p. 144, the distinction of *cārutva-ṭattvam* from *rūpam*.

PART II

THE PLACE OF THE LOTUS-THRONE

THE PLACE OF THE LOTUS-THRONE

"Where is the navel of the world?"—*Ṛg Veda*, I, 164, 34.
"Quivi è la Rosa, in che il Verbo divino carne se fece; quivi son li Gigli, al cui odor si prese il buon Cammino."—Dante, *Paradiso*, XXIII.[84]

In early Buddhist art, as is well known, the Buddha is constantly represented by a simple seat or throne (*pallaṅka*) situated at the foot of a Mahābodhi-tree, the Prince of Trees, *duminda*. After the second century A.D., in the case of *māra-dharṣaṇa* images (recognizable by the *bhūmi-sparśa-mudrā*), the manifested form of the Buddha, himself, seated on a lotus-throne, or combined lotus- and lion-throne, has become the most prominent feature of the whole, the Wisdom-tree being now reduced from its original supremacy to a function merely indicative of place and event; or if some other of the *aṣṭasthāna* is in question, or indeed any scene from the Life, the Buddha is seated on a lotus-throne, or stands on a lotus-pedestal, the representation including at the same time the necessary indications of place and event. In just the same way the anthropomorphic figure displaces the Wheel, which is relegated to the pedestal as an indication of the event of the First Preaching; though it appears also as *lakṣaṇa* on the soles of the feet and palms of the hands, for the Buddha even in human form *is* essentially the Wheel, his Existence *is* its revolution.

In other words, anthropomorphic elements have now been combined with the earlier and more abstract symbolism; that was an inevitable result of the emergence of Buddhism as a popular religion, its extension as an emotional (*bhakti-vāda*) persuasion. That may have been just what the Buddha is said to have prophesied with regret on the occasion of the admission of women to the monastic order; and as we have seen a use of anthropomorphic images had been condemned as "groundless and fanciful." Even if this is not original, as it may well be, at least it represents an iconoclastic tendency, subsequent to the development of the anthropomorphic imagery. Not that monastic orthodoxy could really have feared "idolatry" in the fetishistic sense, but that he who had denied that he was either Gandhabba, Yakkha, or Man, asserting thereby his Principal essence, might have sensed, or been thought of as sensing, a psychological danger in the use of a cult image in the form of a man, danger in fact in any sort of cult susceptible of an "animistic" interpretation. Nothing, however, is really changed in principle; the "anthropomorphic" image in India remains "abstract,"[85] and rightly understood is merely as means to the realization of a given station of consciousness. Actually, in the theological development, the Principal Essence of the Tathāgata is more and more strongly emphasized, the content of the iconography, anthropomorphic or otherwise, becomes more and more ontological, less and less historical. It is just this emancipation from the historical point of view which determines the character and permits the expansion of Mahāyāna art, preoccupied as it is with the concept of the Buddha's transcendental Perfection: when it is realized that the Buddha's Comprehension (Sambodhi) dates from the beginning of time, and was merely "displayed" at Bodhgayā, and that he "has never left his seat on Mt Gṛdhrakūṭa," a mistaken attachment to his human personality is precluded.[a] The mediaeval development of Christianity and of Christian art after the decline of Iconoclasm presents an exact analogy; here likewise it was realized that "Christ's birth is eternal," and so there came into being an art that emphasizes the Perfection of his being in Glory, far more than the course of his earthly ministry.[86]

Beneath the Bodhi-tree, within the Bodhimaṇḍa, Gautama is said to have accomplished the Great Awakening, Mahāsambodhi, becoming Buddha, "Comprehensor"; That was an attainment of Nirvāṇa, though other terms for this condition attainable by a still existent being, particularly the term Arahatta, "Perfection," are more frequently employed in the canonical Pali texts. What was then this "Full Attainment" (*samāpatti*)? Nirvāṇa is literally "despiration," but in Buddhist usage more specifically "Extinction," viz. extinction of the flame of Will. Most significant for us is the distinction of Nibbāṇa as *sa-upādi-sesa*, "having a residual existential ground," from Parinibbāṇa as *an-* or *nir-upādi-sesa*, "without any residual ground of existence";[87] for these interpretations coincide with the doctrine of the *Saddharma Puṇḍarīka* that the Buddha, though omniscient, though "extinguished," is not yet "absolutely extinguished" (*aparinirvāyamāṇa*, see p. 64). The Mahāsambodhi, Great Awakening, displayed at Bodhgayā was not then a "Drowning" in the utterly Unknowing and Unknown,[88] but the realization of a paradisiac, super-individual state of pure Being, realization of sovereign personality as Cakravartin and Dharmarājā. A transformation (Pali *vikubbana*, Skr. *parāvṛtti*, *abhisambhava*) is necessarily involved, which can only be described in terms of Paradise and Vision, Buddha-saukhya-vihāra (*Mahāyāna Sūtrālaṁkāra*, IX, 46).

[a]*Pāṭika Suttanta* (*D*.III.2.20, text p. 28). "The ultimate beginning of things (*Dialogue*, Pt. III, p. 25) (*aggañña*).

So according to the *Nidānakathā*, *J.*, I, 75-76, "... throughout the universe flowering trees put forth their blossoms, and fruit-bearing trees were loaded with clusters of fruit ... hells, whose gloom the rays of the seven suns had never dispelled, were filled with light[89]. . . the blind from birth received their sight. . . ." But this experience was not an effected miracle (*pāṭihāriya*, *inda-jāla*) made visible to any spectator: "the Great Person (*mahāpurisa*) sat there alone," *J.*, I, 72, and if he beheld the ten thousand world-systems, the "World-picture" (*jagac-citra*, *Svātmanirūpaṇa*, 96),[90] none therein beheld *him*, unless it were in a likeness, *pratibimbavat*. Paradise is ever present to the transcendental Buddha, but naturally it was not supposed that the vision remained or could have remained present to the empirical Buddha in subsequent daily life, and indeed he is made to say that were he to repeat elsewhere the Full Attainment reached in the Bodhimaṇḍa, "Wisdom-circle," earth could not sustain him (*J.*, IV, 229).[91]

Now to consider the position of the Bodhimaṇḍa, and continuing with the *Kāliṅga-bodhi Jātaka* (*J.*, IV, 228-9): with the Buddha's approval, as already explained above, Mogallāna fares through the sky[92] to the Bodhimaṇḍa, and there procures a seed of the Wisdom-tree, and brings it back. Anāthapiṇḍika plants it in the place prepared for it at the gateway of the Jetavana, and there it springs up immediately, a full-grown "Forest-Lord," Vanaspati.[93] A Wisdom-festival (*bodhi-maha*) is held, and a railing (*vedikā*) and enclosing walls (*pākāra*) are built, clearly in imitation of those on the original site. Ānanda then prays the Buddha to repeat "at the foot of this Bodhi (-tree) that Full Attainment (*samāpatti*) to which you attained at the root of the Mahābodhi (-tree)." The Buddha replies that this is impossible, "for should I accomplish here what I accomplished in the Mahābodhimaṇḍa, the earth will not be able to sustain it"; he consents, however, to achieve during one night such a measure of Attainment as the site can support.

It is thus apparent that a particular significance attached to the (Mahā-) Bodhimaṇḍa with respect to its position in the Universe. We have already understood that the Wisdom-circle is an extent ideally equivalent to that of the whole Universe, and in gnosis realized as such. Now the meaning of a circle is with respect to its centre, which is a mathematical, and undimensioned, point, not with respect to its actual extension in physical space. It is in fact precisely at the centre of the Bodhimaṇḍa that the Bodhisattva took his seat. As related in the *Nidānakathā*, he first essays to find a seat on the north, south, and west of the Tree, but in each case the Great Earth (*mahā-paṭhavī*) fails to maintain its level, it seems to move up and down, like a great carwheel lying on its hub (*nābhi*, "navel," "nave") when the circumference is trodden on; only when he takes his stand to the east of the Tree, that is evidently *on* the hub of the "wheel," is the level maintained.[94] Here there rises up a seat (*pallaṅka*) called "Unconquerable" (*aparājita*), and "of impartite, or admantine, form" (*abhejja-rūpa*), and the Bodhisattva takes his seat with his back to the Tree. Māra, embodying the Will to Life, *libido, lubet*, claims the throne;[95] he assaults the Bodhisattva with every weapon known to him, but every weapon is transformed and reaches the Great Person in the form of a flower. Māra's daughters present seduction in all its most attractive forms; the Bodhisattva is equally unmoved, he does not "look," for he has passed beyond "affection" to "perfection."[96]

The location of the Buddha-seat at the navel of the World-wheel is emphasized again in the *Buddhacarita*, XIII, 68; "This is the navel of the earth-plain (*nābhir vasudhā-tala*)[a]; it is possessed of transcendent entirety (*parama-kṛtsna*[97]); no other place on earth but this is the realm of At-one-ment or Consummation (*samādhi*), the situation of the Goal (*hita*)." By the same token, this "unmoving site" (*acalaṭṭhāna*) has been occupied by all previous Buddhas (*J.*, I, 71), by every Bodhisattva "on the day of his Great Awakening" (*abhisambujjhana*, *J.*, I, 74, cf. *Buddhacarita*, XIII, 67).

The seat itself (*pallaṅka*, *patta-pallaṅka*) is spoken of as unconquerable (*aparājita*), impartite or adamantine (*abhejja*), and as a Waking-seat (*bodhi-*) and Victory-seat (*jaya-*), J., I, 73-7.[b] It is fourteen cubits in length, and makes its appearance, "is" (*ahosi*), spontaneously; but its form is not emphasized, *pallaṅka* and *patta-pallaṅka* simply denoting a slab of stone, and as such, supported by a plain rectangular base, the seat is represented in the early art. In *Theragāthā*, 1095, however, we find it spoken of as a "lion-throne," *sīhāsana* (glossed *thirāsane aparājita-pallaṅke*, "unconquerable seat of firm séance"); this lion-throne is the form actually favored in the case of the oldest representations of the Buddha in human form at Mathurā, and it long survives in literature and art, often in combination with the lotus. Other royal types of seat or throne are met with at Amarāvatī. It is here also, as well as in the art of Gandhāra, mostly of the second century A.D., that the characteristic lotus seat (*padmāsana*) or lotus pedestal (*padma-pīṭha*) first appears.

[a] On the significance of the navel of the earth see commentary given on *ŚB* 1.1.2.20: See also *Guenon, L'esoterisme de Dante.*

[b] Cf. *TS* IV.2.9.5 (r, s) "Sit down as ancient Hotṛ . . . on this seat and on the one which was *apratima*".

We also find the term *vajrāsana*, "adamantine throne," applied to the Buddha's seat. This term does not occur in the Pali texts, but is common in the Mahāyāna sūtras. The word and notion led no doubt to the occasional representation of actual *vajras* on the pedestal of the Buddha throne, as at

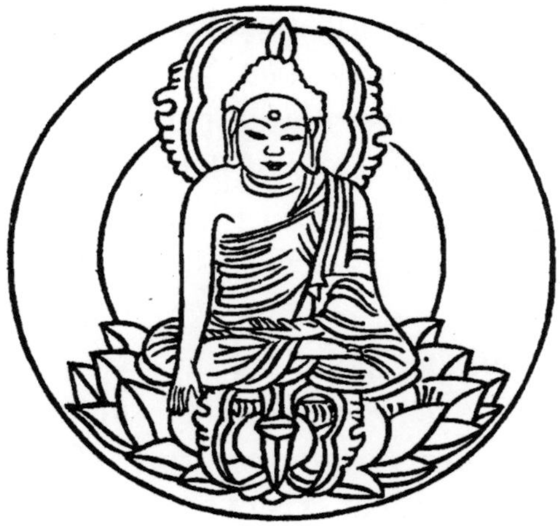

Fig. G. Vajra-dhātu form of the Dhyāni-Buddha.
After Ōmura Seigai, *Sanbon Ryōbu Mandara.*

the Gal-vihāre, Poḷonnāruva, in the twelfth century; such representations are rare.[a] In certain Shingon Buddhist representations (Fig. G) the *vajra* is combined rather with the body of the Buddha than with the throne, and this is probably to be connected with the late Tantrik form of Buddhism known as Vajrayāna, the designation of the Principal plane as Vajradhātu, Dharmakāya as Vajrakāya, and the personification of Vajrasattva = Vairocana, Ādi-Buddha. It will be remembered also that long before this (*Dīgha Nikāya*, I, 95, *Majjhima Nikāya*, I, 231, and in the *Lalita Vistara*) a Yakṣa Vajrapāṇi, a guardian angel and not to be confused with Indra, is closely associated with the Buddha during his ministry; and that this Vajrapāṇi, "who bears a *vajra* in his hand," soon becomes the Bodhisattva of the same name.[98] From the standpoint of Vedic angelology such a figure must be regarded simply as an externalization of the Buddha's own adamantine power, personified as an angel attendant upon him.[99]

Although the term *vajrāsana* is not directly represented in Pali texts, the idea is clearly present by implication. The throne is in fact spoken of

[a] In *J.* VI. 2 the Bodhisattva Temiya in his mother's womb, which was filled as if with diamond. *Deviyā kucchi vajirapuṇṇa viya ahosi.*

J. 1.135 Bodhisattva concerned. *Bodhisatto tassa kucciyaṁ yeva patisandhiṁ gaṇhi. Tāvad eva tassa vajrapūrita viya garuka kucchi ahosi.*

as *abhejja-rūpa*, i.e. as of impartite or adamantine form, *abhejja* being equivalent to Skr. *abhedya*, "indivisible," and also a kenning for *vajra*, "diamond," "adamant." We have also already seen that the Buddha's seat is at the centre, on the navel of the World-wheel, i.e. also centred on the axle-tree (*akṣa*), which is also the World-axis; and it may be noted that *akṣa-ja*, "axle-born" or "axis-born," is again a kenning for "*vajra*," while Kṛṣṇa's *cakra* is said to be *vajra-nābha*.[100]

The *vajra* (Jap. *kongō*) plays a large part in Shingon symbolism and ritual (Figs. G, H). A detailed study of the symbolism of Shingon ritual and implements is much to be desired.[101] However, it is evident from the representations and objects themselves, in the light of what has been shown above with respect to *akṣa*, *vajra*, and *cakra*, that the point or end of the *vajra* corresponds to *āṇi*, the "point" of the axle-tree that penetrates the nave of the Wheel, Dante's *punto dello stelo a cui la prima rota va dintorno*. In the ordinary double *vajra*, *kongō-sho* (Figs. 26, 27), then, the stem or handle corresponds to the vertical axis of the Universe, extending between Heaven and Earth, which are represented by the two ends, one- or three-pointed as the case may be, each in the image of (*anurūpam*) the other. That is as pure Being, *Ding an sich, in principio*, and motionless, *pūrṇa apravartin, acala, abhedya*. On the other hand the fourfold (crossed) *karma-vajra, katsuma-kongō* (Fig. 28), corresponding to Dharmacakra, *rimbō*, represents the movement or operation of this exemplary Principle either universally or on any given plane of being, as already explained in connection with the symbolism of the Wheel. Hence we find the spokes of the World-wheel not infrequently and quite naturally represented as *vajras*, extending from centre to felly; in the *rimbō* (Fig. 25), for example, the "earth-points" of the eight *vajra*-spokes are seen in contact with the felly, but it must be understood that the unseen "heaven-points" meet at the common centre, within the lotus-nave. From the point of view of anyone "on earth" the corresponding *vajra*-spoke extends as before from Earth (the felly) to Heaven (centre). From this point of view it will also be apparent why in Shingon symbolism the *vajra*, *kongō*, is always represented as "supported" by a lotus, that is, by a universal "ground," the relation of *vajra* to lotus being that of "impartible essence" to "universal substance"; and it is in the "middle region," i.e. "round about" the axis of the *vajra*, between the center and the felly of any Wheel, that all existence is extended. It should not be overlooked that *kongō-sho* and *katsuma-kongō*, the former vertical, the latter in a horizontal plane, considered together represent the poles of the Universe in the form of a three-armed cross: and as we have seen, the Buddha's throne is situated in the centre, at the intersection of the arms.[a]

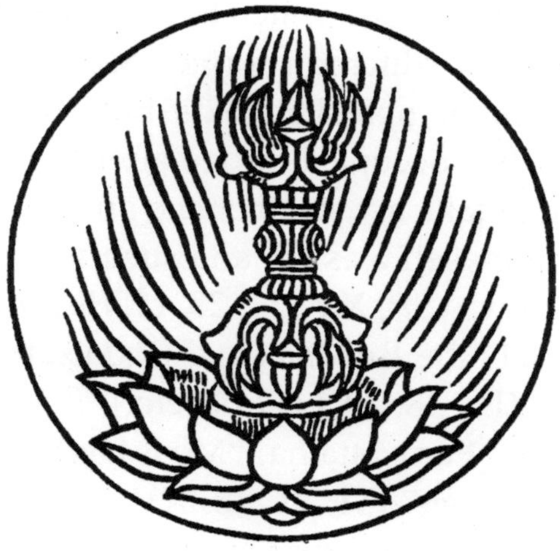

Fig. H. Vajra-dhātu symbol of the Five Dhyāni-Buddhas.
After Ōmura Seigai, *Sanbon Ryōbu Mandara.*

Furthermore, the origin of the term *vajrāsana* can also be explained psychologically, with reference to the mentality of him who sits thereon:[102] in the *Anguttara Nikāya*, I, 124, the highest type of consciousness is termed *vajirūpama citta*, "heart like adamant,"[103] he having such a heart or mind "who by the destruction of the foul-issues[104] and the vision of Dhamma (principle) has verified the gnosis of issue-free heart-and-mind-release (*vimutti* = *nibbāṇa*), and having won it abides therein. Just as, Brethren, there is nothing, whether gem or rock, which a diamond cannot cut (*vajirassa . . . abhejjam*) . . . such is one of the three types of man (*puggala*) to be found in the world." In Hinduism such a one is styled Jīvan-mukta, Freed in Life, or Vidvān, Gnostic, in Buddhism Jina, Conqueror, or Nirvāta, Extinguished, in Christianity Comprehensor. Such undoubtedly was the Mahāpurisa, Tathāgata, Buddha, Devātideva; appropriate to him whose heart is like a diamond, adamantine, or as we should now perhaps express it, "of steel," is an admanatine throne, immovable as himself.

In the *Saddharma Puṇḍarīka*,[105] not later than A.D. 250, the Buddha doctrine is completely emancipated from its historical setting, which is

[a]Cf. *padma* = *bhaga*; *vajra* = *linga*. See Shahidullah, *Chants Mystique*, p.10; Poussin, *Bouddhisme*, p. 154 note.

preserved only with respect to the "traces" (*dhatū*) of Gautama on earth, and in the iconography in so far as the monastic type is still adhered to. The Buddha himself becomes as transcendental principle, Dharma, Logos, awakened (*abhisambuddha*) from the beginning of time (*SP*, XV, 1). Not merely is his throne (*āsana*), upon which he is never weary of sitting (*SP*, V, 23),[106] the same as that which all former Munis have occupied (*SP*, XIII, 67), as was also taught in the Pali texts, but he is from the beginning one and the same who has occupied throne after throne in time and time again: "again and again I take my stand on the ground of the living world" (*SP*, XV, 7), "showing myself as such and such forasmuch as men have fallen into sin and sorrow" (*SP*, XV, 22, 23, cf. *Bhagavad Gītā*, IV, 7 and 8); being thus not merely the Buddhas and Bodhisattvas of the past, but those yet to come (*SP*, XIV, 38, XVI, 59-62, etc.).[107] As Dharmarājā, "King of the Word" (*SP*, V, 1), Puruṣottama, "Most High Person" (*SP*, II, 41), *Svayambhū*, "Self-subsistent" (*SP*, II, 48, XV, 21), Lokapitā, "Father of the World" (*SP*, XV, 21), and Sarvaprajāna Nātha, "all-fore-knowing Lord" (*SP*, XV, 21, cf. "Prajāpati"), "I display return (*nirvṛta*) who am not myself returned (*anirvṛtaḥ*)" (*SP*, XV, 21).[108] "I reveal the Ground of Extinction (*nirvāṇa-bhūmi*), speaking by accommodation for the edification of living beings, though I was not Extinguished (*na . . . nirvāmi ahu*) at that time, but am ever revealing the Dharma here. . . . Believing that my spiritual-nature (*ātma-bhāva*)[a] was Wholly Returned (*parinivṛta*), they worship variously the traces (*dhātu*), but see not Me. . . . I have not left this Gṛdhrakūṭa . . . the duration of my life is an interminable aeon" (*SP*, XV, 3, 5, 10, and 17). Again, "The Threefold World is seen by the Tathāgata,[109] not as childish worldlings see it, but immediately as Principles (*dharmā*); varily the Principles are not remote from the Tathāgata in the station where he is. . . . The Tathāgata who was Awakened (*abhisambuddha*) so long ago, and the measure of whose life is incalculable, is continuously (*sadā*) existent (*sthita*). . . . My ancient Bodhisattva course is not yet run, the measure of my life is not fulfilled. . . . I announce an Absolute-Extinction (*parinirvāṇa*) who-am-not-by-way-of-being-Totally-Extinguished (*aparinirvāyamāṇa*) . . . lest those whose virtuosity (*kuśala*) is insecurely rooted, thinking 'the Tathāgata is alive" (*tiṣṭhati*), should fail to exert their manhood (*vīrya*) towards a Negation-of-the-flux (*niḥsaraṇa*) of the Threefold World" (*SPt*, pp. 318, 319).[110] And as for those Comprehensors

[a] *ātmabhāva*, essence, existence, individuality. Cf. Abhidh. II.45; Poussin, p. 120; *A*. II.159 'personality', etc. - substance?

who may in future take their place at the foot of the Wisdom-tree, "there have I taken my seat, where that Son of Buddha is, there am I" (*SP*., XVI, 59-62); "moved by compassion, like a father's for his dear and only son, he appears (*avatīrya*, i.e. as *avatāra*) in the Threefold World, seeing with the eye of wisdom that living beings are revolving (*paribhramataḥ*, cf. *paribhramati* in *Maitri Up*., III, 2) there in the Wheel of the World-flux (*saṁsāracakra*) and laboring without discovering a Negation of the Flux (*niḥsaraṇam*). . . the Tathāgata who thus beholds the deep principles (*gambhirān dharmān*) sees without seeing (*paśyaty apaśyanayā*)[111] the Threefold World that is the crowded home of multifarious living beings" (*SPt*, pp. 135-7).

The Buddha as Supreme Person (Puruṣottama, etc.) of incalculable but not infinite age, whose enlightenment dates from the beginning of the world, is thus from the standpoints of ontology and psychology, as well as by verbal correspondences (Lokapitā, Svayambhū, Prajānanātha, etc.), virtually identified with Brahmā-Prajāpati, who is the Father of the World.[112] This virtual identification of Buddha and Brahmā appears already in certain passages of the Pali books, for example in the equation of Dhammakāya and Brahmakāya (*Dīgha Nikāya*, III, 84), or again in the Tevijja Sutta,[113] where it is affirmed that the enlightened Bhikkhu may well attain to union with Brahmā, "who is the same." As we shall presently see, this virtual identification of Buddha with Brahmā has also its equivalents in iconographic representation.

It will be understood, of course, that in the *Saddharma Puṇḍarīka* the Buddha is speaking (Fig. 30) throughout not as the Word, for the Word (Dharma) is without origin (*anutpattika*), and non-existent, not like the Sambhogakāya Buddha manifested as it is in itself, which would be impossible. The Word does not speak, it is moved or taught (*pravartita, deśita*); [114] Buddha as Cakravartin is not the permissive, but the immediate, cause of the Turning of the Word-wheel. As Crowned King of the Word, *dharmarājā paṭṭabaddha* (*SPt*, p. 417),[115] and Universal Sovereign, *cakravartin* (Maitreya-Asaṅga, *Uttaratantra*, I, 150), he displays to the assembled congregation of his spiritual sons the likeness of a Nature (*svabhāva*), Suchness (*tathatā*), Quiddity (*tattva*),Void (*śūnyatā*), Sameness (*samatā*), and Logosity (*dharmatā*) that are ineffable. That is, his manifestation in the station (*sthāna*) where he is, one Mt Gṛdhrakūṭa where he is always, is not of the Dharmakāya as such, but of the Dharma in a likeness, in the likeness of a Wheel, or the likeness of Gautama. What he reveals to his children, the Bodhisattvas, who alone are competent to the vision, is his Person in Majesty, the Sambhogakāya. That reflection (*pratibimba*) is in fact all that can be revealed to the angelic eye, for the attachment of *-kāya* to *dharma* is purely analogical, and must not be understood to mean that the Dharma has a form. At the same time his appearance in a designated body, Nirmāṇakāya, displaying the drama of Awakening eventfully, is for the sake of those living in the flesh in that day, or who may after the "Parinirvāṇa" (here the temporal and analogical equivalent of a Return at the End of Time) find their way to Awakening by means of the "traces" of the apparition.[116] Such temporal manifestations by way of *avatarana* are rare and precious, but he will "come again" as Maitreya Cf. Vedic Mitra as "Agni when enkindled," *Ṛg Veda*, III, 5, 4 and V, 3, 1.

The foregoing evidences of the virtual identification of the Buddha in Majesty with Brahmā-Prājapati enthroned in the supra-mundane Empyrean heavens are paralleled by the iconographic prescription of the *Bṛhat Saṁhitā*, LVIII, 44, "The Buddha is to be shown seated on a lotus, like the Father of the World" (*padmāsanopaviṣṭhaḥ piteva jagato bhaved buddhaḥ*).[117] The Buddha is in fact represented *padmāsana*, *kamalāsana*, from late Āndhra times onwards, that is almost from the beginning of the anthropomorphic inconography. In the common representation of a Buddha triad, the Buddha being seated or standing between a pair of Bodhisattvas, the latter are supported by paired lotuses springing from the same stem, and such triads may be compared from more than one point of view with the Several Angels (*viśve devāḥ*) of the Upaniṣads and Vedas, where the Unity of the primordial Agni is represented in a trinity of aspects; the Buddha triads, for example, corresponding iconographically to such representations of the Trinity as appear in the Burmese relief (Fig. 16). The ontology is the same, whether the stem of the Buddha-lotus be prolonged downwards and there supported by paired Nāgas representative of the Waters (as at Kārlī) (Fig. 29), or the stem of the Brahmā-lotus rises from the navel of Nārāyaṇa (Fig. B, p. 36), originally Varuṇa, recumbent on the Waters.

An equivalence can be demonstrated also from many points of view between the Buddha paradises (Sukhāvatī, etc.) and the Brahmalokas,[118] and more specifically between the thrones of Buddha and of Brahmā when the throne is thought of as *pallaṅka*, Skr. *paryaṅka*, rather than as *padmāsana*. Thus, access to the Brahmaloka is by a crossing of the river Vijarā, "casting off of change-and-decay," which crossing must be effected "only be the Intellect" and involves a shaking off of all the pairs of opposites, including good and evil; the city of Brahmā is called Sālajya, his abode (*saṁshtāna*) Aparājita ("Unconquerable"), the throne-room (*pramita*) Vibhu ("Space"). The *Kauṣītaki Up.*, I, 3, and 5, further describes the footstool (*āsandī*)[119] and the throne (*paryaṅka*) of Brahmā: the former is called Vicakṣaṇā, "Discernment" and is explained as Prajñā, "Omniscience" or "Perfect Wisdom," the latter is called Amitaujas, "Limitless Splendor" or "Limitless Power" (the designation applies to Indra in *Ṛg Veda*, I, 11, 4), and explained as Prāṇa, "Spirit" or "Life," and it is "only by Prajñā that one ascends the throne."[120] Here the last assertion corresponds to *SP*, V, 75, "no Extinction without Omniscience," as cited below; and the name of the throne is equivalent to Amitābha, a Buddha name denoting "Limitless Light," and its nature, Prāṇa, to Amitāyus, "Limitless Life," which is another epithet of the same Buddha, who represents the Sambhogakāya aspect of Gautama.

The Buddha throne, however, is usually a lotus, or lotus- and lion-throne combined; the Boddhisattvas, and all who are born again in Buddha paradises, are similarly lotus-supported, but on smaller flowers. So the predications of future enlightenment generally include such promises as "shall appear seated in the cup of a lotus on a lion-throne in Paradise" (*SPt*, p. 419); "there the Leader Amitābha is seated in the lovely glistening cup of a lotus (*padmagarbhe*),[121] on a lion-throne (*siṁhāsane*) . . . there the Sons of the Conqueror come into existence (*upapāduka*) seated in the pure cups of lotuses" (*SP*, XXIV, 31, 32, cf. *Mahā-Sukhāvatī-vyūha*, 16, 40 and 41).[122] In these passages, *upapāduka* has generally been rendered "miraculously born," but the direct sense of *upapad* is simply "to enter into any state," "to appear," "come into a given mode of existence"; it is not miraculously but inevitably that a certain degree of enlightenment results in a future birth in a Buddha paradise. On the other hand, *upapāduka* contrasts with *anutpattika*, "unoriginated," applicable to the Dharma as being precisely that which does not come into existence, the Buddha being merely an image, *ākṛti*, of the Dharma, existent in the world, like the *mūrta* Brahman, viz. Brahmā. The primary ontological significance of the lotus is precisely with respect to this existence *astitva*, *sthāyitā*, *sthiti*, a being "firmly grounded in the possibilities of existence," commonly called the Waters, *padmāsana* and *vajrāsana* are equally symbols of the *sthāyitā*: both express visually *sadā sthita*, and *tiṣṭhati*, with respect to the Buddha or any Angel; both differentiate the station of Sambhogakāya from that of the Dharmakāya, which is inaccessible even to the angelic eye.

Sthāyitā in any Buddha paradise, whether with respect to the Buddha there manifested, or to his sons and disciples the Bodhisattvas and Pratyeka Buddhas, is an immortality until the end of time, viz. until the lifetime of the Buddha lord of the field or cosmos is fulfilled, not the absolute eternity of the Dharmatā, Parinirvāṇa, which never having come into existence can never pass away. The Bodhisattva in whom the Wisdom-heart (*bodhicitta*) has opened (*utpanna*), and who is thereby born (*upapāduka*, *upapattika*) in the pure cup of a paradisiac lotus, whence he beholds the Buddha face to face, is indeed no longer involved in the world-flux (*saṁsāra*), but neither has he reached *nirvāṇa*, much less *parinirvāṇa*, however he may imagine: "that is a resting-place (*viśrāma*), not a Return (*nirvṛti*); it is by accommodation (*upāya*) that the Buddhas teach this doctrine (*naya*, viz. of a Paradise), actually there is no Extinction (*nirvāṇa*) without omniscience (*sarvajñatva*), strive for That" (*SP*, V, 74, 75).[123] Only when that Omniscience has been attained can the disciple be said to have become a Buddha, *the* Buddha; then like Prabhūtaratna he sits with the Buddha on one and the same throne, being in fact the Buddha, Tathāgata, though intelligibly and apparently to the angelic eye still "himself." As a Buddha, *the* Buddha, he is still existent, *sa-upādi-sesa*, until the end of time, *kalpānta*, in saecula saeculorum. But his appearance as a Crowned King of the Word is but the presented aspect of this being; in reality he faces both ways, like Agni *pathāṁ visarge* (RV X.5.6; cf. *Dhammapada*, 282, *dvedhāpatha*) seeing at once the operation of and the Sameness of All Principles. Not Absolutely Extinguished (*parinirvāta*), nor beyond the ken of the angelic eye, he "sees without seeing" (*paśyaty apaśyanayā*), or sees ideally, the Threefold World "as is" (*yathābhūta*); he is not merely Mover of the Wheel (*dharmacakravartin*), but also "has the Word as his intrinsic nature," *svabhāva-dharma-samanvāgata* (*SPt*, p. 481). He sees that Nirvāṇa and Saṁsāra are the same, he knows, he is the Sameness of all Principles (*dharmā*);[124] he is omniscient of the identity of the world and the abyss, actuality and possibility, active and passive aspects of the infinite, though he has still a "residual existential element." He has become the Universal *jīvanmukta,* super-individually existent as the One Great Person.[125]

From the one point of view he sees only the "patient-stillness of the unoriginated Word" (*anutpattika-dharma-kṣānti*), from the other and same point of view he sees the same Word in rotation (*pravartana*) or procession (*prasaraṇa*) as the causal world of birth and death, the wandering-place of living beings ignorant of a reversion (*nivṛtti*) or recession (*niḥsaraṇa*).[126] So feeling a great tenderness (*karunā*) towards his world, his "Buddha-field," he reveals the Word by means of various alternative-formulations (*dharma-paryāya*), either directly, or by means of other teachers; for he is infinitely skilful (*kuśala*) in the use of convenient means (*upāya*) adapted to the capacity (*bala*) of every auditor.[127]

The *Saddharma Puṇḍarīka*, summarized above, may be described as the most important of the Mahāyāna *dharma-paryāyas*, equally from ontological and iconographic points of view. But that is not all. An understanding of the ontology is essential also for the student of "art," who must realize that a work of art cannot be "understood" or rightly "valued" or "criticized" apart from the form which is its *raison d'être*. Content is not *post factum*, but *causa faciendi*; the significance of things well and truly made is with respect to the end for which they are made.[128] As religious art is never an end in itself, but always a means of communication, it can only be called "good" or "bad" in so far as it actually expresses and conveys as given "idea"; rational judgment of a given work can only be based on a comparison of the substance with its determining form. How then can one who ignores the idea or form embodied in a work of art be qualified to "criticize" it? All that such a one can do is to say that he knows nothing of art, but knows what he likes.

Let us admit the possibility of "aesthetic experience," and that this possibility is independent of the theme, whatever it may have been. This experience will be realized in an assimilation of the perceiving consciousness to the form of the thing considered. Inasmuch as "Buddhism" is the "form" of Buddhist art, it follows that an understanding of Buddhism is indispensable, not only for a rational interpretation of the iconography, in which the logic of the work is expressed, but also as prerequisite to "aesthetic experience." To assert that "aesthetic experience" of Buddhist art is possible without an *a priori* knowledge of Buddhism embodies this element of truth, that the content of Buddhism is not merely specific, but also universal, and that in so far as our experience is not, for example, merely specifically Christian, but Christian universally, we do already possess an *a priori* knowledge of Buddhism; one does not know who, however, can lay claim to so profound an understanding of any religious art as to enable him to say that he knows so much of the form of religious art that he need know no more.

Returning now to the iconography or symbolism of our art: we read in Hsüan-tsang, *Life*, Ch. III (Beal, p. 103), that the adamantine throne (*vajrāsana*) which is in the centre of the Bodhimaṇḍa was perfected at the beginning of the Bhadra Kalpa, the present aeon, and rose up when the world was brought into existence. It is at the very centre of the Universe, and extends downwards to the "golden wheel"; it is about a hundred paces round. That it is called adamant means that it is pure and indestructible. Without its support the Earth could not endure; were the seat not admantine, there would be no place in the world that could support the Adamantine At-one-ment (*vajra-samādhi*). Here whoever desires to conquer Māra and to attain to perfect wisdom must take his seat; were it essayed elsewhere, the Earth would be overturned. The thousand Buddhas of the present aeon have all attained their emancipation here. If the world were shaken to its foundations, the Bodhimaṇḍa would not be moved.[129]

Here the only important point added to what we already knew from texts previously cited is the explanation that the Bodhimaṇḍa represents a section on the terrestrial plane of the axis of the universe, which axis extends downwards to the "golden wheel," and on which the stability of the Earth depends. What is meant by that "golden wheel" may be learnt from Vasubandhu's *Abhidharmakośa*, III, 45 ff., Poussin, II, 138 ff., where the "world-receptacle" (*bhājanaloka*) is described.[130] The Universe is conceived of as consisting of so many superimposed "circles" (*maṇḍala*): nethermost is the circle of Space (*ākāśa-maṇḍala*), "solid" and of "immeasurable" circumference, and 1,600,000 *yojanas* in thickness; over and on this rests the circle of the Waters, 1,120,000 *yojanas* in thickness and 1,203,450 in circumference.[131] The surface of these Waters, just as in the Brahmanical cosmology and in Genesis, is stirred by the dawn wind of creation, which is impelled by the latent causality of past events. The foam of the Waters[a] solidifies to form the golden circle (*kañcana-maṇḍala*) or "Land of Gold" (*kañcana-bhūmi*),[132] the same as Hsüan-tsang's "golden wheel" and representing the "foundations of the earth" firmly established amidst the possibilities of existence. The Land of Gold has a diameter equal to that of the Waters, and displaces 120,000 *yojanas* of their depth. The surface of the Land of Gold is the Round of the World, with its mountains (Meru, etc.), continents (the four *dvīpas*), seas, and outwall (*cakra-vāḍa*). Of these continents, or rather "islands," our terrestrial world Jambudvīpa lies to the south of Meru, which rises in the centre of the whole Universe, and extends from the Waters below to Heaven above, as world-pillar and world-axis. "Midmost in Jambudvīpa, and resting on the Land of Gold, is the *vajrāsana* on which the Bodhisattva takes his seat to realize the *vajropama samādhi*[133] and so become an Arhat or Buddha: no

[a] Foam of the waters: *SB* VI.1.3, cf. NA notes p. 14.

other place, no other person, could support the Bodhisattva's *samādhi*."

It is clear that Hsüan-tsang merely repeats the ancient tradition of the Buddha-throne as it had been told to him, or as he might have read it in the texts from which we have quoted above. It is true that the centre of Jambudvīpa cannot be regarded, unless analogically, as the actual (local) centre of the entire Universe, for that centre is on the axis of Mt Meru. In the same way with respect to this world, which is the particular Buddha-field of the Tathāgata *quo* Śākyamuni, it will be remarked that the Bodhimaṇḍa at Bodhgayā, and the summit of Mt Gṛdhrakūṭa where the Sambhogakāya is "always" revealed, are not locally on one and the same axis or meridian. That should serve to remind us that the "centre of the Universe" is not a spot fixed in space, but (as will be further shown below) as psychological centre, the focal point of consciousness, not *bahir-* but *antar-bhūtasya.*[134]

In actual iconography, the axial extension of the Buddha's throne or footstool may be clearly shown. In the case of a *padmāsana* or *padmapīṭha* the supporting axis, viz., the stem, extends downwards through the Earth into the depth of the Waters, where it is upheld by paired Nāgas, as representative genii of the nether Waters.[135] Of this we have an excellent example in the Sambhogakāya relief of Gupta age at Kārlī (Fig. 29, also Bachhofer, *Early Indian Sculpture*, Pl. 68, central panel). Here, within a pillared structure which may be compared to Brahmā's throne-room Vibhu, the Buddha is seated on a lion-throne, with his feet supported by a lotus. To left and right are the Bodhisattvas Avalokiteśvara and Maitreya, representative of the congregation assembled on Mt Gṛdhrakūṭa; they are standing upon lotus supports. Immediately below the Buddha's lotus is a Dharmacakra, flanked by paired deer, indicative of place and event, viz. the Deer Park at Sārnāth and the First Sermon, *prathamadeśanā*. At this level is represented the earth-plane (*vasudhā-tala*), extending horizontally to left and right, but interrupted centrally where the descending axis penetrates it. The "lotus-capital" of the descending axis has now a more bulbous form, but taking wheel and pillar together, we recognize without difficulty an original formula constantly met with in the earliest Buddhist art. The rounded masses under the earth-plane correspond in position to the "foundations of the earth," the Land of Gold. All below this represents the Waters, the support given by the paired Nāgas indicating the firm establishment of the cosmic pillar in the nether sea of possibility. Above the Buddha's head, supported by angels commonly spoken of as Vidhyādharas (Cherubim), is *stūpa*,[136] symbol of the Parinirvāṇa, and that it is thus above and removed from him corresponds to the fact that he is not yet transcendentally *parinirvāta*, for as we have seen, the temporal decease represented not the realization, but only the analogy, of the final Parinirvāṇa. There is a similar relief at Kondivte.

When the throne is alternatively a *paryaṅka* and thought of as the *vajrāsana*, a condition corresponding to Hsüan-tsang's conception, the supporting axis is shown as extended downwards into the Land of Gold, and there supported by a Guhyaka Yakṣa.[137] An admirable illustration of this can be cited in the case of the pedestal (Fig. 41) of the Yakushi Buddha of the Kondo, a Japanese work of the eighth century (*Japanese Temples and Their Treasures*, Pl. 206: *Yakushiji Ōkagami*, II, Tokyo, 1922). Here the flat surface of the rectangular throne is an earth-plane (*vasudhā-tala*), the solid body of the pedestal corresponding to the Land of Gold. On the front side of the pedestal is represented a vertical axis extending downwards to the lower margin of the block, where it is supported by a crouching Yakṣa Atlant.[138] This representation is exactly analogous to that of the Guḍimallan liṅgam (Fig. 43 and my *History*, Fig. 66), nor need the point be labored here that the Śiva liṅgam, established in the Land of Gold (Hāṭaka) and extending thence to Heaven above, represents another aspect of the one axis of the Universe. The ornamental form of the Yakushi axis recalls that of the Dharmacakra pillars represented at Amarāvatī (cf. Figs. 2, 3, 12) (e.g. my *History*, Fig. 136, right and left), and shows clearly the jointed structure of the axis. On the side of the Yakushi pedestal (Fig. 41), right and left of the axis, and as though to emphasize the character of the central supporting Atlant Yakṣa, are other figures of the same type, crouching within and peering out of caverns, which are their chambers in the bowels of the earth; similar representations are to be seen on the other faces of the pedestal. Below the level representing the base of the Land of Gold are four strata representing the Waters; on the uppermost of these, centrally on each side, are theriomorphic emblems of the Four Quarters, those on the front side being a tortoise and a snake, representing the North (the Buddha therefore "is" in the North and faces South); the lowest stratum consists of a lotus-petal moulding, which may here be understood to mean the nethermost Waters as the ultimate "ground" of all that is above them and established in them.

A part of what has been independently deduced and demonstrated above has also been stated by M. Mus in his admirable monograph, *Le Buddha paré*, etc., previously cited. For example, "The throne of the Law is the symbol par excellence of the teaching, and even of the state of Buddhahood" (p. 243); "It cannot be conceived that the Body of Beatitude (Sambhogakāya) could have been seated anywhere else than on the angelic lotus, far above the throne to be seen in the holy place (Bodhgayā)" (p. 204); "The holy throne combines in itself three appearances, corresponding to those of the Three bodies" (p. 272); "The prolongation of the stem, which is the axis of the sensible world, bears at the summit of the universe the spiritual lotus-throne of the Sambhogakāya" (p. 243).[139] M. Mus points out further that the lotus-throne which supports the Word as it is in itself can be imagined only analogically; that transcendental throne could no more than the Word itself be conceived of as visible even to the angelic eye, for the being of the Word is strictly noumenal, *un être verbal* (*nāmavat*), not contained by, only indicated by, the thought and spoken words.[a]

We have thus discovered in the texts a sufficient explanation of the most characteristic formulae of the iconography. We now return to and conclude with the problem of the place of the Buddha's throne; i.e., of course, a special case of the general problem of the meaning of "immanence." We have already surmised that by the centre of the Universe, the navel of immortality, and similar expressions there is to be understood not a determinable spot, but a spiritual centre and point of consciousness "where every where and every when is focussed"; that the traditional cosmology is in fact far more pneumatology than a cosmic geography. That is explicitly enunciated in the pre-Buddhist doctrine of the Lotus of the Heart, as ground whereon and space wherein all existence is unfolded. It seems that no use of this significant image was actually made in Buddhist texts, but it can easily be shown, and has indeed already been shown in other ways, that Buddhahood, Nirvāṇa, is not in any place, but represents a state of being, viz. being universally; the Buddha-throne can only be established "within you," *antarbhūtasya*. The adamantine throne is the stability of the adamantine intellect. Knowledge of the Buddha is not the knowledge of any "thing," but a consummation of the process of de-

[a]Mus, 1934, p. 263 "texte et images devraient ainsi être considérés comme l'empreinte dans des matières diverses d'un même archétype transcendent."

"text and image should thus be considered as the imprint of a same transcendent archetype in diverse materials".

Mus, p. 158 . . . "aucune réalité ne réside dans l'aspect que le Buddha prend aux yeux d'une créature . . . cette apparence exprime, en tout cas, un rapport, une relation entre l'auditoire et la réalité qu'il preçoit dans la personne de son maître."

"there is no reality in the aspect which the Buddha assumes in the eyes of a creature . . . anyway, this appearance expresses as an alliance and relationship between the audience and the reality which it perceives in the nature of its Lord."

mentation of discriminative perception, *viññānassa nirodha* = *ceto-vimutti*, *Dīgha Nikāya*, I, 223, and *Anguttara Nikāya*, I,124, cf. *mano niroddhavyaṁ hṛdi*, *Maitri Up.*, VI, 34 and *amani-bhāva* in *Maitrī Up.* VI. 34 "Never again shall thou build me a house". So in his "Song of Victory" (*Nidānakathā*, I, 76 = *Dhammapada*, 154) the Buddha exclaims, "The key-plate of the roof has been shattered, intellect has reached the dissolution of its composite formulations."[140] That is to say that the Comprehensor, emancipated from all dialectic understanding, knows and is the Only Principle; in the Act-of-Identity (*samādhi*) he is the Sameness of All Priniciples.[141] He is *nibbuta, nirvāta,* the Supreme Identity has been touched, the Buddha essence is liberated from duration; yet speaking *qua* the Great Person; he cannot say that he is Absolutely Extinguished, he must say that he is not "yet" Absolutely Extinguished, *quâ parinirvāta*, he would not be a Person. The unity of Being and Non-being can *speak* only as Being, only as Being can he be *spoken of* or represented in a likeness.

One further word on Buddhahood and the concepts of Nirvāṇa and Parinirvāṇa. Negative expressions are inevitable, merely because all affirmation is the enunciation of a limiting condition; denial is a double negative, affirming absence of conditions, whereof the In-finite *qua* in-finite, is necessarily indigent. That has been recognized again and again also in Europe; cf. Maimonides, *Guide for the Perplexed*, I, Ch. 59, "Supreficial thinkers . . . ask "Is that thing existing in the Creator, or not?' . . . by each additional negative attribute you advance toward the knowledge of god"; Eckhart, I, 87, "Nothing true can be spoken of God"; Dante, *Convivio*, III, 15, ". . . certain things which our intellect cannot behold . . . we cannot understand what they are except by denying things of them." There is nothing here that the adamantine mind can fear; in the words of the *Taittirīya Upaniṣad*, II, 7, "Truly, when one finds a fearless foundation (*pratiṣṭhā*) in that which is invisible (*adṛśya*), not-selfed (*anātmya*), ineffable (*anirukta*), homeless (*anilayana*), then has he attained to fearlessness (*abhayaṁ gata*)." Cf. *ŚB*, VII.2.2.14, "What is silent (*tūṣṇīm-maunam*, the characteristic state of the *muni*) is unexpounded (*aniruktam*), and what is unexpounded is everything (*sarvam*)."

Eckhart and Blake alone should have sufficed to demonstrate the naïveté of the view that Buddhism is proven "atheistic" by its negative phraseology. According to Eckhart, "It is more necessary to perfection that the soul lose God than that she lose creatures . . . the soul honors God most in being quit of God (I, 274) . . . the fastidious soul (cf. Buddhist *ariya*) can rest her understanding on nothing that has name. She escapes from every name into the nameless nothingness (I, 373) . . . this is the death of the spirit . . . the spirit puts its own self to death . . . and remains in the unity of the divine nature. . . . These are the blessed dead. . . . No one can be buried and beatified in the Godhead who has not died to God (I, 411) . . . the Godhead is as void as though it were not. . . . In this state we are as free as when we were not: free as the Godhead in its non-existence (I, 381-2). . . . She (the soul) sinks for evermore in the depths of this naught. She sinks and drowns: she drowns to her own aught. But the naught that sinks can never comprehend the naught it sinks in (I, 373)."[a] So also Blake, "I would go down unto Annihilation and Eternal Death, lest the Last Judgment come and find me Unannihilate, and I be seiz'd and giv'n into the hands of my own Selfhood." Those who cannot bear with such thought as this can never bear with Buddhism, nor understand the ultimate significance of Buddhist art.

Any change of state is a death. Christian tradition alludes to "three deaths of the soul," namely (1) the death to self-will, which death implies the attainment of angelic being, a state of grace, (2) the death of the soul to its own separate form, implying a conscious conformity to the Principal Being, and (3) a death, called a Drowning, in Waters where God is unknown to himself, unknown as oneself; there as Eckhart expresses it the soul is "free as the Godhead in its non-existence." In corresponding Buddhist formulation we have a lower mortification, (1) that of the man who adopts the homeless life, and attains to so much Awakening as to ensure his birth in a Buddha paradise, (2) the attainment of Buddhahood, Nirvāṇa, extinction of self, but with residual existential elements; and (3) Extinction Absolute, Parinirvāṇa without residual factors of existence. To any of these deaths can be applied the thought of Chuang Tzŭ, "How do I know that he who dreads to die is not as a child who has lost the way and cannot find his home?" He who shrinks from the Drowning, from Death, Privation, Extinction, Night, may reflect, *Mors januva vitae*. Unitary Beings, that is only One, both His and ours, even a stone has being, is at the same time fontal and inflowing, *saṁsaraṇa, niḥsaraṇa*[142] "He who is Death is likewise the Year, the Father of his children,"[143] "Pillar of Life, at the parting of the Ways . . . there, where Life was erst, insists our Agni, First-born of the Law,"[144] "born ever and again."[145] If then we lay aside all thought of temporal succession, all considerations of mortality, viz. of eventful birth and death, we shall understand that Life and Death, Being and Non-being,

[a] Eckhart 1.149 "The kingdom of God is for none but the thoroughly dead".

Nirvāṇa and Parinirvāṇa, are incessant aspects of That which is emancipate from all possible contingency, even from such accidents of Being as the phrase "not yet Absolutely Extinguished" implies. "That" is neither "here" nor "there," but "within you," *antarbhūtasya khe*, in the Calyx of the Heart.

All this the Buddha refused to discuss. His business was to proclaim as Way (*mārga, pantha*), he would not speak of That, the Goal (*artha*) whereof nothing can be spoken truly or intelligibly. How indeed, as Confucius expresses it, should those who have not yet understood Life, aspire to comprehend Death? Whilst we are on the way, we are not there. We can then only take the Buddha as he *is*, as manifested operative presence, and strive to realize ourself as Same, by following his or any alternatively formulated Way, taught by himself or any "other" Comprehensor. That Way is mapped, not only in spoken words, but equally in painted or sculptured iconographies. These "works of art"[146] are footprints of the Law," "traces of the Buddha," which we cannot say that we have really heard or seen, otherwise than by merely animal perception, unless we have seen through them at least a shadow of the form by which they are what they are. Let us not forget that the Brahmanical or Buddhist craftsman was required to *be* that which he was commissioned to *represent*, and that only in so far as we can be again the Same, can we begin to understand his operation.

To resume: it has been shown by reference to chapter and verse of canonical texts, both Buddhist and pre-Buddhist, that the Buddha, humanly presented, is in fact connatural with the Vedic Agni, and that Buddhist symbolism, far from being an isolated language, is proper to the one great tradition which has persisted from the Vedic or a pre-Vedic period until now. The lotus denotes ontologically a firm establishment amongst the possibilities of existence, denotes a birth and manifestation primarily in the intelligible, or also and consequently in the sensible, world; while it denotes ethically, detachment, as of one who is in the world but not of it. The throne of deity is a lotus-throne from the foregoing points of view; as impartite and immovable, it is adamantine; as royal, it is a lion-throne. The Tathāgata, Buddha, seated on such a throne, standing on such a pedestal, affirms an infinite negation, a sable stillness against which his golden Person shines resplendent, unconfined by any form, but omniform. As crowned King of the Word he utters to angelic ears as much as can be spoken of the silence, that is our existence.[147] As an individual teacher with a given name, he plays a part and proclaims a Way. From any point of view his intellect is adamantine, regal, and intangible. The foundations of his manifestation are established in the depths of the upper and the nether seas: he is the Axis of the Universe, in whom it comes to be and goes to be not. By whatever name, personal or essential, the Spoken Word, the Wheel in Revolution, the Tree of Life, or Fiery Pillar, he may be called, in whatever form he may be imagined, who surely takes the forms imagined by his worshippers, for all convenient means are at his command, he, Tathāgata, Agni Vaiśvānara, Brahmā-Prajāpati, Christ, or Idea of Muḥammad, is one and the same, his throne is single. As Kabīr expresses it, echoing classic formulae in what is still the lingua franca of a hundred million speakers:

> What a wonderful lotus it is that blooms at the heart of the wheel; who are its comprehensors?
> There in the midst thunders the self-supported lion-throne, there the Great Person shines resplendent.[148]

NOTES

NOTES

1 (*page 21*). The likeness of any thing as such, presented to the eye's intrinsic faculty, is merely an occasion of sensation, and necessarily without meaning, recognition being an animal, not an intellectual operation.

2 (*page 21*). In one sense, though not essentially, the aniconic image may be regarded as *more* a likeness of Him, that is in so far as it reminds us of the relative unimportance of the human mode, as merely a particular case amongst the possibilities of existence.

3 (*page 21*). Cf. *Jaiminīya Upaniṣad Brāhmaṇa*, III, 32, "This the Sātyakīrtas say: 'As to the Angel whom we worship, of him we say that there is one aspect in the cow, another in beasts of burden (horses), another in the elephant, another in man (*puruṣa*), another in all existences; such is the Angel's omni-aspectuality (*sarvaṁ rūpaṁ*).' That same single aspect is the Spirit (*prāṇa*)."

"Just as little" should be noted, for this is not a pantheistic point of view, it is merely "not anthropocentric." St. Francis also preached to the birds and fishes, for "the whole creation groaneth and travailleth together."

4 (*page 22*). A prohibition of this kind is alluded to in Ch. 48 of the *Vinaya* of the Sarvāstivādins. See Waley in "Mélanges chinois et boudhiques," *Inst. Belge des Hautes Études Chinoises*, I, 1932, 352. Compare Nanda's refusal to provide biographical material for the representation of the events of the Buddha's life in a drama, related in the Kah-gyur (Schiefner, *Tibetan Tales*, no. xiii). With *tathāgata*, or *tathâgata* cf. *ā agāt*, *Ṛg Veda*, X, 53, 1, with reference to Agni.

5 (*page 22*). That of Strzygowski's "Mazdean art," but this is no more Iranian than Indian.

6 (*page 22*). A *cetiya*, as appears from the present text and elsewhere, is not primarily a building, but any object made use of as a sacred symbol or cult object. A shrine in the sense "temple" is *cetiya-ghara*. Cf., my *Yakṣas*, I and II, *passim*, and B.C. Law, "'Ċetiya' in the Buddhist Literature," *Studia Indo-Iranica*, 1931, pp. 42-48. For derivation of *Caitya*: "That which has been thought of", "imagined", "built in imagination" See *SB* VI. 2.3.1 *cetayadhvaṁ* i.e. *citiṁ icchate* "bethink ye i.e. "wish for a feeling". *RV* VI.1.5 agni, *cetyaḥ*, "to be known as" or "to be thought upon as".

7 (*page 22*). From *paribhoga*, objects used by or in connection with the person; thus equally in the case of the dead or absent person, traces or relics other than any part of the body itself. In the present case, for example, the Buddha's begging bowl, garments, the tree under which he attained enlightenment, the hut occupied by him; and probably, though more abstractly, such "things" as the wheel which he set in motion in Benares. The *sārīraka* and *pāribhogaka cetiyas* are then precisely those symbols which are alluded to as "traces" (*dhātu*) in the *Saddharma Puṇḍarīka*; the term *dhātu* appearing also in *dhātu-gabba* = *dāgaba* = *thūpa* = *stūpa*, "tope."

8 (*page 26*). *Ṛg Veda*, I, 24, 7; IV, 13, 5; X, 82, 5 (?); *Atharva Veda*, X, 7, 38; *Chāndogya Up.*, VI, 8, 4; VI, 11, 1; VI, 12, 2; *Śvetāśvatara Up.*, III, 9; *Taittirīya Up.*, I, 10. For the pre-Buddhist tree cults and their survival in Buddhist ritual see my *Yakṣas*, Pts. I and II, Washington, 1928 and 1931, and "Early Indian Architecture, II, Bodhigharas," in *Eastern Art*, III, 1931.

9 (*page 26*). Regarding the "up" or "down" of the roots and branches, it should be observed that this is not a question of local direction: if certain texts say "down" as if from Waters enclosing the *brahmāṇḍa*, and the representations are of upward growth, as if from a given platform of being, both are equally correct, in that the Waters are no less omnipresent substance than the Self is omnipresent essence. There is no question so far of "aerial roots"; these are alluded to only in the *Aitareya Brāhmaṇa*, VIII, 31, and *Bhagavad Gītā*, XV, 2, where they are explained as the "bonds of works."

10 (*page 26*). Śaṅkarācārya interprets *rerivā* (*Taittirīya Up.*, I, 10) as either "mover" or "remover" (for the latter implication cf. *Bhagavad Gītā*, XV, 3, *aśvatthaṁ . . . chittvā*): "mover" is most appropriate in our text, but either sense would be intelligible, inasmuch as *pravṛtti* and *nivṛtti*, outflow and inflow, spiration and despiration, are simultaneous movements of the cosmic "puls" of the Self.

Vedic "*yakṣa*," in its general application to Varuṇa, latter Brahman, represents in our view an essential name of the manifested deity as mover in the Tree of Life.

11 (*page 28*). The tree itself is analogically the Great Awakening, not merely the sign of the place where the Awakening was accomplished, which from the standpoint of the developed Buddhology was not an event in Time. Cf. *pratyabudhyata*, "awakened," "illuminated," with reference to angelic, prophetic, or human knowledge of Brahman, whereby the one awakened is identified with That, *Bṛhadāraṇyaka Up.*, I, 4, 10; and *pratibodhaviditaṁ matam amṛtatvaṁ hi vindate, ātmanā vindate vīryam vidyayā vindate amṛtam*, "It (brahman) is thought of as known with Awakening, for thus one finds what is deathless; by the self one finds the virile-strength, by knowledge one finds the Deathless," *Jaiminīya Upaniṣad Brāhmaṇa*, IV, 19.

Budh is primarily "to awaken," and metaphysically, from the sleep of potentiality to actuality of operation; in this sense we find in the *Ṛg Veda* not only *uṣarbudh*, but the verbal form *abodhi*, "awakened" (I, 157, 1; III, 5, 1; V, 1, 1; VII, 9, 1), applied to Agni, who is the Enlightener rather than the Enlightened. Hence we prefer to the familiar "Great Enlightenment" the rendering "Great Awakening" for *mahāsambodhi*; and for *bodhi-vṛkṣa*, "Tree of Awakening" to "Wisdom-tree." If it be desired to retain the notion of illumination, which is inherent in this sense that the awakening is a beginning to shine, it should be with full awareness that the Great Awakening is with reference not only to him who wakes, but also to those on whom he shines. The Mahāsambodhi is in fact the Buddha's true birth into the worlds, all that precedes properly belonging to the Interior Operation, though developed in the texts quasi-historically.

Pali Commentators explain *budh* by *avagamane*, "coming down," tantamount to *avacaraṇa*, "descent," cf. *avaś caran*, of Agni, *Ṛg Veda*, VI, 9, 3, by *bodhane* "awakening"; and as "to rise up" (*uṭṭhahati, Atthasālinī*, p. 217: cf. *ud asthāt*, of Agni, *Ṛg Veda*, IV, 18, 5; Sāyaṇa on V, 19, 1, *sthitaṁ padārthajātam*, "*sthā* means to be born"; and *ṭhitako . . . paṭhaviyaṁ patiṭṭhāya, Nidānakathā*, p. 53) from the sleep of the kindred of the slime (*kilesa-santāna-niddāya*), or to understand the Four Ariyan Truths, or to realize *Nibbāna*." Here it can be clearly seen how edifying secondary meanings have been given to the root which meant originally to "come into existence," or "be manifested," thus preserving the concept of *upodsarpaṇa*. *Kilesa* (Skr. *kleśa*) has generally in fact a moral value in Pali Buddhism, but the fundamental sense of "slime," and the involved notion of "germinal heat" (*kilissati* = *upatāpe*, *Dhtp.*, 445 and *Dhtm.*, 686), cf. *kliś*, "to suffer," and *ciklīta* = "slime" in *Śrīsūkta*, 12, and the imagery of the lotus, born in the mud and yet unstained (p. 39), whereas in the *Śrīsūkta*, 11 and 17, we have merely *kardamena prajā sraṣṭā sambhūtiṁ gamayāmasi* "we thy children emanated from the mud would go forth into existence." The force of these comparisons is to show that the language of Pali Buddhism is inherited directly from Vedic sources, though generally with an ethical in place of the originally metaphysical application. In the *Ṛg Veda*, the Awakening is to Existence, in Buddhism to Non-existence. The contrast is less than might appear at first sight, for the "Turning of the Principal Wheel" has neither beginning nor end (*dharmaṁca deśemyahu nityakālam, Saddharma Puṇḍarīka*, XV, 1, or as *Ṛg Veda*, V, 58, 5 expresses it, "none of the spokes is last in order"); Dawn and Sunset, Life and Death, follow each other in unending sequence, and from the standpoint of the Understanding of Sameness (*samatājñāna*) this is not really a sequence but an act in simultaneity.

12 (*page 28*). On *tejas* in Buddhism see J. Ph. Vogel, "Het Sanskrit woord tejas (= gloed, vuur) in de beteeknis van magische kraft," *Med. K. Akad. Wet., afd. Letterkunde*, 70, B, 4, Amsterdam, 1930. An error should be corrected here, viz. p. 107 and Pl. II, for on the occasion of "Indra's visit" the Buddha's grotto is illuminated, not by his own *tejas*, but by that of the visiting angels, as expressly stated in *Dīgha Nikāya*, II, 264 and 269. *Tejas* as one of the "five elements" (e.g. in *Śvetāśvatara Upaniṣad*, VI, 2) corresponds to "phlogiston," Böhme's "ignited air."

13 (*page 28*). Also Fergusson, *Tree and Serpent Worship*, Pl. LXVII, mid-left, and LXX, top-centre and mid-right; Bachhofer, *Early Indian Sculpture,* Pl. 114, left-centre.

14 (*page 28*). The fiery pillars are mentioned by Kramrisch, *Indian Sculpture*, 1933, note 209. The importance of the fiery element in Buddhist symbolism was recognized by Maisey, *Sanchi and its Remains*, 1892, Ch. X, and later by Foucher and Vogel in connection with the representation of shoulder-flames, the double miracle, etc. I have argued elsewhere (*A New Approach to the Vedas*, 1933, p. 43) that Agni Vaiśvānara, Christ, the idea of Muḥammad, and others, are ontologically identical Persons. The historical narrative of the Buddha's "life," for example, like that of the Christ's, must be regarded as a contraction or reflection of the cosmic relations; the Buddha as Gautama is an *incarnation* of Agni. Assuming that a historical Gautama may really have taught, the mere "man" is altogether hidden by the aegis of divinity, and surely would have willed it to have been so.

15 (*page 28*). In *Ṛg Veda*, I, 59, 1 and 2, Agni is "a pillar (*sthūṇa*) supporting the kindreds" (*janān*, viz. angels and men); in IV, 13, 5, "established as an angelic pillar (*skambha*) he rules-and-wards (*pāti*) the firmament" (*nāka,* that Middle Space, *antarikṣa,* in which all existence is extended); *ibid*., X, 5, 6, "He is a pillar (*skambha*) of life at the parting of the ways"; *ibid*., V, 29, 4, "Heaven and Earth he pillars-apart" (*vitaraṁ viṣkabhāyat*). That axis of the Universe is also, as stated explicitly in *ibid*., X, 89, 4, the axle-tree of the Solar Car, "by the axle of his wheeled car he indeed by his powers pillars-apart heaven and Earth" (*akṣeṇeva cakriyā śacībhir viṣvak tastambha pṛthivīṁ uta dyām*). In *Atharva Veda*, X, 8, 2, the pillar (*skambha*) is "all that is enspirited" (*sarvam ātmanvat*), and the entire hymn, X, 7, lauds the same pillar wherein all existence (*bhuvana*) is infixed (*ārpitā*);

this axis of the Universe (which is also the axle-tree of the Solar Car and the trunk of the Tree of Life), though single in its proper form (*svarūpa*, Dante's *forma universal, Paradiso*, XXXIII, "one simple Light, that in its depths encloses, as in a single volume, all that is scattered on the pages of the Universe)," is also the form of very different things (*viśvarūpa*). The Scholastic notion of *exemplarism* is implied, cf. Eckhart, I, 182, "Everything is pictured in His Providence," which corresponds again to the notion of the world-picture, "painted by the Self on the canvas of the Self," Śaṅkarācārya, *Svātmanirūpaṇa*, 95.

The axis of the Universe is coincident also with the fiery Śiva-liṅgam set up, according to the Devedāruvana legend, in the foundations of the Earth (*Hāṭaka*, the Land of Gold, see p. 531) and extending upwards to Heaven, see F.D.K. Bosch, "Het Linga-Heiligdom van Dinaja," *Tijdschr. K. Bat. Genootschap van Kunsten en Wetenschapen*, LXIV, 1924. The axis in its most general aspect corresponds to the vertical of the Cross, as to which, and for further details of application, see M. René Guénon's admirable treatise, *La Symbolisme de la Croix*, Paris, 1931. See also notes 100 and 139.

16 (*page 29*). Also Fergusson, *Tree and Serpent Worship*, cut on p. 114. At the very summit of the jewelled tree, hardly visible in the reproductions, is represented a royal umbrella, comparable to those which are seen above contemporary more realistically depicted Bodhi-trees, or stood over the early anthropomorphic Buddha images, and to the more elaborate baldachins of Far Eastern art. Considering the symbol of royalty above, and the marks of the *dharmacakra* on the feet, it could not have been more clearly asserted, "This is the anointed King of the Word."

17 (*page 29*). The formula is not remote from that employed in the representations of the Tree of Life in Assyrian art, cf. for example *Propyläen Kunstgeschicte*, II, Pls. 498, 499.

18 (*page 30*). Māra, Will-spirit, Kāmadeva, angel of love and death, Vedic Gandharva (whose "daughters" are three forms of the Vedic Apsaras), is the indwelling Yakṣa of the Tree itself. It is at the foot of the tree that any Yakṣa has his seat or altar (cf. my *Yakṣas*, I, Pl. 20, lower-left), where his presence is to be inferred or may be manifested in an image made with hands. So when the Bodhisattva takes his seat at the foot of the Wisdom-tree "with his back to its trunk," *bodhikhandam piṭṭhito*, *J.*, I, 71, he is trespassing on Māra's ground, and Māra naturally lays claim to and defends the throne as his by right, as well he may, who is the "first born of the angels," the Will to Life, Eros, *causa causans* of the world, prime mover of the Tree, autonomous in the realm of existence, inasmuch as all existences live-dependent on (*upajīvanti*) their such-and-such desired ends (*Chāndogya Up.*, VIII, 1, 5).

It should be observed that the "Awakening" of the *Ṛg Veda* is from potentiality to act and with respect to works; while in the Upaniṣads and Buddhism, the "Awakening" is from activity to understanding, and towards a cutting off of the will to experience. These opposite points of view, though both at one and the same time inherent in the ultimate reality, correspond to those from which, on the one hand, the Tree of Life is regarded as a manifestation to be fostered, and, on the other, as one to be cut off. The conflict is precisely between those principles which are represented by Māra and Buddha; who however opposite in nature are one in essence, and therefore at one beyond experience where "all principles are same." Cf. the characteristic Mahāyāna text *saṁsāraṁ caiva nirvāṇam manyante tattvadarśinaḥ*, "Those who have vision of the Quiddity do not distinguish between the Vortex of Life and the Extinction." (*Cittaviśuddhi*, attributed to Āryadeva, see H. Shastri in JASB., LXVII, p. 178). Cf. Prajāpati identified with Death, etc. *SB* X. 4.3. 3; no conflict with Death *JB* II 69-70 and passim.

In Christian terms, *saṁsāra* is "storm of the world-flow" (Eckhart, I, 192).

19 (*page 30*). As the *Saṁyutta Nikāya*, IV, 102, very correctly expresses it, "even the king of the Angels (*devānām inda*) is not emancipated so long as there remains in him any occasion of existence," and this must hold for the Buddha himself, "Angel of Angels" (*devātideva*), whose *nibbāṇa* is by definition *sa-upādi-śeṣa.*

Will is the cause of existence (*Ṛg Veda*, X, 129, 4; *Mahābhārata*, III, 313, 98, *kāmaḥ saṁsārahetuḥ*); Buddhism makes its goal not the *saṁsāra*, but *nissaraṇa*. A Jātaka preserved only in a Chinese text, but illustrated at Mathurā, has for its motif that "existence is the worst of all evils" (Foucher in JBORS., 1920, pp. 47-53, Vogel, *La Sculpture de Mathurā*, Pl. XVI, a).

Those who attempt to show that Buddhism does *not* teach the extinction of all desire miss the point: that Bodhisattvas and those like them are moved by what we believe are *right* desires, commendable ambitions, concerns the Way, and not the Goal. The very fact that the Buddha speaks to "others" reminds us that "whiles we are on the way to God we have not gotten him." All traditions as to the last death of the soul are in agreement that that is a total death with respect to all self-willing and self-thinking: "prudence (*adhyavasāya*), conception (*saṁkalpa*), and notion of I-and-mine (*abhimāna*)," *Maitri Up.*, VI, 30, must be destroyed, the "last way" (*parama-gati*) implying a state of "de-mentation" (*amanībhāva*) and a "self-naughting" (*nirabhimāna*), *ibid.*, VI, 30 and 34. Our resistance to these points of view, our reluctance to admit that Nirvāṇa implies a super-individual existence, Parinirvāṇa a total release from existence, is purely sentimental; actually, existence of any kind is being in a mode, therefore indigent and unifinite, less than the *summum bonum.* On "de-mentation" see also note 128.

20 (*page 31*). On the other hand, we must not be disconcerted if these distinctions are not always rigidly maintained; they are, in fact, "logical, not real." Buddhahood is virtually, if not actually, Parinirvāṇa; God is virtually Godhead; the *jñāna-* and *svabhāva*-aspects of the Dharmakāya are not divided.

21 (*page 31*). According to the well-known Aupaniṣada aphorism, the Ultimate Reality is "Not so, not so"; cf. Böhme, "God is properly to be spoken of as No Thing," Dante, *Convivio*, III, 15, "Things which our intellect cannot behold . . . we cannot understand what they are except by denying things of them," and Maimonides, *Guide for the Perplexed*, 1, 59, "By affirming anything of God you are removed from Him." Hence the Buddha's refusal to discuss Nirvāṇa.

22 (*page 32*). Cf. also my "Notes on Indian Coins and Symbols," *Ostas. Zeitschr.*, N.F. IV, 1927/28, pp. 180, 181.

23 (*page 32*). The *vajra* of iconography represents the axis with its two three-pointed ends. Comparison of *Ṛg Veda*, I, 51, 10, and I, 121, 12, gives us the synonymy *vajra* = *sahasa*, "strength": in the former passage, it is by the "strength" found by Kāvya Uśanā ("the Poetic Will") that Indra with strength holds Heaven and Earth apart (*rodasī vi bādhate*—Sāyaṇa glosses *vibādhate* by *te bibhīte, a ity arthaḥ*, "are afraid," an interpretation to be correlated with *abībhatsata* and *te vyadravatām* in *Jaiminīya Upaniṣad Brāhmaṇa*, I, 50, and 54). Indra is here acting instead of or on behalf of Agni, whose function it is to divide or pillar-apart (*viṣkabh*, etc.)

Heaven and Earth throughout the Cosmic Day, and is often called the "Son of Strength," *sahasaḥ putraḥ* or *sūnuḥ*. Thus *sahasaḥ putra* = *akṣa-ja* = *vajra*, and we have proof that the *vajra* originally represented "Fire"; and at the same time another link between Agni and the Buddha, with his "adamantine" nature.

24 (*page 32*). The sacrificial post as a *vajra* is eight-angled, "for the attainment of all desires" (*aṣṭāśrir, AB* II.1. better. yūpa = *vajra* in both, *Kauṣītaki Brāhmaṇa*, X, 1), which form might be expected in connection with (1) the notion of eight directions meeting at a common centre, and (2) the known prevalence of eight-sided pillar forms in early Indian art, cf. *aṭṭhaṁsā sukatā thambhā, Jātaka*, VI, 173. Cf. descriptions of Figs. 3, 13.

Account should also be taken of the history of the "thunderbolt" in Western Asiatic iconography, see Jacobsthal, *Der Blitz in der orientalischen und griechischen Kunst*, Berlin, 1906; Jacobsthal's Figs. 1, 2, 4, 5, for example, depict single, bifurcated "vajras."

25 (*page 33*). Indraji, "Antiquarian Remains at Sopārā and Padaṇa," *J. Bombay Br. R.A.S.*, XV, 320 and Pl. 3.

26 (*page 33*). "Notes on Indian Coins and Symbols," *loc. cit.*

27 (*page 35*). E.g. at Bhitargaon Cunningham, *A.S.I. Reports,* XI, 1880, Pl. XVII; at Bādāmī, *Mem. A.S.I.*, XXV, Pls. XI and XXIIa; also at Elūrā, in the Daśavatāra cave.

28 (*page 35*). Temple, "Notes on Antiquities from Ramannadesa," *Indian Antiquary*, 1894, also Ray, *Brahmanical Gods in Burma*, 1932, Pls. 4, 5, cf. Kak, *Ancient Monuments of Kashmir*, 1933, Fig. 39.

The Birth of Brahmā compositions (as well as older representations of lotus forms arising from a Yakṣa's navel) are very like, and may be the source of, the Tree of Jesse formula which appears in Christian art towards the close of the eleventh century; the example which forms a pulpit panel in the Church of S. Leonardo at Arcetri may be cited as showing very clearly the equivalence of western Rose and eastern Lotus, the Mother of God, who is the central flower on the stem that rises from the navel of the recumbent Jesse, corresponding to the Indian Māyā-Lakṣmī; see my "The Tree of Jesse and Indian Parallels or Sources," *Art Bulletin*, XI, 1929, and further discussion in *Parnassus*, Jan. 1935.

29 (*page 36*). Cf. Dante, *Paradiso*, XXX, 116, 117, *quant'è la larghezza di questa rosa nell' estreme foglie*?

30 (*page 36*). Vasiṣṭha: *Ṛg Veda*, VII, 33, 11, cf. *Bṛhad Devatā*, V, 154-5, *Nirukta*, V, 14, *Sarvānukramaṇī*, I, 166. Agni: *Ṛg Veda*, VI, 16, 13. *Atharva Veda*, X, 8, 34, where the Year- or World-wheel is supported by a lotus, will be discussed later. Another version of the same myths is represented in the legend of Purūravas and Urvaśī, and their son Āyus. In each case we are concerned with a primordial trinity of Father (Mitra-Varuṇa, Heaven), Mother (Urvaśī, Earth), and Son (Vasiṣṭha, Agni, Āyus, Life) of God. Identification of Agni Vaiśvānara with Vasiṣṭha and Āyus is further implied by *Atharva Veda*, X, 8, 20, where the expression "churned, or rubbed, forth" (*nirmanthate*), appropriate to Agni, is used with reference to Vasu (= Agni or Vasiṣṭha), and *Ṛg Veda*, I, 31, 5, I, 67, 5, I, 68, 3, etc., where Agni is spoken of as "Single Life" or "Universal Life" (*ekāyu, viśvāyu*). Our present concern is with the ontological equivalence of the Buddha with Agni, Āyus, etc.; we have already recognized the Buddha in the form of a fiery pillar supported by a lotus, and seen that this corresponds to a Vedic image of Agni.

Note that in *Bṛhad Devatā*, V, 154, *puṣkare sthitaḥ* need not mean "standing up in the Lotus," but rather "insistent in the Lotus," *sthitaḥ* being virtually the same as *pratiṣṭhaḥ*. Just as in *Bṛhadāraṇayaka Up.*, II, 3, 1, *sthitaḥ*, applied to the *mūrta* Brahman, i.e. Brahmā, means "existent," and as *sthitaḥ* is used in the *Saddharma Puṇḍarīka* to express that the Buddha is still living, not yet Wholly Extinguished. Similarly, *sthāyitā*, "persistence," "continued subsistence," is used of the relative immortality of the "angels with respect to works," such as Indra. *Sthitaḥ* is thus by no means contrary to *padmāsana*; in the *Bhagavad Gītā*, XI, 15, Brahmā is *kamalāsana-sthaḥ*, that is "present," "born," or "manifested"—not "standing"—on a lotus-throne. Cf. my *New Approach to the Vedas*, 1933, note 111 (*sthā* is *existare*, or as Sāyaṇa says, "to be born"). The *Gopatha Brāhmaṇa*, I, 16, has *brahma ha vai brahmāṇam puṣkare sasṛje*, rendered by Bloomfield "Brahman created Brahmā on the lotus." This is scarcely more than a paraphrase of *RV*, VII, 33, 11, where Vasiṣṭha, child of Mitrāvaruṇau and Urvaśī, as a sperm-drop fallen "by divine efflux" (*daivyena brahmaṇā*), is born in the lotus (*puṣkare*), and is addressed as "priest" (*brahman*). Although we have avoided a tendenzios translation, it can hardly be overlooked that the contrast of *brahman* (n.) and *brahmā* (m.) occurs in both texts, and it would have been very easy to render the RV passage as "Brahmā born in the lotus, drop let fall by Brahman"; as remarked by Grassmann (*Wörterbuch*, s.v. *brahman*, m.), "die Keime der späteren Sonderung (i.e. of Brahmā from Brahman) finden sich schon im RV." Vasiṣṭha corresponds to Agni, *puṣkare*, in VI, 16, 13; and in any case the prototype of the Buddha icnonography is unmistakable in all three passages. *J*.1. 392 as soon as things are born there is what is called a "state" (*tesam uppāde sati yeva thiti nāma hoti*).

"Earliest references" is said with respect to Indian sources. The texts cited from the *Ṛg Veda* can scarcely postdate 1000 B.C., a conservative estimate, not to mention that the Vedas represent an already late and sophisticated tradition. In Egypt, Ḥeru-pa-kharṭ (Harpocrates), the child Horus, son of Isis and Osiris, image of ever-young and self-regenerating life, is represented as lotus-born and lotus-supported throughout the Ptolemaic period, i.e. from about 900 B.C. onwards. See E.W. Budge, *The Gods of the Egyptians*, I, opp. p. 484, and *Book of the Dead*, *Papyrus of Ani*, Pl. 28; *Cataologue générale du Musée de Cairo*, XXIX, Pl. XI, items 38, 221 and 222; *Illustrated London News*, January 21, 1933, p. 84.[a] A head of Tutankhemen supported by a lotus has been interpreted as representing him as "the young Sun-god emerging from a lotus flower which sprang out of the primeval waters when creation took the place of chaos" (*Illustrated London News*, May 23, 1931). See further A. Moret, "Le Lotus et la Naissance des Dieux en Egypte," *Journal Asiatique*, May 1917. The conception of Horus goes back at least to the New Empire (nineteenth century B.C.), but there is no evidence for the representation of the child in or on a lotus until later. Lotus forms are said to appear in

[a] G. Roeder, "Die Kosmogonie von Hermopolis", *Egyptian Religion*, Vol. 1, 1933.

The appearance of the sun from a lotus blossom on the primordial hill, found in section entitled Harpocrates (Horus on lotus).

A. Piankof, 'Nefer-Toum et Mahas' *ibid* Nefer Toum is a form of Horos. Nefer-toum's symbol is the lotus. He is a "personified and divinized" lotus. Heliopolis the sun is described "the lotus bed appearing in the flood as child of Methyr". King Mahas identified with N. Mahas = "lion of the dread look".

Plutarch Moralia 400 A.B. "The Egyptians to show the beginning of sunrise, paint a very young baby sitting on a lotus flower."

Mesopotamian art "only with the pressure of Egyptian influences, from the middle of the second millennium" (B.C. onwards), Andrae, *Coloured Ceramics from Ashur*, p. 5; but Indian sources would be equally conçeivable. We can only assert that lotus symbolism must date back at least to the second millennium B.C., without being able to determine its precise origins.

31 (*page 36*). For they are of mutual origin, *anyonyayonitā, itaretarajanmānā, Bṛhad Devatā*, I, 71, and *Nirukta*, VIII, 4. The trinity of the Several Angels who are thus of one and the same sphere and birth (*sālokyatva, ekajātatva, Bṛhad Devatā*, I, 98) corresponds to those numerous Buddha trinities in which the Buddha stands between two Bodhisattvas, supported by three several lotuses springing from a common stem, which rises from the Waters.

32 (*page 37*). I.e. Agni as First Principle is embodied as Agni Vaiśvānara, the "Distributive Fire" "grandson of the Waters."

33 (*page 37*). By no means necessarily in the terrestrial mode; in fact, the lotus is generally employed to denote a universal, or at least angelic, existence.

That the "Earth" is not merely our terrestrial land, but any "ground" of life (cf. Böhme, "even thy own earth, that is thy body"; *puṇḍarīka* as human body, e.g. in *Atharva Veda*, X, 8, 43, *puṇḍarīkaṁ navadvāram . . . tasmin yad yakṣam ātmanvat tad vai brahmavido viduḥ*, "the lotus of nine gates, what Self-ish Genius is therein, that only the Comprehensors of the Brahman know," where *yakṣas*, as usually in the Brāhmaṇas and Upaniṣads, Brahman; and *Chāndogya Upaniṣad*, III, 12, 3, "what this earth is, that is the same as what the body in man here is . . . the heart, whereon are established, *pratiṣṭhata*, the breaths of life"), is clearly recognized by Sāyaṇa, commenting on *Ṛg Veda*, VI, 16, 13, where he says "Earth is the support of existences in very world" (*bhūmiśca sarvajagata ādhārabhūteti*), cf. *pṛthivī* used in the dual or plural to denote the Two Worlds or Three Worlds, *Ṛg Veda*, *passim*, e.g. I, 108, 9 and 10; VIII, 104, 11; X, 59, 4. Cf. also *Majjhima Nikāya*, I, 421, *ajjhatikā paṭhavī-dhātu*, "the personal earth-element."

34 (*page 37*). Vasiṣṭha, primarily an aspect of Agni (as was recognized by Siecke, *Liebesgeschichte des Himmels*, 1892, p. 73), is also rightly identified with Prajāpati and Dakṣa, *Śatapatha Brāhmaṇa*, II, 4, 4, 2, and called a Prajāpati, *Mānava Dharmaśāstra*, I, 34. Prajāpati is Brahmā, *padma-ja*; cf. *Bhāgavata Purāṇa*, III, 20, 15-16, "From the navel of the Lord sprang up a lotus, resplendent as a thousand suns, the abode of all living things (*sarva-jīva-nikāya*) where the Ruling Power (*svarāj*) himself of himself came to be (*svayam abhūt*, cf. "*svayambhū*" = Brahmā)." It may be observed that *svayambhū*, characterizing Prajāpati as demiurge, corresponds to the conception of Agni as "self-lighted" (*agninā agniḥ samidhyate*, *Ṛg Veda*, I, 12, 6): and this idea in the *Ṛg Veda*, where Agni is typically *punar punar jayamānaḥ*, "constantly reborn," underlies the Buddhist comparisons of rebirth as the lighting of one flame by another without "individual" identity of the substance enflamed.

35 (*page 37*). Summarized more fully, "the lotus-leaf is a basis (*pratiṣṭhā*), for it is this earth (*pṛthivī*), and earth is a basis . . . this same earth is Agni's womb (*yoni*) . . . one who is not thus supported (*pratiṣṭho na bhavati*), he is as it were unsupported in a far country." Cf. the epithet *supratiṣṭhapāda*, "with firm-based feet," applied to the Sambhogakāya Buddha, Maitreya-Asaṅga, *Uttaratantra*, II, 16, where it may be taken for granted that the Buddha is understood to be lotus-seated. Cf. *J.*, I, 53, *paṭhaviyaṁ patiṭṭhāya*, "standing on the ground," corresponding to the

iconography of the Nativities, in which the infant Boddhisattva is usually represented as standing on a lotus.

In connection with the phrase "extended on the back of the Waters" it should be noted that some of the commonest designations of "Earth," e.g. *pṛthivī*, *urvī*, *uttānā*, imply precisely "extension," and further that it is expressly stated that the extent of Earth is necessarily equal to that of Heaven, for the Sun, though represented on earth by Fire, cannot be thought of as confined, "for he fills all these worlds" (*Śatapatha Brāhmaṇa*, VIII, 7, 2, 1 and X, 5, 2, 8).

36 (*page 37*). In the older texts we find simply *puṣkara*, "lotus," which may imply the whole plant or only the flower. In *Atharva Veda*, X, 8, 34, the flower is specifically mentioned (*apām puṣpam*); in *Maitri Up.*,VI, 2, cited above, the mention of petals implies "flower," as do the later terms *padma-kośa* and *padma-garbha*. In any case, the expanded flower is the immediate support, through the whole plant, consisting of stem, leaves, and flower, is often represented. In *Jaiminīya Upaniṣad Brāhmaṇa*, IV, 3, the "flowers of aeviternity" (*amṛtasya puṣpāṇi*) are no doubt lotuses.

37 (*page 38*). It is by no means intended to assert that the chthonic basis of existence can be or is *only* indicated by the Lotus. On the contrary, the Earth may be represented by the spirits of the Earth, viz. the Guhyaka Yakṣas, or Bhumma Devas, cf. my *Yakṣas*, I, 8, my *HIIA*, Figs. 38, 66, and the Yakushi Buddha pedestal described below cf. Fig. 41. Or various animals may be the supporting bases of angelic beings, their "vehicles"; or the ground may be represented simply by a plane surface or platform.

In *Ṛg Veda*, VII, 88, 3 and 4, by a closely related image, the support of Vasiṣṭha in the Waters is called a ship (*nau*), wherein he, Varuṇa's Son, appointed Prophet (*ṛṣi*), rises gladly with Varuṇa in mid-ocean "when first the heavens were spread out and dawns outstrung," that is when time began, the ship of life left port, the Flower of the Waters showed above the waves. That image of a ship wherein the Universal Man and Progenitor sails upon the Waters is clearly an aspect of the Vedic *devayāna* and *pitṛyāna*, and corresponds to Manu's voyage in an ark (*nau*) in the Indian form of the Flood Legend; and provides an archetype for all that Buddhist imagery of a voyage across the sea of life which is implied in the terms Hīnayāna and Mahāyāna, the Lesser and the Greater "Voyage" (not, as generally translated, "Vehicle"), which are at the same time one and the same voyage, Ekayāna. The Lotus is the vehicle of life: for him who understands (*vidvān*) bearing him on toward a known port, but for the foolish (*avid*) storm-driven to an unknown landfall. Cf. *Ṛg Veda*, VIII, 42, 3, and 72, 3.

38 (*page 38*). In the present monograph we have not emphasized the distinction of Upper (*para*) from Nether (*apara*) Waters, representing respectively the possibilities of existence "above" and "below," in yonder world and this world, Heaven and Earth. It may, however, be remarked that the Lotus nearly always appears in the glory or nimbus (*prabhā-maṇḍala*) of the Buddha and other celestial figures (cf. Fig. 36) of the Buddha or other angelic figures; then two flowers, one behind the "head," the other beneath the "feet," and each a reflection of the other, representing the "grounds" (*pṛthivī*) of existence *in extenso* (*rājasika, antarikṣhe*) between them. Cf. *Śatapatha Brāhmaṇa*, IV, I, 5, 16, "Agni is verily the lotus of this Earth, the Sun the lotus of yonder Sky" : and *ibid.*, VII, 1, 1, 24, Upper and Nether Waters.

39 (*page 38*). The version of Caland, *Pañcaviṁśa Brāhmaṇa*, 1931, p. 494, is too specific: *nakṣatra* in the plural need not mean only "stars," cf. *Ṛg Veda*, X, 55, 4, where the first of lights (*vibhānām*, glossed by Sāyaṇa as *grahanakṣatrādīnām*) by its shining brings to birth (*ajanayaḥ*) the *puṣṭasya puṣṭam*, tantamount to the *apāṁ puṣpam* of *Atharva Veda*, X, 8, 34. Nor need *avakāśa* imply a light shining only at night; Caland himself cites *Mānava Gṛhyasūtra*, II, 1, 5, where *avakāśe* = "at daybreak." *Nakṣatra* designates the Sun in *Ṛg Veda*, VII, 86, 1; X, 88, 13, and X, 156, 4.

40 (*page 39*). Apart from this hermeneutic etymology, the more strictly correct derivation of *puṣkara* is from root *puṣ*, to grow or increase, be nourished, etc., cf. *Ṛg Veda*, X, 55, 4, where *puṣṭasya puṣṭam*, "the amplitude of increase" or "growth of growth," which is brought forth by Dawn, is tantamount to *puṣkara*, the World-Lotus rising from the Waters at the dawn of creation, just as the day-lotus opens at sunrise in actual experience. Cf. Yāska, *Nirukta*, V, 14, *puṣkaram antarikṣam, poṣati bhūtāni*, "The Lotus is mid-space, it propagates beings," and *Viṣṇu Purāṇa*, I, 8, 23, *padmā svadhā śāsvatapuṣṭidā*, "The Lotus-lady is intrinsic power, the constant giver of increase."

41 (*page 40*). *Śrī*, "glory," "beauty," in the *Ṛg Veda*, is constantly an "attribute" of Agni; *lakṣmī*, "auspicious sign," is mentioned only once. In the Brāhmaṇas, Upaniṣads, and later, Śrī-Lakṣmī is usually one angel (*devī*) and corresponds to the Vedic Apsaras, and other aspects of Aditi. The description of Śrī-Lakṣmī in the *Śrī-sūkta*, of Brāhmana-Upaniṣad period, corresponds in all respects with the iconographic formula as found in Early Indian art (see my "Early Indian Iconography," II, in *Eastern Art*, I, 1928); here again the close connection is with Agni (Jātavedas). The following is abbreviated and condensed from the full text as given by Scheftelowitz, *Apokryphen des Ṛgveda*, 1906, pp. 72-9: "Who is gladdened by elephants . . . bathed by elephant-kings, with golden vessels (*gajendrair . . . snāpitā hema-kumbhair*) . . . Mother Śrī (cf. Sirimā at Bharhut) . . . the lush, in the lotus lake, the pillar (*yaṣṭī*), golden . . . we, thy children, coming forth from the mire (*kardamena prajā sraṣṭā*, cf. the human body as "*puṇḍarīka*"), have proceeded to existence. . . . Lotus-faced, lotus-shouldered (*padma-ūrū*), lotus-eyed, lotus-born, darling of Viṣṇu . . . Mahālakṣmī, lotus-wonted . . . set down thy lotus-foot within my heart (*hṛdi saṁ ni dhatsva*)." The cult of Siri-devatā is referred to in *Milindapañha*, 191, her followers being spoken of as *bhaktas*. Gerta Hartmann, *Beiträge zur Geschichte der göttin Lakṣmī* (Contributions to the History of Goodess Lakṣmī) Wertheim, 1933.

Lakṣā (Śrī, Lakṣā, listed amongst the *brahmavādinī*, or feminine seers, in *Bṛhad Devatā*, II, 84) is evidently synonymous with *Lakṣmī.*

42 (*page 40*). See my "Early Indian Iconography, II, Śrī-Lakṣmī," *Eastern Art*, I, 1929; "Notes on Indian Coins and Symbols," *Ostas. Zeitschr.*, N.F., IV, 1927/28; and "Archaic Indian Terracottas," *I pek*, 1928, Figs. 25, 30.

43 (*page 40*). "Images indiennes de la Fortune," *mem. conç. l' Asie Orientale*, I, 1913; and "The Buddhist Madonna" (in *The Beginnings of Buddhist Art*, 1917).

44 (*page 41*). Lakṣmī's own "lotus-birth" is thus not exactly the same thing as Agni's or Vasiṣṭha's, for she is the Lotus as well as Sirī-mā; mother, not sister, of all those whose coming to be is from a lotus-womb, *abja-yoni*. It may be noted that Lakṣmī as Goddess of Fortune consistently preserves her fickle *āpsaras* character, reminiscent of Urvaśī; it is only as the Earth, as Bhūmi-devī, that she stands firm.

45 (*page 41*). In *Ṛg Veda*, I, 164, 8, if we accept the interpretation of Sāyaṇa, we have "the germ (*garbha*) was in the cloud" (*vṛjanī*); but it would be more natural to take *vṛjanī* as "holy site," hortus inclusus (cf. *vrajaḥ . . . sapariśrayaḥ, Bṛahdāraṇyaka Up.*, VI, 4, 23, where cosmic analogies are applied to human generation). In any case, the Mother (Earth) is here associated (*yukta*) with the Father (Heaven) and it is made quite clear that she is fertilized by an essence that can only have fallen from Heaven as rain; "she the shy one was penetrated by the tincture (*rasa*)," cf. *Ṛg Veda*, VII, 101, 3, "The Father's juices (*payaḥ*) grasped (*prati-gṛbhṇāti*) the Mother, thereby are increased both Father and Son," *Ṛg Veda*, I, 164, 51, "the rain-clouds (*parjanyāḥ*) animate (*jinvanti*) the Earth," and similar passages. It is the descent of the *rasa*-bearing rains that is represented in the Gaja-Lakṣmī composition, which is rather a Conception than a Nativity. But that Conception, being of Life universally, may well have been thought of as Siddhārtha's, whose name signifies "Accomplishment of Purpose." The notion of impregnation by a cloud or rain is present even in the more familiar Buddhist Conceptions, where the Boddhisattva descends in the form of a white elephant, though this is rationalized by calling it a "dream." Cf. the elephant Paccaya, of sky-faring descent, connatural rain-giving talisman of the Bodhisattva in the *Vessantara Jātaka*, which is certainly not a tale of human happenings (incidentally, *vessa* = *viśva* rather than *vaiśya*; the "*vessa*-street" is not the merchant's street but "Everyman's Way").

The Gaja-Lakṣmī composition further corresponds (1) to Christian Annunciations, where the descent of the Spirit is indicated by rays of the Supernal Sun, and by the Dove (birds, *suparṇa*, representing also in Vedic symbolism, e.g. *Ṛg Veda* I, 35, 7, and I, 164, 47, rays of the Sun), and (2) to Danae's conception of Perseus, if we substitute for the Sun, Agni with his golden seed.

In Buddhist legend, the Nativity has been so far rationalized that no great stress is laid on virgin birth, though both conception and birth are in other respects miraculous. As to the virgin birth, "on n'a jamais cru que Çâkyamouni fût né des oeuvres de Çuddhodana," de la Vallée Poussin, *Le Dogme et la Philosophie du Bouddhisme*, p. 57, and his notes. Indian tradition, however, knows a virginity of the Mother, Aditi, calling her *anarvā, apravitā, kumārī, mātā yuvatī, kanyā, yoṣā*, etc. An ultimate "virginity" of both parents is indeed a metaphysical necessity, for the twin poles of being, the unmoving centres of the Principal and World Wheels, act only by their presence and not by local movement: "He" is undiminished by his largesse, "She" by her parturition.

46 (*page 41*). The analogous lustration of Siddhārtha by two Nāgas, genii of the *nether* waters, is represented on the well-known stele from Sārnāth, see Foucher, *Beginnings of Buddhist Art*, Pl. XIX, Fig. 1, lower-left panel.

47 (*page 41*). On this meaning of Māyā see my "On translation: *māyā, deva, tapas*," in *Isis*, No. 54, 1933. *māyā nirmalaṁ iva bimbaṁ, māyā nāma*.

48 (*page 41*). The name Māyā-devī occurs in *Dīgha Nikāya*, II, 7; Mahā-Māyā in the *Nidānakathā* (J., I, 52 etc.). That the name of Māyā-devī's sister, co-wife of Śuddhodana, should have been Prajāpati is equally significant; as remarked by de la Vallée Poussin, *Le Dogme et la Philosophie du Bouddhisme*, 1930, p. 188, "Jamais femme indienne s'est nommée Māyā . . . Mahāpajāpatī n'est pas non plus un nom" though this is not quite true as regards Māyā-devī. See P.D. Shastri, *The Doctrine of Māyā*, 1911, p. 28.

The various accounts of the Buddha's birth are conveniently assembled in Windisch, *Buddha's Geburt*, Leipzig, 1908.

In the *Buddhacarita*, I, 16-18, Māyā is *uttama devatā*, which may be freely rendered "Queen of Heaven," and as regards her earthly being, is said to have "abandoned, in accordance with the Law (*dharma*), her subtle nature (*sūkṣmāṁ prakṛtim*)."

Māyā-devī who bears and her sister Pajāpatī who fosters the Bodhisattva correspond, in fact to the Vedic sisters Night and Day, the two mothers of Agni, cf. *Ṛg Veda*, I, 95, 1, "Two of unlike aspect, each in succession cherishes the Babe," III, 55, 4 "One mother bears, another cherishes the Calf," and V, 2, 2, the *mahiṣī* and *peṣī* as mother and nurse. Māyā-devī corresponds also to Aditi, Indra's mother whose death is caused by his birth full-grown from her side, *pārśvāt tiraścatā*, *Ṛg Veda*, IV, 18, see Sieg, *Sagenstoffe des Ṛgveda*, Stuttgart, 1902, 76 f. It is noteworthy that the name of the seer of this hymn is Vāmadeva Gautama (*gautama* being patronymic, as in the Buddha's case), to whom also there is attributed a lateral birth from his mother's side, this birth taking place in a wood (*vana*, cf. Lumbinī-vana), as related in Sāyaṇa's introduction to *Ṛg Veda*, IV, 18. It may be remarked that in *Jātaka*, I, 52, Māyā-devī is already on her way to Devadaha, her ancestral home, when the child is born in the Lumbini grove, which was common ground to the people of both cities, Kapilavatthu and Devadaha. Now *devadaha* *devahrada*, "angel-pool," and must surely be the same as the *hrada* or *śaiśava* of the Sarasvatī which is "as far from here as Heaven" (*Pañcaviṁśa Brāhmaṇa* XXV, 10, 12-18), and is the same "source" as that in which the aged Cyavāna was restored to youth by the Aśvins (*apaḥ, ibid.*, XIV, 6, 10, *hrada*, *Śatapatha Brāhmaṇa*, IV, 1, 5, 12, *śaiśava*, *Jaiminīya Brāhmaṇa*, III, 120 and 125 expanding *Ṛg Veda*, I, 116, 10), likewise Varuṇa's abode "at the source of the rivers of life," *sindhūnām upodaye*, *Ṛg Veda*, VIII, 41, 2, the Fountain of Life (*utsa, Ṛg Veda, passim*). That the Bodhisattva is conscious, and speaks, while yet in the womb is anticipated also in the *Ṛg Veda* with respect to Agni, Indra, Gandharva. Correspondences of this kind could be cited without end; cf. my *Ṛg Veda* as *Land-náma-bók*, London, 1935. For the shining in the womb (*Jātaka* I, 52, *Buddhacarita*, I, 22) see *Ṛg Veda*, VI, 16, 35, and cf. the Pseudo-Matthew, Ch. XIII.

49 (*page 41*). In metaphysical formulation, lateral procession is an inevitable concept; the branches of the tree, or arms of the cross, proceeding from the vertical laterally. Cf. Also the origin of Eve from Adam's side; and the Caesarian birth of Rustam.

50 (*page 41*). *Megha*, from root *migh* = *mih*, to sprinkle, micturate, emit; cf. *mīḷhuṣa*, outpouring, bountiful, applied to Varuṇa and Agni, *Ṛg Veda*, *passim* (VII, 88, 1; IV, 5, 1, etc.).

51 (*page 41*). *Anguttara Nikāya*, I, 145 (III, 38).

52 (*page 42*). Omcron, *Letters from Paulos*, 1920, p. 219.

53 (*page 42*). Just as in mediaeval Christianity it was asserted again of him who said of himself, "Before Abraham I am," that "Christ's birth is eternal."

54 (*page 43*). For the Sārnāth capital see Sahni, *Catalogue of the Museum of Archeology at Sārnāth*, 1914, Pl. IV and p. 28. This and corresponding reliefs are further discussed below. Note that from the standpoint of a more metaphysical Buddhology the "first turning of the Wheel" must be thought of as not first eventually, but first primordially, *in principio, agre*. For the pillared wheel as a representation of the

sun, see P.E. Dumont, "The Indie God Aja Ekapād, the One-legged Goat," *JAOS*, 53, 326 f.

55 (*page 43*). In more detailed exegesis: *Bṛhadāraṇyaka Up.*, I, 5, 15, "Self (*ātman*) the nave (*nābhi*), properties (*vitta*) the felly (*pradhi*)", *Śvetāśvatara Up.*, I, 4, "we understand him as with one triple (*trivṛt*) felly (*nemi*) . . . one mystery (*moha*) dually manifested (*dvinimitta*)"; *Praśna Up.*, VI, 5 and 6, "on whom the parts (*kalā*) rest firm, like the spokes on the nave (*nābhi*) of a chariot (-wheel), Him I deem the Person to be known."

56 (*page 44*). It is not at all unlikely that the notion of the revolving well-wheel may also be present; cf. citations in my "The Persian Wheel," *JAOS*, LI, 283.

57 (*page 44*). We do not mean to exclude particular adaptations, as when the *cakra* becomes the "weapon" of a given deity, e.g. Viṣṇu, though even in this case the Wheel could be understood to mean "time," as a destructive power. The use of the *cakra* as a divine weapon is analogous to the similar use of the *vajra*.

Nor is the symbol of the World-wheel by any means exclusively Indian. It is constantly employed, for example, by Dante. It survives even today in the semi-pagan, semi-secular form of the "Wheel of Fortuna." To be "broken on the wheel" represents a form of martyrdom which, like a death on the Cross, is not without its cosmic analogies. We cannot pursue these considerations further here, nor discuss the ultimate origin of the symbol (observe that the *svastika* antedates the wheel), but may remark that the wheel appears also in Greek symbolism, where it is probably of Oriental origin (see Cook, *Zeus*, I, p. 198 f., and Roes, *Greek Geometric Art*, 1933, especially p. 46). Here too the Olympians are "only spokes in the great wheel of nature, not the driving force that sets and keeps her going . . . India and China best help us to the understanding of Dike as the *way* of the world and also as Right and Justice," J. Harrison, *Themis*, pp. 464 and 523-527, cf. also Jackson in *JAOS*, XXI, 171, and Kaegi, *Rig Veda,* note 85. Dike = *aša* = *ṛta* = *dharma* = *tao* as "Way."

58 (*page 44*). Most of the confusion which has been introduced into discussions of Nirvāṇa and Parinirvāṇa has arisen from a failure to distinguish between the non-entity of the irrational (viz. very *impossibility* of existence) and the non-existence of the non- or supra-rational (viz. very *possibility* of existence).

59 (*page 45*). *Ekībhūtaḥ prajñāna-ghanaḥ, Māṇḍūkya Up.*, 5; *sarūpeṇa jyotiṣā vivratena, Ṛg Veda*, X, 55, 3; *viśvam satyam*, II, 24, 12; *viśvam ekam*, III, 54, 8; *sarvadharma-samatā*, *SPt*, 133, etc.

60 (*page 45*). In many of the early Buddhist Dhammacakkas, the nave or hub (*nābhi*) of the wheel is represented either as an open lotus (petals indicated) or as the pericarp (*kaṇṇikā*) of a lotus (the characteristic circular marks being shown on its surface). Cf. Śaṅkarācārya's gloss *pṛthivī-padmamadhye merukarṇikāsanastham* on *kamalāsanastham* qualifying "Brahmā" in *Bhagavad Gītā*, XI, 15; *kaṇṇikā* as the key-plate of a domed roof, the sole support of its rafters, *Jātaka*, III, 317-19; and in connection with these passages, *Ṛg Veda*, I, 35, 6 "as on the chariot's axle-point depend the deathless (principles)," and VIII, 41, 6, "in whom all creative-utterances (*kāvya*) inhere as does the nave within the wheel."

61 (*page 45*) E.g. I, 9, 2, "Let flow the soma to Indra, the instigator (*cakri*) to the operator (*cakri*) of all things (*viśvāni*)"; III, 16, 4, where Agni, "who conducts (*cakri*) the offering amidst the Angels, is the maker (*cakri*) of the several worlds (*viśvāni bhuvanā*) and has full power over them"; cf. IV, 2, 9, and VIII, 31, 9.

62 (*page 45*). Varuṇa, Indra etc., are Kṣatriya, so too is the Buddha by birth; he does not think of himself as a "priest," but as militant. The "Buddha-field" (*Buddha-kṣetra*) is at the same time in this sense a "field of battle" and also a trackless wilderness wherein he alone can point out the Way (*mārga*). In the latter connection we find again the reflection of Vedic concepts of Agni, *vidvān pathaḥ pura-etā*, *Ṛg Veda*, V, 46, 1, *kṣetravit, ibid.*, IX, 70, 9, and X, 32, 7 (Indra), *niyānam saṁjñānam*, X, 19, 4 (in I, 164, 47 *niyānaṁ . . . divaṁ ut* contrasts with *āvavṛtran . . . vi ut*, in V, 46, 1 *vimucaṁ* with *āvṛtaṁ*, hence *niyāna* = *devayāna*), etc. In *Ṛg Veda*, I, 45, 9, the "field" (*kṣetra*) is the extended world over which the sun passes with his seven horses; *ibid.*, X, 32, 7 those that are not way-wise therein seek to be taught by him that is the knower of the field (*akṣetravid kṣetravidam hy aprāṭ*), cf. *Majjhima Nikāya*, No. 108 "revealed a path until then unrevealed" (*asañjātassa maggasa sañjānetā*); in the Upaniṣads similarly *kṣetra* is "world," e.g. *Śvetāśvatara Up.*, VI, 16, and *Maitri Up.*, II, 5. Agni is typically *viśpati*, "Lord of the dwellers in this field."

63 (*page 45*). "The chariot is the Year," *Atharva Veda*, VIII, 8, 23.

64 (*page 46*). In making the use of the symbol of two wheels, progressive enlightenment must be represented by a simultaneous contraction (con-centration) of the circumference of each (cf. *Maitri Up.*, VI, 1), and by a contraction (con-centration) of the axis, resulting as before in the inconnumerable unity of the single point, viz. Ātman *quā* Iśvara, Cakravartin. That is the meeting point of all the spokes, and also the intersection of the arms of the two- or three-armed Cross. Cf. Chuang Tzŭ, II, 3, "When subjective and objective are both without their correlates, that is the very axis of Tao. And when that axis passes through the centre at which all indefinites converge, positive and negative alike blend into an infinite One . . . viewed from the standpoint of Tao, the (horizontal) beam and the (vertical) pillar are identical." In Giles' translation I have substituted "Indefinites" for "Infinities."

Where there is a question of three wheels, of which the third is known only to the adept, it will be evident of course that this hidden wheel, of which there is no extension, must be thought of as coincident with the one "point" (intersection of all axes) which represents principially the two manifested wheels.

65 (*page 46*). Cf. Dante, *Paradiso*, XIII, 21-2, *punto dello stelo a cui la prima rota va dintorno*, and *ibid.*, XVII, 28, and XXVIII, 16 and 41-2; and *Jaiminīya Upaniṣad Brāhmaṇa*, I, 3, where the way out of the worlds, by which one "wholly escapes" (*atimucyate*) (= *loka-dvāra* in *Chāndogya Up.*, VIII, 6, 6, "I am the Door" in John, x, 9), viz. the "hold in the sky" (*divaś chidram*), "at the place of meeting in the Sun" (*ādityam samayā*), is very correctly symbolized by the "space" (*kha*) of a cart (*anas*) or chariot (*ratha*), that is the space at the centre of the wheels, and "that is seen to be all covered over by rays" (*raśmi*). Cf. St Thomas, *Sum. Th.*, III, Q. 91, A.1, "things belonging to the state of glory are not *under the sun*." (My explanation of *ratha-chidra* in *JAOS*, LI, 172, should be rejected.)

66 (*page 48*). For the opposing points of view in dramatic contrast, cf. *Bhagavad Gītā*, III, 16-25, and *Anugītā*, Ch. XXX. The contrast, however, is more apparent than real: what is taught in the *Anugītā* and in early Buddhism is indeed the stoppage (*nissaraṇa, nivṛtti*) of the Bhavacakra, but the real meaning of abstention is better expressed in the *Bhagavad Gītā* and in later Buddhism as a transformation of action, or perfected facility in action, achieved when the action is performed willingly but not from will.

67 (*page 48*). The Angels whose existence is as yet merely potential are thought of as fearing lest being should not flow out into existence. The fear is needless, since in him potentiality and act are indivisible, he works willy nilly, doing what must be done. That the Buddha remains in seclusion during the period of hesitation corresponds to the occultation of Agni (*tamasi kṣeṣy agne*, *Ṛg Veda*, X, 51, 5; *gūḷhaṁ sūryam tamasāpavratena*, *ibid.*, V, 40, 6, etc.) antecedent to the dawn of a creative cycle. That seclusion (in Christian terms "interior operation" or "eternal rest," *solus ante principium*) is the same as the "pleroma non-revolving" (*pūrṇam apravartin*) of *Kauṣītaki Up.*, IV, 8.

The hesitation corresponds in the life of Chirst to the Passion in the Garden of Gethsemane, "O my Father, if it be possible, let this cup pass from me"; and when he adds, "nevertheless not as I will, but as thou wilt," that corresponds to Agni, who performs what is required of him (*Ṛg Veda*, I, 165, 9, *kariṣyā kṛṇuhi* . . . , VI, 9, 3, *vaktvāni* . . . *vadāti*, VII, 20, 1, *cakriḥ* . . . *yat kariṣyan*), and the Buddha, who does what must be done (*kartavyaṁ karoti*, *SPt* Ch. XV). This is, technically, "*necessitas infallibilatis*."

In the individual, it is represented by everyman's idleness, who will not put his shoulder to the Wheel (*evaṁ pravartitaṁ cakraṁ na anuvartayati*, *Bhagavad Gītā*, III, 16), or speaking Christianly, will not take up his Cross.

"Let the Four Quarters bow before thee": as in fact the Four Great Kings ward the unborn Boddhisattva, and receive him when he proceeds from the Mother's side. It is often overlooked that the notion of the Four World Warders is met with already in the Vedas and Brāhmaṇas, for example *Ṛg Veda*, VIII, 28, 2-3, where the *gopāḥ* are Agni (E), Mitra (N), Varuṇa (W), and Aryaman (S); *Kauṣītaki Brāhmaṇa*, VII, 6, with Agni (E), Soma (S), Savitṛ (W), Pathya Svasti, i.e. Vāc (N), and Aditi (Zenith); and *Jaiminīya Upaniṣad Brāhmaṇa*, I, 28, with Agni (E), Manas (S), Cakṣu (W), Śrotra (N), and Prāṇa (Zenith).

That the Bodhisattva stands erect and takes seven steps as soon as he is born corresponds to numerous Vedic texts in which Agni is described as great (*bṛhat*, IV, 5, 1), erect (*ūrdhva*), and strong the moment he is born (*sadyo jātasya dadṛśānam ojaḥ*, IV, 6, 1 and IV, 7, 10).

68 (*page 48*). *Ṛg Veda*, II, 38, 6, "The seeker, having gone forth, returns; home is the desire of all things that proceed (*car*); abandoning his never-completed task, he comes back again, according to the rule of Savitṛ"—with reference primarily to the close of a cosmic day, the end of time, and analogically to the fall of night on earth. Cf. *Jaiminīya Upaniṣad Brāhmaṇa*, I, 3, "Having slain by food this and that hunger (i.e. sated by experience) . . . he is utterly-released (*atimucyate*)."

69 (*page 49*). This must follow in any case directly from the principle "as above, so below," as e.g. in *Aitareya Brāhmaṇa*, VIII, 2.

70 (*page 49*). Cf. the use of *skandha* in *Maitri Up.*, VII, 11, where the proliferation of the World-tree is *skandhāt skandham*, "branch after branch."

71 (*page 49*). See Suzuki, *Outlines of Mahāyāna Buddhism*, pp. 352 ff., and similar passages cited by de la Vallée Poussin, "A propos du Cittaviśuddhiprakaraṇa d' Āryadeva," *Bull Sch Or Stud*, VI, 1931.

72 (*page 49*). See Anesaki, *Buddhist Art* . . . , 1915, p. 39; Ōmura Seigai, *Sanbon Ryōbu Mandara*, Tokyō, 1913; Getty, *Gods of Northern Buddhism* (2nd ed.), pp. 28 ff.

73 (*page 51*). A text significant also in connection with the later virtual identification of the Buddha with Brahmā. In *Majjhima Nikāya*, I, 69, we have *brahmacakkaṁ*

pavatteti, synonymous with *dhammacakkaṁ pavatteti* (cf. *yenedaṁ bhramyate brahmacakraṁ*, *Śvetāśvatara Up.*, VI, 1), and in *Saṁyutta Nikāya*, V, 5-6, "This Ariyan eightfold Way may be spoken of as Brahmayāna or as Dhammayāna." Cf. also Keith, *Religion and Philosophy of the Veda*, p. 550, and de la Vallée Poussin, *Le Dogme et la Philosophie du Bouddhisme*, 1930, p. 186, "le nirvāṇa, c'est-à-dire . . . le *brahmaloka* des bouddhistes."

74 (*page 52*). Ōmura Seigai, *loc. cit.*, XV, 3, 4.

75 (*page 52*). In addition to the Sārnāth pillar are the various representations at Bhārhut, Bodhgayā, Sāñcī, and Amarāvatī, and the large and elaborate Dharmacakras from Siam; see Cunningham, *Stupa of Bharhut*, 1879, Pl. XXXIV, 4 (cf. Pl. VII, showing a Dharmacakra supported by a lotus palmette); Bachhofer, *Early Indian Sculpture*, Pls. 44, 46, 55, 66, 104, 110, 152; my *History*, Figs. 45, 136, 144, 318, also the Sun-wheel pillar on an early coin, Fig. 112; Salmony, *Sculpture in Siam*, Pls. 3a and 5a.

For the fundamental symbolism see Mus, "Barabuḍur . . . ," Ch. III (Le Pilier de Sārnāth et le Problème des Cinq Orients), in *BÉFEO*, 1932, pp. 413 f.

76 (*page 52*). See my "Origin of the Lotus (so-called Bell) Capital," *Ind. Hist. Qtly.*, VI, 1930, 373-5, and "Origin of the Lotus Capital," *ibid.*, VII, 1931, 747-50 (827-30). A.K. Mitra, "Origin of the Bell Capital," *ibid.*, pp. 213 f., and "A further note on the Origin of the Bell Capital," *ibid.*, X, 1934, 125 f., and G.L. Fabri, in *Études d'Orientalisme*, 1932, p. 249, disagree. (Althtough Mitra argues as if against my interpretations, I cannot see any difference between his explanation of the lotus as being primarily a symbol of divine or "miraculous" birth, and of fertility, and my own of the lotus as representing the universal Ground—*pṛthivī, bhūmi*—of existence and as at once the birthplace—*yoni*—and indispensable support—*pratiṣṭhā*—of Life in the Worlds. Dr Mitra seems scarcely to understand the use of the expression "Ground" in metaphysics and theology, where it corresponds to "Substance" as opposed to "Essence." As to the derivative application of the lotus symbol in architecture and ornament, I see no reason to modify views already expressed; and as to the supposed "mystery" will only remark that an established symbol can easily become a *cliché*, and may be used as such without conscious reference to its ultimate significance; the Greek "Egg and Dart," really a lotus-petal moulding, affords a good instance of such usage.) J. Przyluski, "Le symbolisme due pilier de Sarnath," in *Études d'Orientalisme*, pp. 481 f., and Dumont, *loc. cit.* note 54, deal with other symbolic aspects of the Sārnāth capital.

We have deduced elsewhere (*New Approach to the Vedas*, note 67) that conch (*śaṅkha*) and lotus (*padma*), as a formulation alternative to that of paired lotuses (one in the nimbus, the other beneath the feet, or both in the hands of the Sun, *padmahastau*), stand for the powers derived respectively from the Upper and the Nether Waters. As the Nether Lotus is the Earth, the substance of things, so the Conch or Upper Lotus is their form; in other words, while the lower symbols stand for means or ground of utterance, the upper symbols stand for the power of utterance, all that is uttered (*vyāhṛti, deśita*) coming into existence between them. And although I cannot cite a text, it will not be rash to regard the conch as a symbol of the Spoken Word. On these lines the symbol of a conch supported by a lotus which occurs at Ajaṇṭā (Yazdani, *Ajaṇṭā*, Pt. II, p. 53 and Pls. XLVIIa, XLIXd), but is not to my knowledge represented elsewhere, can be explained as an alternative formula equivalent to that of the *sūtra* supported by a lotus, discussed above.

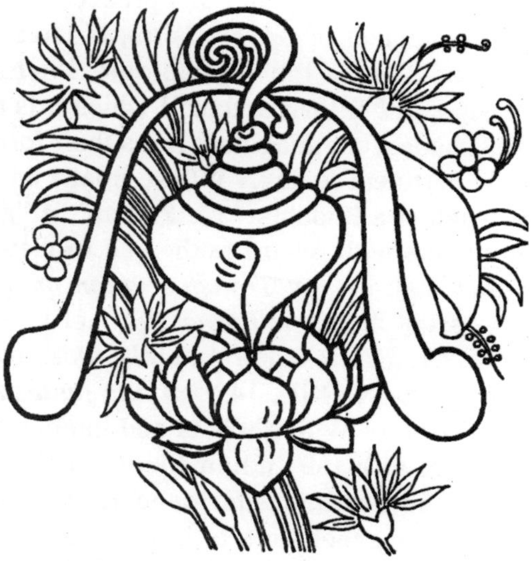

Fig. I. Conch and Lotus, are represented at Ajaṇṭā.
After Yazdani, as cited in note 76.

77 (*page 53*). The connection of *nābhi*, nave and navel, with *nabha*, space or firmament, is anything but accidental, cf. *Maitri Up.*, VI, 6, with respect to Prajāpati's world-form, "the firmament (*bhuvas*) is his navel." Observe that from the Vedic-Aupaniṣada point of view "Space' (*ākāśa*) is an elemental substance, cf. our "ether": "Space (*ākāśa*) is the permissive cause or necessary medium (*nirvahitṛ*) of name-and-aspect (*nāma-rūpa*, i.e. individuation)," *Chāndogya Up.*, VIII, 14. This Space should not be confused with the Void, *śūnya*, although in Buddhism, which is an atomistic system, a confusion is unavoidable; actually, it is correct to speak of the Space-body (*ākāśa-śārīra*) of Brahman, where it would not be correct to speak of a "Void-body."

78 (*page 53*). Note that *kha* is used both with respect to space in the inner man, and to denote the space within the nave of a wheel, into which space fits the point (*āṇi*) of the operating axle (*akṣa*), see above, note 65. *Kha* is at once "void" and "plenum."

79 (*page 53*). For this use of *nīḍa* as "place of being," cf. Dante, *Paradiso*, XVIII, 110, *virtù ch'è forma per li nidi*, "power that is form unto the nests," cf. *nīḷa* and *kulāya* in the *Ṛg Veda* and Brāhmaṇas, *passim*, e.g. *Ṛg Veda*, VI, 15, 16, and X, 5, 6, *Atharva Veda*, IX, 3, 19-20, *Pañcaviṁśa Brāhmaṇa*, XI, 15, 1, and *Maitrāyanīya Up.*, III, 12.

80 (*page 53*). The Buddhist doctrine of the heart (*cit, bodhi-citta*) is already developed not only in the Upaniṣads, but also in the *Ṛg Veda*, where *hṛt*, *hṛdaya*, correspond to *bodhi-citta*. For example, in *Ṛg Veda*, IV, 58, 11, Agni *antaḥ samudre hṛdy antar āyuṣi*; X, 177, 1, the Sun-bird, *hṛdā paśyanti manasā vipaścitaḥ*; I, 65, 1, and 67, 2, Agni, *guhā catantam, niṣīdan*; VII, 76, 4, *gūḷhaṁ jhotiḥ*; VI, 9, 6, *jyotir hṛdaya āhitam.*

81(*page 54*). Cited in the *Kokka*, No. 198, and Sirén, *History of Early Chinese Painting*, p. 101.

82 (*page 54*). Cf. *Divyāvadāna*, XXVI, ed., Cowell and Neill, p. 363, where it is taken

for granted that "those who venerate earthen images of the Angels do not revere the clay, but the Immortals thereby represented." A great part of the modern "love of art" is a veneration of the clay, and this preoccupation with sensible shapes and materials, to the neglect of *raison d'être*, is tantamount to idolatry in the religious sense, fetishism in the psychological sense (fetishism being an attachment to the sign, rather than to that of which it is the sign). The shapes of images are not His shapes, but imagined; He is their form, not they his. Before a Buddhist icon, it is pertinent to ask, "Whose image and superscription is this? We cannot know whether a Buddhist "work of art" is "good" or "bad," that is to say well and truly made with regard to the end in view, so long as we remain in ignorance of that end; cf. my *Transformation of Nature in Art*, 1934, and "Understanding the art of India," in *Parnassus*, April, 1934.

83 (*page 54*). *Inferno*, IX, 61, *Mirate la dottrina, che s'asconde, sotto il velame degli versi strani*; cf. *Paradiso*, XXXIII, 142, *all'alta fantasia qui mancò possa*, and *Taittrīya Up.*, II, 4, "Before Whom words and intellect turn back, not reaching Him." In accordance with the Indian theory of aesthetic experience, the accomplishment of the aesthetic act depends not on the accidents of the representation, but on the spectator's or hearer's own effort or energy. In other words, iconography can be regarded only as a curious and sterile science, a cataloguer's art, until we proceed from the denotation to a realization of, and assimilation to, the ultimate significance (*paramārtha*) of the symbols (*pratīka*) employed. But, as the *Tao Teh Ching* expresses it, "There are but few in the world who attain to the teaching without words."

84 (*page 57*). "There is the rose wherein the divine Word was made flesh; there are the lilies by whose fragrance the Right Way is found"; or to venture a Sanskrit version, replacing "rose" by "lotus," *Tatrāsty apāṁ puṣpaṁ yasmin saddharmo 'nnamayaḥ samabhavat, tatra puṣkarāṇi yesāṁ gandhenāryo mārgo labhyate.*

85 (*page 58*). It is taken for granted that "those who venerate earthen images of the Immortals do not revere the clay, but the Immortals thereby designated," *Divyāvadāna*, XXVI (ed. Cowell and Neill, p. 363).

Cf. Zimmer, *Kunstform und Yoga im indischen Kultbild*, 1926, p. 31, "Das Kultbild ist ein *yantra* und nur ein *yantra*." A *yantra* is a "device" of any kind, here a "piece of psychological apparatus."

86 (*page 58*). Cf. "his manhood is a hindrance so long as they cling to it with mortal pleasure; they ought to follow God in all his ways and not keep solely to his way of manhood who reveals to us the way of Godhood," Eckhart, I, 187.

87 (*page 58*). For the textual references see the *PTS* Pali Dictionary, s.v. *upādi*.

88 (*page 58*). "Where God gives up the ghost, darkness reigns in the unknown known unity. This is hidden from us. . . . Plunge in: this is the drowning," Eckhart, I, 368.

89 (*page 59*). The "Harrowing of Hell," cf. St Thomas, *Sum. Th.*, III, Q. LII. It must be assumed from the Buddha's point of view that Māra himself was not merely defeated, but transfigured and restored, just as the weapons with which he had assaulted the throne-sitter had been transformed. For angels are fallen, not in nature (*svabhāva*) but in grace, their divine prototypes cannot be affected; and what the Buddha sees is things in their perfection; he who attains Perfection sees only perfection, neither good nor evil having any place in the perfectly simple understanding (*samatā-jñāna*).

Just as in Islam, the curse laid upon Iblīs (Satan) lasts only until the Day of

Judgment, and at the End of Time he will be restored to his place with Allāh. It cannot be supposed that the Great Person "now" sees things differently from the manner in which he "will" see them at the End of time, for to him all time is simultaneously present; so Māra, who plays the part of Satan in relation to the man Gautama, by the omniscient Buddha could have been seen only in his eternal perfection.

90 (*page 59*). The World-picture is the "Eternal Mirror," cf. Augustine, *De Civ. Dei,* lib. xii, c. 29, *speculum eternum mentes se videntium ducit in cognitionem omnium creatorum* (here "mens" = *manas* = *daiva cakṣu,* "the angelic eye," as in *Chāndogya Up.*, VIII, 12, 5), and Chuang Tzū, "The mind of the sage, being at rest, becomes the Mirror of theUniverse."

91 (*page 59*). "The moment of supreme illumination is short-lived, and passes like a flash of lightning," Eckhart, I, 255, cf. *svaprakāśa, camatkāra,* in *Sāhitya Darpaṇa,* III, 2.

92 (*page 59*). *Ākāśena . . . gantvā,* which some might well have understood to mean *hṛdayākāśe*. For "Sky" (*ākāśa*) is also "space in the lotus of the heart"; and the "place prepared" may be regarded as the ripened consciousness of the Individual being, in which the planted seed of the Wisdom (-tree) springs up full-grown.

93 (*page 59*). "Vanaṣpati," in the Vedas, commonly designates Agni as the Tree of Life.

The "springing up immediately," as is also outwardly symbolized in the mango trick, cf. *Dhammapada Atthakatha,* III, 207, and in *Jātaka,* No. 489, "Vessavaṇa's Mango" (the same is attributed to Manannan mac Lir, God of the Sea, in Irish myth, see O'Grady, *Silva Gadelica,* 1892, p. 321), is characteristic for any manifested deity or "Hero."

94 (*page 60*). The (Mahā-) Bodhimaṇḍa is *paṭhavī-nābhī* also in *Mahābodhivaṁsa*, 79. The notion of the navel of the earth, which is also a point on the axis of the universe, is found again and again in the Vedas: for example, *Ṛg Veda*, I, 59, 1-2, where "Agni, navel of the earth (*nābhir āgniḥ pṛthivyāḥ*)," is compared to a "column (*sthūṇa*) supporting the kindreds," *i.e.* all the hierarchies of exsistence; X, 1, 6, where Agni is again *nābhā pṛthivyāḥ*; X, 5, 3-6, where Agni is the navel (*nābhi*) of all that proceeds or is concrete, a pillar (*skambha*) at the parting of the ways (*pathāṁ visarge*); X, 82, 5-6, where "the Waters held that same Germ (*garbha*) in which the Several Angels appeared together (*samapaśyanta*, cf. *paryapaśyata* in *Pañcaviṁśa Brāhmaṇa*, VII, 8, 1), on the Navel (*nābhāv adhi*) of the Unborn, and wherein stood (*tasthuḥ*, from *sthā*, to exist) inherent (*arpitam*) the Several Worlds (*viśvā bhuvanāni*)"; IX, 72, 7, where Soma, *nābhā pṛthivyāḥ*, sustains the Mighty Heaven; X, 13, 3, "At the centre (*nabhau*) of the Law (*ṛta*) I make all things clean (*sampunāmi*)"; X, 64, 13, "Where we are met together at the navel (*nābhā*, here the place of Sacrifice), there Aditi confirms our uterine relationship (*jāmitva*)"; *Maitri Up.*, VI, 6, where *Svar* is the head, *Bhur* the feet, and most significant, *Bhuvas* (Space) the navel, of Prajāpati. *Mund.* II. 2.6 *rathanābham . . . Antaścarte bahudhā jāyamānaḥ.*

For the navel of the earth in universal tradition cf. O. Rank, *Art and Artist,* New York, 1932, pp. 138 f. and 189 f., and references there cited, especially W. Roscher, *Der Omphalosgedanke . . .*, 1918 ("The whole of antiquity seems to have thought . . . that the navel of the earth was also the starting point of the world's creation").

As to the primordial importance attached to the East, which at first sight seems to contradict the notion of "centre," a careful comparison of Vedic texts (see my *New Approach to the Vedas*, note 65, and Appendix) shows that by successive analogical transpositions the "East" implies "North," "Zenith," and "Within," i.e. ultimately the "centre of consciousness," centre of life, *amṛtasya nābhi*.

95 (*page 60*). As well he may, who is the "wise, indestructible, undying Mover" of the Tree, *Taittirīya Up.*, I, 10, (*rerivā*), one with the Buddha himself as Pravartin of the Bhava-cakra. Dhamma-cakka and Bhava-cakka are sharply distinguished in Pali texts from the standpoint of edification (especially in the phrase *dhamma-cakka-pavattana*, where *dhamma* has the restricted sense of "Gospel"), but in reality the Principal and Existenctial wheels revolve on a common axis, the omniscient eye perceives their identity, he who moves and he who stays the Wheel are one. The Māradharśana is thus not an external conflict, but simply the involution (*nivattana, nivṛtti*) of the Buddha's own Will. All redemption is God's redemption of himself, every Passion a sacrifice unto the Sacrifice.

96 (*page 60*). Exegesis ordered to edification has missed the point here. "Evil" is that by which existence is diminished or denied: "Good," that by which existence is enhanced or affirmed. Evil is what a given being would naturally avoid, good that which a given being would naturally possess. That is all a matter of the affections, and relative. The point here is not that the Great Person is "good" as other than "bad," viz. morally, but that he is transcendent equally with respect to evil and to good. Māra assaults the Bodhisattva with every weapon in the category "evil"; Māra's daughters present the category "good" in all its most attractive forms. Māra's weapons are transformed into offerings of flowers: the Boddhisattva does not look at Māra's daughters, he remains un-affected. Cf. *Saddharma-Puṇḍarīka*, V, 22-7, like *Bhagavad Gītā*, V, 15, and XII, 17; also the discussion in my *Buddha and the Gospel of Buddhism*, II, 5, and Eckhart, I, 272, "God is neither good nor true." In the Christian "Temptation," Jesus is equally immune to "good" (the kingdoms of the earth) and to "evil" (the being cast down from the mountain) cf. Guénon, *Le Roi du Monde*; this temptation corresponding to Māra's of the Boddhisattva when he offers him the lordship of the world, *J.*, I, 63. It may be noted that in all Messianic concepts, the possibility of an exercise of either the temporal (*kṣatra*) or spiritual power (*brahma*) is presented, and that in the type of the priest-king these are united. In the *Ṛg Veda* the dual powers are represented in the dual Indrāgnī or Indrābrahmaṇaspatī. The spiritual power having precedence (*Aitareya Brāhmaṇa*, VIII, 1, 5, and *Śatapatha Brāhmaṇa*, IV, 1, 4, cf. *Ṛg Veda*, IV, 50, 9), Agni is said to choose Indra for himself, and to have given the *vajra* to his hands (*Ṛg Veda*, X, 124, 4 and X, 52, 5) followed by the ritual in SB where the Brahman gives the king his sword, with the words Indra's are the sins (*kilbiṣāni*) involved in the establishment of the temporal power, Agni the Redeemer (*kilbiṣas-pṛt*).The Buddha plays the part of, and strictly speaking "is," Agni.

97 (*page 60*). *Kṛtsna* (Kṛtsna = 'holy' as a "whole'—see Jacob Böhme, *Of the Incarnation of Jesus Christ*, London, Constable & Co. 1934) is the term employed in the *Bṛhadāraṇyaka Up.*, I, 4, 17, to denote the entirety and plenitude of the Self, Ātman, in contrast to the privation (*akṛtsna*) out of which it proceeds. Depsite the dialectical antithesis, this "Pleroma" is not other than, but is the affirmation of, the "Void" of the Śūnya-vādin. Just as in Christian theology the omnipotence of God springs from the unground (= *abudhna*) of the Godhead, "which is as though it were not,"

so also in our own experience, the source of our highest powers is "unconscious."

98 (*page 61*). See my *Yakṣas*, I, 30-31.

99 (*page 61*). See *Bṛhad Devatā*, I, 73, and IV, 143: the weapon of any Angel is his Fiery Energy (*tejas*), and conversely, the Angel is the Self (*ātman*) of the weapon. Reitzenstein, Bibliothek Warburg, *Voiträge* 1924/25, pp. 1, 19 (Teubner 1927) regards him in an Orphic hymn 'fires radiate from his body . . . the earth is his abdomen, his navel a mountain peak with the ocean above it, as of Indian origin. The Buddha employs his own *tejas* directly as a weapon when he overcomes the Nāga on the occasion of the Conversion of the Jaṭilas, and perhaps also in his conflict with Māra, cf. description of Figs. 8-9; the *vajra* only indirectly, through Vajrapāṇi, cf. *Ṛg Veda*, X, 52, 5, where Agni entrusts the *vajra* to Indra. In Buddhism, the "Angel with the flaming sword" is specifically *Mañjuśrī*, cf. Fig. 39.

100 (*page 62*). Axle-tree and axis are the same, of course, as the trunk of the Tree of Life, the stem of the Lotus of Space, the vertical of the Cross, and with the Liṅgam based in the "Land of Gold"; also with the Fiery Pillar, and with the Sacrificial Post when universally considered. Cf. R. Guénon, *Le symbolisme de la croix*, Paris, 1931; E. Rouselle, "Die Achse des Lebens," *Chinesische-Deutsche Almanach*, 1933; J. Strzygowski, *Asiatische Miniaturmalerei*, 1933, pp. 102, 170.

Islamic theology has also its exactly equivalent expression in the doctrine of the Quṭb, the axis and pole or centre of the Universe. This pole, primarily the Divine Idea (*ḥaqīqa*), Word (*amr* = Logos, Fiat), and Spirit (*rūḥ*), is an aspect (*wajh*) of Allāh, and called the Premier Angel, on him "turns the mill-stone of created things" (= Skr. *bhavacakra*), he has dominion over heaven, earth, and hell. To that same Idea also the Saint and Comprehensor attains, "he becomes the Pole on which the Universe revolves." Furthermore, the throne (*'arsh*) of Allāh is supported by eight Angels (presumably guardians of the quarters and inter-quarters) who are the "powers" of this axis or pole. See R.A. Nicholson, *Studies in Islamic Mysticism*, 1921, pp. 105-14, 194, 195, and D.B. Macdonald, "Development of the Idea of Spirit in Islam," *Acta Orientalia*, IX, 1931, 346, 347. Guénon writes: Er-*Rūh* (Arabic for the spirit of God) is identified with the metatron of the Kabbala. It's "place" is at the centre of *El-'arsh*, represented by a circular figure. The eight angles that support *El-arsh* correspond to the four cardinal points and the four intermediate points [of a compass] but at the same time they also correspond to certain groups of letters of the Arabic alphabet in accord with their numerical order, which are also related to these same regions. [tr. ed.]

101 (*page 62*). Amongst the Japanese sources may be mentioned Ōmura Seigai, *Sanbon Ryōbu Mandara*, Tokyō, 1913; Mossaku Ishida, *A Study on the Excavation of Buddhistic Remains at Nachi*, Tokyō Imperial Household Museum Investigation Series, No. 5, Tokyō, 1927; and Takakusu and Ono, *Taisho Shinshu Daizōkyō Zuzō* (the Tripitika in Chinese, picture section), Tokyō, 1934. See also Anesaki, *Buddhist Art* (1st ed., 1915), pp. 38 f. and Pl. XVI, and Getty, *Gods of Northern Buddhism* (2nd ed., 1928), pp. 28 ff., and s.v. *tri-koṇa* and *vajra* in Index. (In Anesaki, Pl. XVI, the places of the illustrations A and B are reversed.)

102 (*page 63*). "In material seats is displayed strength, forasmuch as a person sits firmly thereon. But here the reverse is the case; for the Angels themselves are made firm by God," St Thomas, *Sum. Th.*, I. Q. 108, A. 5.

103 (*page 63*). *Citta* corresponds to Brahmanical *hṛdaya*, Islamic *qalb*, Christian "soul,"

the "heart" psychologically. Cf. Bodhi-citta, "heart of awakening," or "wisdom mind,' the virtual Buddhahood in every consciousness. *SB* III. 8.3.16 heart is the ātman of the creature.

104 (*page 63*). The four *āsavas*: generally will (*kāma*), contingency (*bhāva*), opinion (*diṭṭhi*), and empiricism (*avijjā*). *Avijjā* (*avidyā*) is "knowledge of," to be contrasted with *vijjā* (*vidyā, jñāna*), which is "knowledge as."

105 (*page 63*). Translation in SBE, XXI; text, *Bibliotheca Buddhica*, X. References given here as *SP* are to the verses, and those given as *SPt.* to the prose text of the edition. By far the best interpretation of this fundamental Mahāyāna Sūtra, both from the theological and the iconographic standpoint, appears in A. Mus, "Le Buddha paré . . . ," in *BÉFEO*, 1929. For the Prabhūtaratna section, in which the identity of present and past Buddhas is demonstrated, see H.E. Fernald, "An Early Chinese Sculptured Stele," *Eastern Art*, III, 1931.

106 (*page 64*). "It is an unthinkable number of myriads of aeons (*kalpa*), whereof there is no measure, since I was first awakened (*prāptā mayā eṣa tadāgrabodhiḥ*, cf. Vedic *uṣarbudh*), and I proclaim the Dharma eternally (*dharmaṁ deśemy ahu nityakalam*) . . . My standing-place (*adhiṣṭhāna*; also in *Ṛg Veda*, X, 81, 2, and *Chāndogya Up.*, VIII, 12, 1, *adhiṣṭhā Śvet.* 1.1 in the same way, as ground or platform of the Self) endures for inconceivable myriads of aeons, such is my quality (*etad īdṛśam*), nor do I move from this Gṛdhrakūṭa downward to any other seat (*śayyāsana*) during myriad ages," *SP*, XV, 1 and 10. Maitreya's bewilderment at the Buddha's assertion, voiced in *SP*, XIV, 44-54, exactly parallels Arjuna's in the *Bhagavad Gītā*, IV, 4, "Later was thy birth, how then am I to understand that thou sayest "in the beginning'?" In the Christian Gospels, cf. "Before Abraham I am."

107 (*page 64*). This point of view seems to be reflected iconographically in the Buddha-Maitreya types of Mathurā, which are called "Bodhisattva" in the inscriptions.

The statements as to the Buddha's repeated messianic "descents" are to be reconciled with his perpetual and real presence on Mt Gṛdhrakūṭa (*SP*, XV, 10) by the doctrine of Nirmāṇakāya, the earthly likeness being merely a shadow or reflex of his being in majesty.

108 (*page 64*). Note that *nivṛtti*, "return" (to unconditioned being), *nirvṛtatva* in *Maitri Up.*, VI, 22, is here equivalent to Parinirvāṇa; elsewhere also in the *SP*, Nirvāṇa is often used where Parinirvāṇa is to be understood. Actually, the Great Person stands "where void looks into void, equally spirated, despirated"; what he reveals, even to the Boddhisattvas on Mt Gṛdhrakūṭa, is necessarily his face, his light directed towards the world, not that aspect which faces the unknown darkness of the altogether inexpressible, with respect to which he is from the beginning silent, for "this Brahman is silence." Hence the necessary frontality of the worshipped icon, for no man worshipping objectively can see the back of the deity (that Moses is said to have seen God's "back," Exodus, xxxiii, 23, implies that Moses was more than a man, *amānava*, like Agni and Buddha). Cf. *Ṛg Veda*, IV, 1, 2, where Agni is besought to "turn hitherward thy brother Varuṇa" (*ā vavṛtsva*, and Sāyaṇa's gloss, *abhimukhī kuru*, "make him to face towards us"), which is effectively a prayer to Agni to reveal himself, who is in fact Varuṇa's "face" (*anīka*, VII, 88, 2).

The contrary of *nivṛtti*, "return," is *āvṛtti*, "hither-turn," or *pravṛtti*, "out-turn," towards existence and embodiment (cf. *āvavṛtran* contrasted with *niyāna* in *Ṛg*

Veda, I, 164, 7, *vimucam* with *āvṛtaṁ punah* in V, 46, 1). *Niḥsaraṇa* and *prasaraṇa* = *pravartana* are similarly contrasted; though *pravartana* is often used with respect to Dharma in the restricted sense of "Gospel," and is then an operation undertaken solely to the end that *niḥsaraṇa* may be accomplished.

109 (*page 64*). In Hīnayāna and Mahāyāna Buddhism, "Tathāgata" or "-āgata" is the most usual designation of the Buddha.

Presumably compounded of *tathā* + *āgata,* the meaning is either "he who has reached Suchness," or "He who has thus attained," i.e. has reached the goal. The Commentary on *Dīgha Nikāya*, III, 84, very well explains *tathāgata* as *dhamma-sabhāva*, "having the Word as his intrinsic nature," cf. *svabhāva-dharma-samanvāgata*, "having gotten to the Word as his intrinsic nature," *SPt*, p. 481, and *dharmatā*, the "Wordness," *SP*, II, 34. Dharmakāya and Svabhāvakāya are interchangeable terms (*Bodhicaryāvatāra*, III, 16), essence and nature being indivisible in pure Being. For this identity see also Maitreya-Asaṅga, *Uttaratantra*, I, 149. Synonyms of *dharmatā* are *tathatā*, "suchness," and *bhūtatā*, "is-ness." On *dharma* and *dharmatā* as essence and nature see also Maitreya-Asaṅga, *Dharma-dharmatā-vibhaṅga*, as analyzed by E. Obermiller, "The Sublime Science of Maitreya," *Acta Orientalia*, IX, 1931, 87, 88.

Svabhāva in Mahāyāna texts has been well and more fully discussed by St. Schayer, "Die mahāyānistische Kritik des hīnayānistischen Pluralismus (im Anschluss an das Problem des svabhāva)," *ZDMG,* N.F. IX, 1930, 105. Cf. note 117.

Svabhāva is generally "intrinsic nature" as distinguished from *svarūpa*, "intrinsic form," *nirguṇa* as distinguished from *saguṇa* Brahman, Godhead (which "is as though it were not") from God. Equally correct, though perhaps not stated quite from this point of view, is the comparison of the Absolutely Extinguished (*parinibbuta* = *parinirvāta*) Buddha with the Deep Sea (*gambhīra samudda*), *Saṁyutta Nikāya*, IV, 376: for the Deep Sea is the Waters, the Abyss, cf. *Ṛg Veda*, X,129, 1-3, *gahanaṁ gambhīram . . . ānīd avātam . . . apraketaṁ salilam*; V, 85, 6 and X, 5, 1, Agni as "single sea" (*ekaḥ samudraḥ*); and Eckhart, I, 176, "the sea of his own unfathomable nature."

Some Buddhist scholars use these terms very loosely: Mrs Rhys Davids for example (*Manual of Buddhism*, 1932, pp. 144-6) treats *svabhāva* as "essence," "own-being," and speaks of the body as "giving 'more being' to what we judge we really are," as though a "more" could be added to "being." What is meant is that *the body is that whereby being is manifested in a given mode*; but that neither adds to nor detracts from "being," cf. *Bṛhadāraṇyaka Up.*, IV, 4, 23, "This everlasting omnipotence of the knower of Brahman is neither increased nor diminished by action."

110 (*page 64*). Compare the case of the angel Baka, *Saṁyutta Nikāya*, I, 142 (VI, 1, 4, 2), who labours under the delusion that there is no "further recession" (*uttariṁ nissaraṇam*) beyond the Brahmā-world; and "the light beyond Heaven," *Chāndogya Up.*, III, 13, 7.

111 (*page 65*). Cf. *Ṛg Veda*, X, 129, 2, *ānīd avātam*, "breathes without breathing," *Atharva Veda*, VIII, 9, 9, *aprāṇaiti prāṇena prāṇatīnām*, "moves breathless in the breath of those that breathe," *Maitri Up.*, II, 7, *acala . . . carati*, "moves without moving," *Bṛhadāraṇyaka Up.*, VI, 3, 23, *paśyan vai tan na paśyati*, "sees but does not see," *Śvetāśvatara Up.*, III, 19, *paśyaty acakṣuḥ*, "sees without looking," etc.

112 (*page 65*). Verbal and ideological correspondences between the *SP* and the Upaniṣads and *Bhagavad Gītā* abound. We do not, however, by any means intend by what is said above to imply that an identification of the Buddha with Brahmā was ever accepted by Buddhists literally; Brahmā by name is never from the Buddhist point of view, whether Hīnayāna or Mahāyāna, more than the wisest and best of the Brahmanical Angels.

Cunningham, *ASR*, III, Pl. 18, illustrates a Buddha image having the inscription *bhagavato pitāmahasya*, "of the Bhagavata Grandfather."

113 (*page 65*). *Dīgha Nikāya*, I, 252, "There is agreement and likeness between the Bhikkhu and Brahmā . . . it is in every way possible that the Bhikkhu should be united to Brahmā, who is the same," i.e. in purity and wisdom. The adjective *brahma* is freely used in Hīnayāna texts (e.g. *brahma-vihāra*, with reference to the four stages of Jhāna which lead to rebirth in the Brahma-worlds), but generally in a specifically ethical rather than theological sense, so that "*brahma*' is made to mean "sublime," rather than "of or belonging to Brahmā." Buddhism in fact preserves the older Ṛg Vedic meaning of *brahma* as spiritual power contrasted with *kṣatra* as temporal power. With Buddhist usage cf. *brāhmaṇa* in *Bṛhadāraṇyaka Up.*, III, 5, and the special use of Brahman to mean not any priest but that priest who "voices the lore of Genesis," *vadati jātavidyām*, *Ṛg Veda*, X, 71, 11.

114 (*page 65*). The "utterance" of the Word may be understood (1) with reference to the manifestation and exposition on Mt Gṛdhrakūṭa, and (2) with reference to the manifestation and preaching on earth, the one being heard by the angelic, the other by the sensible, ear. In either case the teaching is not the Word itself, but merely an echo of the Word; not that anything is deliberately withheld, but that words or other symbols are inadequate. Cf. pp. 35-6.

115 (*page 65*). The Cakravartin and later Sambhogakāya concepts explain the iconographic type of the "Crowned Buddha, " see P. Mus, "Le Buddha paré . . .," *BÉFEO*, 1929.

Observe further with respect to the revelation on Mt Gṛdhrakūṭa that this was a place exactly appropriate to the manifestation of the Buddha in his capacity as Cakravartin and Dharmarājā; for according to Hsüan-tsang it was on Mt Gṛdhrakūṭa that kings were accustomed to announce their accession with great ceremony.

116 (*page 66*). On the "Three bodies of a Buddha," viz. Dharmakāya, Sambhogakāya, and Nirmāṇakāya, see de la Vallée Poussin "Studies in Buddhist Dogma: the Three bodies of a Buddha (*trikāya*)," *JRAS*, 1906, pp. 943 ff.; Masson-Oursel, "Les trios corps du Bouddha," *Journal Asiatique*, May-June, 1913, pp. 581-618; de la Vallée Poussin, "Note sur les trois corps du Bouddha," *Muséon*, 1913, pp. 261, 262; Demiéville, "Les versions chinoises du Milindapañha," *BÉFEO*, 1924, esp. pp. 52-70; E. Obermiller, "The Sublime Science of Maitreya," *Acta Orientalia*, IX, 1931; "The Doctrine of Prajñā-pāṛamitā as exposed in the *Abhisamayālaṁkāra* of Maitreya," *ibid.*, XI, 1933, and Mus, *loc. cit.* In the expositions of Maitreya there is posited a fourth "body," the *svabhāvakāya* or "intrinsic-nature body," as being in potentiality transcendental with respect to the actual (*saṁskṛta*) *dharmakāya*, the "relation" being that of non-being to being, essence to nature, Godhead to God; it is inasmuch as these are one and the same in the Tathāgata that the two aspects of the Dharmakāya (viz. *svabhāva-* and *jñāna-*) are not distinguished in the familiar arrangement in "three bodies" (*trikāya*).

A rendering of *kāya* as "substance" rather than as "body" might be preferable. The "three bodies" (*trikāya*) may be compared to the three modalities of the Self (*ātman*) in the ontology of the Upaniṣads, viz. the *annamaya*, *manomaya*, and *ānandamaya* bodies (*śarīra*) and to the states of "Waking," "Dream," and "Deep Sleep,"; *svabhāva-kāya* to "the Fourth." The four bodies correspond to "states" of non-being, being in the angelic mode, and being in the human mode; only the two latter can be said to "exist" (*existare*). The following may serve to clarify the meaning of the conception of Buddhahood on three distinct planes of being: "There is one Word both thought and spoken: angels, the soul, and all creatures. Another Word, thought but unspoken, I can conceive. And there is still another Word unthought of an unspoken which never proceeds forth but is eternally in him who speaks it," Eckhart, I, 214, cf. Plotinus, *Enneads*, I, 2, 3, "as the uttered thought is the image of the soul-thought, so the soul-thought images a thought above itself and is the interpreter of the higher sphere." Islamic *kalima* includes the Word thought and spoken, and thought but unspoken, these expressions corresponding to an interior Word, *kalām*, unthought and unspoken. The application of the *nirmāṇakāya* doctrine corresponds to that of the Docetic heresy in Christianity.

117 (*page 66*). One should not, of course, be misled by such expressions as "Father of the World," or *prajāpati*, "Lord of his children," to identify Prajāpati with "God the Father" in the Christian Trinity. Brahmā-Prajāpati, Agni, Buddha are the begotten Son, and as such the exemplary cause of the whole emanation; it is precisely their filial relation to the Father that is reflected in the iconography of the lotus-birth, cf. Fig. B, where the recumbent "Father" is Nārāyaṇa.

118 (*page 66*). Max Müller in SBE, XLIX, ii, xxii, rightly derived the Buddhist Sukhāvatī from the Paradise of Varuṇa, but for this the Purāṇas are by no means the oldest sources; see for example *Jaiminīya Brāhmaṇa*, I, 42-44 (*JAOS*, XV, 234-8).

119 (*page 67*). The *Kauṣītaki Up.* description of the *āsandī* corresponds to that of the Vratya's throne in *Atharva Veda*, XV, 3, 3-9, and to that of Indra's throne in the *Aitareya Brāhmaṇa*, VIII, 12. It is moreover quite intelligible that the *throne* of Indra should be the *footstool* of Brahmā. A very near parallel to the Indian *āsandī* and *paryaṅka* can be pointed to in the Muḥammadan conceptions of the Footstool (*kursī*) and Throne (*'arsh*) of Allāh, the former representing the analytical aspect and the latter the synthetic aspect of the Divine Understanding, see Nicholson, *Studies in Islamic Mysticism*, p. 111, note 3.

120 (*page 67*). Observe that union with Brahmā, the sharing of his throne, while it corresponds ideologically to the sitting together of Gautama and Prabhūtaratna in the *Saddharma Puṇḍarīka*, is not *ati-mukti*, "Total Release" (cf. Sāyaṇa on *Aitareya Āraṇyaka*, II, 3, 7, citing also *Bṛhadāraṇyaka Up.*, IV, 1, 2; and Śaṅkarācārya on *Brahma Sūtra*, IV, 4, 22), just as union with the Sambhogakāya Buddha, the sharing of his throne, is not Parinirvāṇa (for the Buddha enthroned is *sadā sthita* (cf. Agni, *anipadyamāna*), not *parinirvāyamāṇa*, *SPt*, pp. 318, 319).

121 (*page 67*). From what has already been deduced, it will be evident that *padmagarbhe* is also *garbhe mātuḥ*, e.g. in *Ṛg Veda*, VI, 16, 35.

122 (*page 67*). The famous Lamaist formula *Oṁ maṇi padme hūṁ*, which may be more or less adequately rendered "Hail, the Jewel in the Lotus," is unquestionably connected with Avalokiteśvara, and in Tibet is understood to refer to his lotus-birth in the Western Paradise of Amitābha (Rockhill, *Land of the Lamas*, pp. 326 ff.). It is also suggested that Maṇipadme can be read as one word, vocative of

Maṇipadmā, who would be the Śakti or Tārā of the Bodhisattva, cf. such other *dhāraṇīs* as *Oṁ vajrapuṣpe hūṁ*, and the discussion by F.W. Thomas, in *JRAS*, 1906, p. 464.

123 (*page 68*). With the notion of the Buddhist paradise as merely a resting place, compare Eckhart (Evans, I, 274, 276) with respect to Heaven and the vision of God, "As this is not the summit of divine union so it is not the soul's abiding place," for the soul in Heaven is "not yet dead and gone out into that which follows created existence." Cf. also Préau, in *Le Voile d' Isis*, XXXVII, 566.

124 (*page 68*). "Extinction (*nirvāṇa*) is indeed an awakening (*avabodha*) to the sameness (*samatā*) of all principles (*dharma*)," *SPt*, p. 133; "Without understanding of the World-Wheel, the Return is not understood," *saṁsāracakra-syājñānān nirvṛtiṁ na vijñānate*, *SP*, V, 50. Cf. "In god all things have the same form, though that is the form of very different things," Eckhart, I, 211, and "Not till she knows all that there is to be known does she cross over to the unknown good. This crossing is obscure to many a religious," Eckhart, I, 385. Whereas "He who sees the principles separately (*dharmān pṛthak*), runs to waste after them" *Kaṭha Up.*, IV, 14. Keith, who is much concerned to show that the texts of the Vedas and Upaniṣads do not mean what they seem to mean, denies the correspondence here, *HOS*, XXXII, 547; but already in *Ṛg Veda*, X, 90, 16, *dharmāṇi* is "principles," *dharma* in all these passages coming very near to *nāma*, "form" in relation to *rūpa*, "thing," or better "phenomenon." As for *dharmya* contrasted with *aṇu*, as "thingish" with "undimensioned," in *Kaṭha Up.*, II, 13, cf. *dharmin* and *dharma* as "thing" and "quality" in *Sāhitya Darpaṇa*, II, 10, that which is qualified being "thingish," while the quality is "essential".

125 (*page 68*). "One and one uniting, void shines into void, equally spirated, despirated, there is the Supreme Being," Eckhart, I, 368. Buddhist scholars apparently ignore that the Upaniṣads (e.g. *Bṛhadāraṇyaka Up.*, II, 3, 1) distinguish the Brahman in a likeness (*mūrta*), mortal (*martya*), selfed (*ātmanvī*), etc., from the Brahman that is imageless (*amūrta*), not-a-self (*anātmya*), immortal (*amṛta*, to be understood absolutely, not as when applied to the Angels, relatively), etc. The Buddhist emphasis on *anatta* cannot have been a purely monastic development, for that would be to assert that the Buddha's Buddhism had been strictly and merely a theistic doctrine. Why does the Buddha teach an Absolute Extinction, who is him-Self merely Extinguished-with-residual-existential-elements (*sa-upādi-sesa*)? Why does Eckhart (Evans, I, 274, 376) assert that it is God's full intention that we should become what He is not, that the soul honors God most in being quit of God? Because there lies beyond the idea (*nāma*) of Buddha, God, Self, Person, Being, the *possibility of these assumptions*; these assumptions are not All that "is" (here "is-ness" can be predicated only analogically). The *bhakta* deliberately rejects this last death of the soul. Nevertheless, in order to attain to the Supreme Identity of that which is the Self, and that which is-not the Self, the soul (individual or super-individual consciousness) must become, be lost in, That of which the Self is the first assumption: the soul, in order to be one with the Supreme Identity, must go beyond its Selfhood to the unselfed source of Self. That is the "Drowning," "Absolute Extinction," from which every individual or even super-individual existence naturally shrinks, which only the adamantine mind (*vajirūpama citta*) dare essay.

126 (*page 68*). Hence the Tathāgata may be represented either in Samādhi, or on the

other hand in one of the customary active poses, e.g. *dharmacakra-pravartana*.

127 (*page 69*). "With-due-regard-to (*vyavalokya*) their faculties and energy he reveals to living beings in each generation his name and his extinction (*nirvāṇa*) and by various alternative-formulations (*paryāya*) gladdens these beings . . . and the Word (*vāc*) that the Tathāgata utters (*vyāharati*) for their instruction (*vinaya, nirṇaya*), whether in his own aspect (*ātmopadarśana*) or another's, whether on his own basis (*ātmārambaṇa* = *ātmālambaṇa*) or under the cloak (*āvaraṇa*) of another, all that the Tathāgata declares, all those alternative-formulations are true," *SPt*, pp. 317, 318. The Bodhisattva Gadgadasvara, for example, is said to have preached the alternative-formulation known as the *Saddharma Puṇḍarīka* ("Lotus of the True Doctrine"), "sometimes in the shape (*rūpa*) of Brahmā, sometimes in that of Indra, sometimes in that of Śiva . . . ," continuing with a list of men and women of various degree, *kinnaras, nāgas*, etc., through all of whom the True Word has been revealed, *SPt*, p. 433. The monastic as distinguished from the dogmatic Buddha is but one such *upadarśana* and *ārambaṇa*. Cf. R.O. Franke in *OZ*, N.F. IV, 1915-16, p. 10, "All the seven Buddhas are only paradigms of the dogmatic Buddha . . . which dogmatic Buddha is the cloudy image of a more ancient concept of the deity"—that is, as has been amply demonstrated, of the Vedic Agni-Sūrya.

128 (*page 69*). We need not consider the case of things made without an end in view, because an activity of that kind can be predicated only of the insane, and enjoyed only by the insane. It is true that Deity in "making" the world "works" without an end in view, and that in so far as man becomes Godlike he too "works" without a purpose. But though there is thus an analogy between insanity and divinity (as when we say that to know Him, the mind must be de-mented), there is no likeness implying as sameness: on the one hand, insanity depends on a defect of substance, not of form, on the other the "work" and "making" of the world by Deity are merely figurative expressions for what is not *working*, but a *being*, not a procedure from potentiality to act, but an identity of "cause" and "effect."

129 (*page 70*). An almost identical account appears in the *Si Yu Ki* (*Records of the Western World*, Ch. VIII, Beal, pp. 115, 116).

130 (*page 70*). This cosmology, in the main of pre-Vedic antiquity, is also outlined in the Pali texts, e.g. *Dīgha Nikāya*, II, 107, and *Milindapañha*. 68. Cf. W. Kirfel, *Die Kosmographie der Inder*, 1920, and S. Beal, *Catena of Buddhist Scriptures from the Chinese*, 1871, pp. 101-16, cf. pp. 11, 12.

131 (*page 70*). Needless to say, these directions and measurements are purely analogical. In any case the Universe is thought of as a sphere or egg, the various circles referred to representing cross sections of this sphere, each such circle having its own characteristic possibilities.

132 (*page 70*). In the *Bodhicarya*, VI, 1, *kañcana-vajra-maṇḍala*. That is, of course, Hsüan Tsang's "golden wheel." This "land of Gold," representing the foundations of the earth, must also be identified with the otherwise unexplained Hāṭaka of the Devadāruvana legend (see my *Yakṣas*, II, 44, 45), where it is Śiva's liṅgam which forms the axis of the Universe. That the first product of the Waters should have been golden is developed also in Vedic cosmology from another point of view, that of the origin of created things from Fire and Water, by either reflection or generation, e.g. *Śatapatha Brāhmaṇa*, II, 1, 15, "Agni at one time cast his eyes upon the Waters, 'May I pair with them,' he thought. He united with them, and what was emitted as his seed (*retas*), that became gold (*hiraṇya*). Therefore the

latter shines like fire, being Agni's seed, hence it is found in water, for he poured it into the Waters." Hence the so often mentioned myth of the search of the Angels for the Sun or Fire "hidden in the Waters," which search is the *Quest of Life*; also the designation of the Person, Self, Brahman, in the mode of Fiery Energy and Life as "germinal" (*raitasa*, from *retas*, "seed"), Life being *found* in the "individual" Self (*adhyātman*) supported by an individual "Earth", *Bṛhadāraṇyaka Up.*, II, 5, 1-2, viz. the body, "lotus of nine gates."

133 (*page 70*). This phrase, "adamantine Identity" or "Consummation" (of *dhyāna*), appears also in the *Mahāyāna Sūtrālaṁkāra*, XIV, 45 and in the *Abhisamayālaṁkāra* of Maitreya; it is proper to the very last stage of a Boddhisattva's course and simultaneous with the "One Instant (i.e. "Eternal Now") Total Awakening" by which he is unified with the Primordial Buddha-Essence. It is evident that for this Adamantine Consummation only the "Adamantine Heart" (*vajirūpama citta, Anguttara Nikāya*, I, 124) is apt.

134 (*page 71*). When a given location, such as the Bodhimaṇḍa at Bodhgayā, or any of the other places for which a similar claim has been advanced (e.g. the Delphic Omphalos, or even Bostonian "Hub"), is identified with the "navel of the earth," or centre of the Universe, that is merely an analogical assumption, not to be literally interpreted. The superimposed centres of the various cosmic circles constitute a common axis, but it must not be understood that they revolve about this axis locally, or that the axis is situated anywhere; the cause of all things is not any one of them.

135 (*page 71*). On the habitat and character of Nāgas, see J. Ph. Vogel, *Indian Serpent-lore*, 1926; also my "Angel and Titan: an essay in Vedic Ontology" to appear in *JAOS*. The Nāgas correspond to the mermen and mermaids of European folklore, as described for example in Fouquet's *Undine*. "They are, *ante principium*, what the Angels are in *principio*."

136 (*page 71*). The Kārlī relief (Fig, 29) is not, as I once thought, a Buddha coronation (*JRAS*, 1928, p. 83); the stūpa is not a crown, though it is not althogether inappropriate that it should seem to be such. Other Indian and Chinese representations of the *stūpa* in its present relation can be referred to, e.g. Sirén, *Chinese Sculpture*, Pls. 242, 245, 246. It may be noted also that in the common Pāla reliefs representing the *aṣṭasthāna* the Parinirvāṇa is always placed at the top of the slab, above the central Buddha's head, e.g. my *History*, Fig. 228.

137 (*page 72*). For Yakṣas as chthonic powers, and specifically as earth-spirits, corresponding to the Germanic dwarfs, elves, and gnomes, see my *Yakṣas*, I, 8, and PTS Pali Dictionary, s.v. *bhumma deva.*

138 (*page 72*). Atlas, in classical mythology, is a real equivalent.

139 (*page 73*). The introductory invocatory verse of the *Daśakumāracarita* mentions amongst the various aspects of the axis of the universe the "stalk of the lotus where Brahmā resides"; other equivalents including "the staff of the umbrella of the world-egg, the mast of the ship of the earth, the flagstaff of the banner of the river of life, the axis of the circle of light (*jyotiś-cakra*, the Zodiac), the triumphal pillar of conquest of the three worlds, the three-strider's (Viṣṇu's) walking-stick," and it is "the rod of death to the foes of the wake" (i.e. of the Angels, the allusion being to the value of the *akṣa* as the *vajra* of Indra's hands.) See also notes 15, 100, and Mus, "Barabudar" in *BÉFEO*, 1932.

140 (*page 74*). Cf. Eckhart, "To find nature herself (*māyā*, *prakṛti*, *svabhāva*) all her

likenesses have to be shattered, and the farther in the nearer the actual thing" (I, 259); "None may attain be he not stripped of all mental matter" (I, 359); "this knowledge de-ments the mind" (I, 370).

141 (*page 74*). Cf. Eckhart, "On coming to one, where it is all one, she is the same" (I, 259).

142 (*page 75*). "Fontal and inflowing": *samānam udakam ut ca eti ava ca ahabhiḥ*, *Ṛg Veda*, I, 164, 51; *viṣvañc, sadhryañc*, ibid., X, 177, 3; *yad vai vāyuḥ parāṅ eva paveta kṣīyeta . . . reṣmāṇaṁ janamāno niveṣṭamāno vāti, kṣayād eva bibhyat . . . yad u ha vā āpaḥ parācīr eva prasṛtās syanderan kṣīyeraṅs tāḥ, yad aṅkāṁsi kurvāṇā niveṣṭamānā āvartān sṛjamānā yanti kṣayād eva bidhyatīḥ*, *Jaiminīya Upaniṣad Brāhmaṇa*, I, 2; that is, "If the Spirit should blow only straight away, it would die away; (but) it blows from all quarters together, winding itself in so as to generate a whirlwind, that it may not die away. And if the Waters should flow streaming only straight away, they would come to an end; but in that they proceed making bends, winding themselves in, and making eddies, that is to avoid a coming to an end." (With the notion *āvarta*, "eddy," here, compare that of "auspicious curls," *nandyāvarta*, and the general value of spirals and "strapwork" in symbolism.)

Pali *uddhaṁsoto*, "Upstreamer," sometimes applied to the religious man, corresponds to the notion of "inflowing"; cf. *Taittirīya Saṁhitā*, VII, 5, 7, 4 "upstream (*pratikūla*) from here, as it were, is the world of heaven," and *Pañcaviṁśa Brāhmaṇa*, XXV, 10, 12-18, where the distance upstream (*pratīpam*) on the Sarasvatī (the River of Life) from the place where it is lost in the desert to its source is said to be equal to that of heaven from earth. It is, in other words, a matter of "inverse thinking" (*pratyakcetanā, Yoga Sūtra*, I, 29). *āvartan*: cf. *JUB* III. 33 *brahmaṇa āvartaḥ*; *CU* IV. 15.6 *mānavāvarta* and *Brahmāvarta*; *RV* X.30.10, where *āvarvṛtaṭiḥ dvidhāraḥ* flows down to the lower pasture; (*pratikūlaṁ* = *brahmāvarta* cf. *JUB* III.33).

143 (*page 75*). *Eṣa vai mṛtyur yat saṁvatsaraḥ . . . Prajāpatiḥ*, *Śatapatha Brāhmaṇa*, X, 4, 3, 1 and 3; *Prajāpatir yaṁ prajāyamānaṁ viśvaṁ rūpaṁ anuprajāyate*, *Aitareya Brāhmaṇa*, II, 17.

144 (*page 75*). [note missing in original also]

145 (*page 75*). *Navo Navo jayamānaḥ*, *Ṛg Veda*, X, 85, 19.

146 (*page 76*). Viz. *nirmitāni*, things designed and fashioned, like the manifested flesh (*nirmāṇa-kāya*) of the terrestrial manifestation, insignificant as they are in themselves, and with respect to which the "lover of art" is no better than the hypothetical "heathen in his blindness" who worships stocks and stones, or those of whom the Buddha said, "They worship variously my traces (*dhātu*), but see not Me" (*SP*, XV, 5). The image is significant only with respect to its form, being His whose image it is, not his who fashions it.

In connection with the "traces," or "Footprints of the Law," discussed above and on p. 33-4, it may be remarked that an almost identical formulation is met with in Scholastic philosophy. The elements of the beautiful in nature and art are unity, order, and clarity: "*Ad pulchritudinem tria requiruntur. Primo quidem integritas, sive perfectio; quae enim diminuta sunt, hoc ipso turpia sunt. Et debita proportio, sive consonantia. Et iterum claritas: unde quae habunt colorem nitidum, pulchra esse dicuntur*," St Thomas Aquinas, *Sum. Th.*, I.Q. 39, A. 8. Now it is precisely these elements of integrity, harmony, and lucidity in things that are called the "traces" (*vestigia*) of God in the world, and as to this, the reader may conveniently consult Gilson, *Introduction à l'Étude de Saint Augustine*, 1931, Ch. III, *Les Vestiges de Dieu.* It is obviously from this point of view that St Bernard could say, what sounds so like a Zen dictum, "*Ligna et lapides docebunt te, quod a magistris audire non posse.*"

Even more remarkable, from the standpoint of comparative symbolism, is the fact that the "trace" is actually spoken of as a "footprint," *vestigium pedis*; cf. Bissen, *L' Exemplarisme divin de Saint Bonaventura*, 1929, pp. 70, 71, citing the Seraphic Doctor as follows: "*Egressus enim rerum mundarum a Deo est per modum vestigii. Unde si pes esset aeternus, et pulvis, in quo formatur vestigium, esset aeternus, nihil prohiberet intelligere, vestigium pedi esse coaeternum.*" It is very evident that to follow in these tracks will be to find their maker.

Mathnavi II 160-1,

Dh A I. 201 Buddha's footprint ineffecable, established for a particular person; Elephant's foot, See *S* I.86.

AV 21 characteristics of all feet are combined in elephant's foot, which is chief in size.

Kūṭāgāra mūle (kūṭaṁ = aggaṁ)

Hatthipadopama fully elucidated in *M*. no. 27,

M.I. 175 f. (*see also M*. 1.184)

. . . *kataṁ karanīyaṁ nāparaṁ itthatāyā'ti pajānāti-idaṁ vuccati brāhmaṇa tathāgata padaṁ iti pi, tathāgata niscaritaṁ iti pi, tathāgatārañjitaṁ* ('furrow'–trace of *rajas*) *iti pi.*

cf. Karlgren, in *Bull, Mus. Far Eastern Antiquities* II, pp. 53-4 (for prints in Sweden and China).

Mus. *Barabudur*, p. 62.

"Giordano Bruno allegorizing the story of Actaeon, decribes Actaeon (the intellect) as letting loose his dogs (thoughts), 'upon the tracks of savage beasts in forests wild.' These 'savage beasts' he continues, are 'the intelligible kinds of ideal conceptions, which are occult, followed by few, visited but rarely, and which do not disclose themselves to all those who seek them.' (*The Heroic Enthusiasts*, translated by Williams, vol. 1, p. 91)".

Nicholson, *Shams. . . . Tabrizi*, p. 32)

Just Bing, *Ipek*, 1926, p. 240, footprints in Norse Archaeology: Müller says

Note *tatpadavyām padaṁ dhā* (to step on another's footprints,) hence "imitate" "equal", *Kāvyād*. II. 64, cf. *RV* I. 146. 4 *cakra-pāda* (1) wheel-footed = chariot (2) elephant, *Mon. Williams.*

A.1.178 cakka = *ratha* in *cakka-samārūḷhā* "mounting their chariots".

M. 1. 176, *Sutta* 37.

A.II. 37 (IV.4. 36) best on padāni "The Brāhmaṇa Doṇa beheld on the footprints (*padesu*) of *Bhagavat* the wheels (*cakkāni*) with their 1,000 spokes (*sahassārāṇi*) with their rims (*sanemikāni*) and hubs (*sanābhikāni*) and all their appurtenances complete. On seeing these he thought thus: It is marvellous indeed! These will not be the footprints of one in human form (*manassabhūtassa*)"

M 346 *yathā pi gajarājassa padaṁ disvāna mānusā anumānena jānanti, mahā eso gaja it.*

Eckart, 1.349 "following the spoor of her quarry, Christ."

Dh. A. III. 194 B° leaves *pada-cetiya* where he has been standing still. The print as such is pada-valañja (*lāñch, lakṣ*), or *pada*.

Dh. A. III. 195 describes the interpretation of character from foot prints (*pada*) – *vivattacchadassa* (*vivaṭacchadassa*) *idaṁ īdisam padam ti.*

Combined with the notion 'traceless'.

Dh. A. III. 179 *taṁ Buddhaṁ anantagocaraṁ apadaṁ kena padena nessatha.*

"that Buddha whose field is endless and who is footless, by what path can you track him?" (cf. *Mund* 1.2.6 *Brahman apāda*).

JUB 1.15.3f (with *SB* X. 4.3.9) "shaking off their *śarīrāṇi*, the verbal tracks (*ṛkpadāni*) that lay strewn (along the *deveyāna*) upto the sky".

III.38.10 death followed up these *ṛcs.* by means of the incorporeal *sāma.*

JUB III.35.7 *padena ha vai punarmṛtyuṁ anveti. . . . na ha vai etāsāṁ devatānāṃ padaṁ asti.*

147 (*page 76*). The utterance (*vyāhṛti*) of the Three Worlds is their existence (*astitva*); the meaning of *ākhyāta* is *pradhāna*; the ground on which we stand is literally the "substance" of a "name" (*nāma*). Note the equivalence of *pradhāna*, "ground," to *pradhi*, "circumference" (of the Wheel of Life).

148 (*page 77*). Kabīr, Bolpur Edition, II, 62:

Cakra kē bich mē̃ kā̃vala ati phūliyā,
Tāsu kā koi santa jānai?
Tā madha adhara siṁhāsana gājai,
Puruṣa mahā tāha adhika virājai.

PLATES

PLATE I

FIGURE 1. The Buddha (Amitāyus) as the Tree of Life. Sāñcī, north *toraṇa*, left pillar, outer face 100-50 B.C. India Office photograph.

Above, *triśūla*, *vajra*, or "*nandi-pada*" symbol forming a head; middle, a column of superimposed lotus palmettes (cf. *skandhāt skandham, Maitri Up.*, VII, 11) forming the trunk; below, the *pādukā*, feet, "firmly established," *supratiṣṭhā*; cf. Figs. 13, 14. Above the "head" will be observed the umbrella (*chattra*, *uṣṇīṣa*) of the Cakravartin; corresponding to the prescription *uṣṇīṣa-śīrṣa* proper to the Buddha's anthropomorphic likeness. The triple division may be compared to that of the cosmic (*lokavat*) aspect of Prajāpati as described in *Maitri Up.*, VI, 6, where the "Three Worlds" constituting this "body" are *svar*, *bhuvas*, and *bhūr*, celestial, spiritual, and chthonic.

The whole is to be regarded as a "support of contemplation" (*ārambaṇa*, *Aṣṭasahasrikā Prajñāpāramitā*, *passim*; *dhīyālamba*, *Maitri. Up.*, VII, 11, see p. 27; *ālamba*, *Yoga Sūtra*, I, 10).

For a description from other points of view, see text , pp. 26-8.

FIGURE 2. The Buddha as Supernal Sun. Amarāvatī, in the Indian Museum, Calcutta, *ca.* 200 A.D. India Office photograph.

Above, the Dharmacakra or Principal Wheel, supported by four lions of which two only are visible in the frontal view.

The nave is lotiform, the eight petals representing directions; there are sixty-four spokes; the triple felly is fringed with twelve *triśūla* symbols, representing solar "months." At this level also are two dancing Apsarases, supported by lotuses (of the "upper waters"). Above the wheel are "cherubim." For the solar significance of the addorsed animals cf. Roes, *Greek Geometric Art*, 1933, pp. 94-122. The wheel is supported by a column, the Axis of the Universe, corresponding to the trunk of the Tree of Life, and the "one leg" of the Sun, when alluded to as *eka-pād*. At the base level there is a throne and footstool, with wheel-marked feet (*pādukā, pada*, Buddha-pada), as in Figs. 1, 13, 14. These, his "traces" (*dhātu*) on earth, are adored by human worshippers.

FIGURE 3. The Buddha as Supernal Sun. Amarāvatī, *ca.* 200 A.D. British Museum (?). India Office photograph.

Similar to Fig. 2, but the pillar is differently treated and the paired riders are replaced by flying angelic types, except at the top, where two riders take the place of the Apsarases. The pillar has three lotiform nodes. The segments (*parva*) between the three nodes are octagonal, and geometrically patterned, with human worshippers at the base level. Such arrangements, indeed, as those of Figs. 2 and 3 correspond exactly to such representations of superimposed worlds as may be seen at Sāñcī, east *toraṇa*, right pillar, front face (Bachhofer, *Early Indian Sculpture*, Pl. 59), where the Brahmaloka is sharply differentiated from the *kāmarūpa lokas* below.

PLATE I

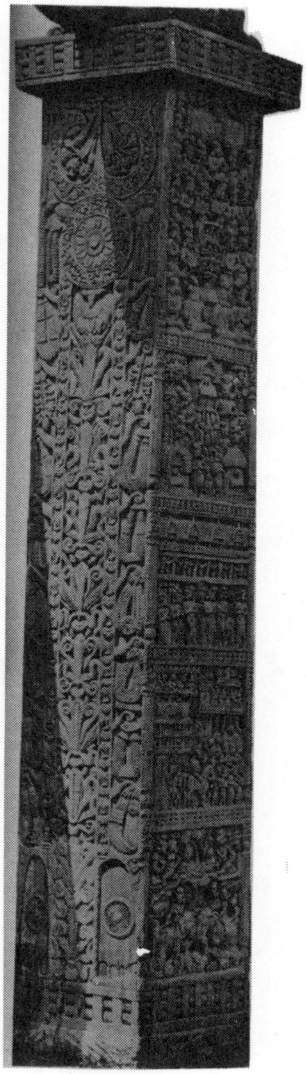

1

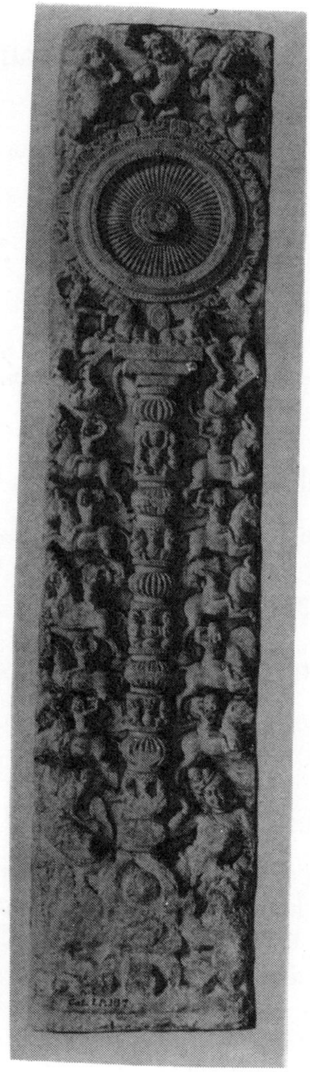

2

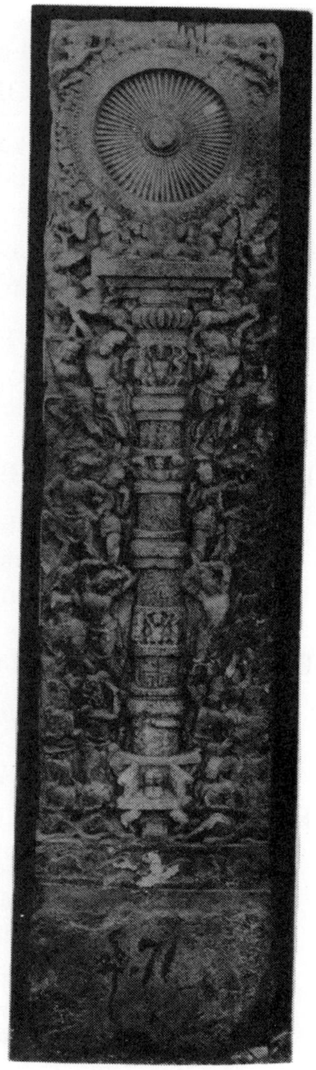

3

Cf. the similar examples, Burgess, *Buddhist Stūpas of Amarāvatī and Jaggayyapeṭa*, Pl. XXXVIII, Figs. 1 and 7. In one of these the Dharmacakra symbol is combined with that of the Cross with equal arms.

PLATE II

FIGURE 4. The Buddha as Pillar of Fire. Amarāvatī, 3rd century A.D. Madras Museum. India Office photograph.

The head and base as in Figs. 1-3, the pillar segmented and fringed with flame. See description in text, p. 28.

FIGURE 5. Scene from a Jātaka (?) Amarāvatī, *ca.* 200 A.D. Madras Museum. India Office photograph.

The Buddha as Pillar of Fire, with human worshippers.

The feet are very clearly lotus-supported (*padma-pīṭha*), and are turned in the direction of movement or response.

FIGURE 6. Cult of the Buddha as a Pillar of Fire. India Office photograph.

Type as before, but the pillar is spirally marked. Amarāvatī, *ca.* 200 A.D. British or Madras Museum. Cf. Fig. 10, upper centre, where the seated Buddha is surrounded by a flaming glory.

FIGURE 7. Scene from a Jātaka (?) Amarāvatī, as Fig. 6.

The feet are *padma-pīṭha*, and seem to be turned in the direction of movement or response.

FIGURE 8. Relief from Amarāvatī, as Figs. 6 and 7.

Perhaps the Offering of Sujātā, and Assault of Māra or that of Aṅgulimāla (cf. relief from Nāgārjunikoṇḍa, reproduced by Bachhofer in *OZ*, NF 10, Abb. 5, a similar scene with the Buddha in human form). In any case, the Buddha, as before, is represented by a Pillar of Fire, with *triśūla* "head" and lotus-supported (*padma-pīṭha*) feet.

For Sujātā = Apālā = Uṣas, see my "The Darker Side of Dawn" (Smithsonian Miscellaneous Publications vol. 94, no. 1, 1935).

FIGURE 9. The same scene as Fig. 8, in an older style. Amarāvatī, *ca.* 100 B.C. Madras Museum. India Office photograph.

PLATE II

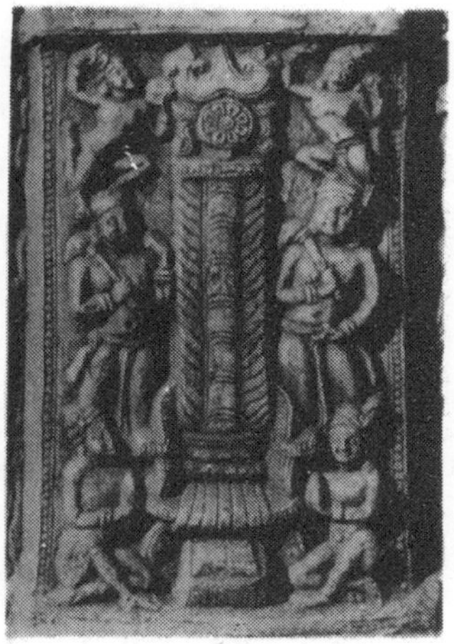

4

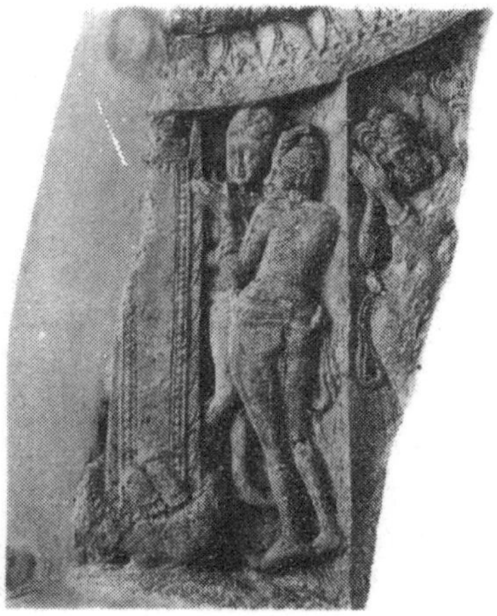

5

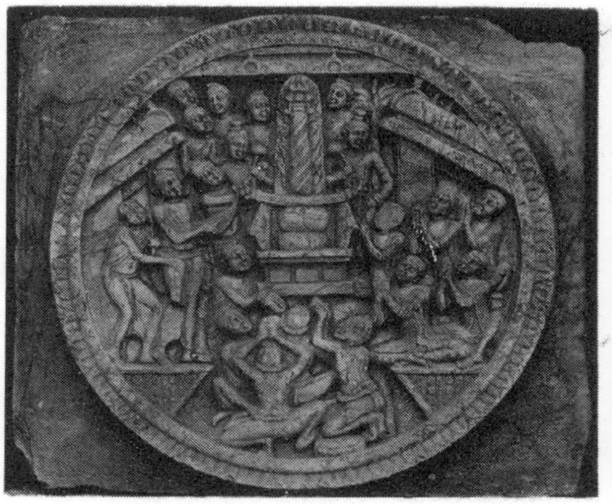

6

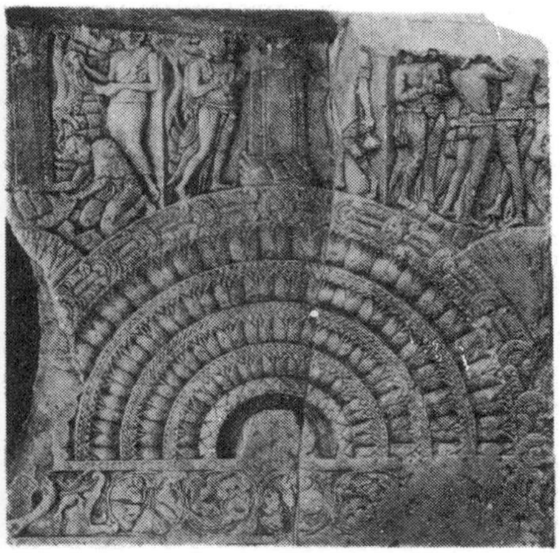

7

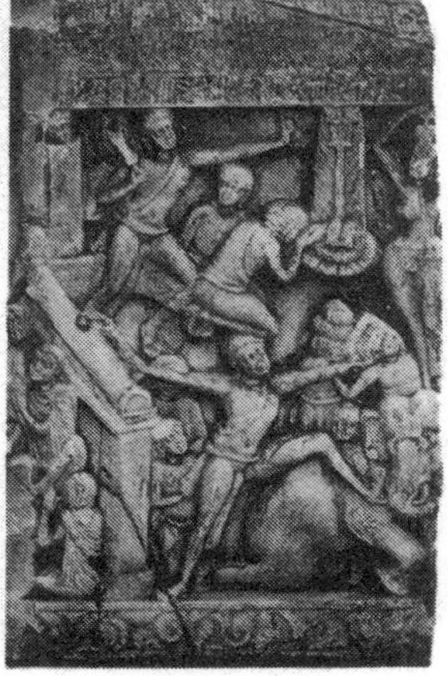

8

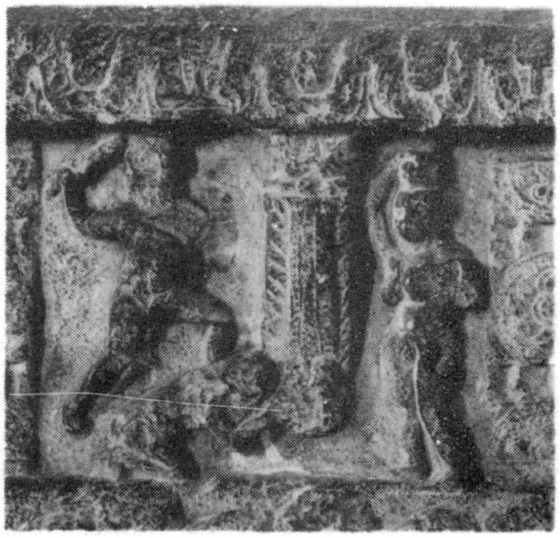

9

PLATE III

FIGURE 10. Above, possibly the same as Figs. 8 and 9; in any case, the Buddha seated with a flaming aura completely surrounding him. Below, Worship of the seated Buddha as a Pillar of Fire (as in Fig. 6), beneath the Bodhi-tree. Amarāvatī, *ca.* 200 A.D. Madras Museum. India Office photograph.

There is some reason to suppose that the Pillar of Fire type is in a special way connected with the Māra Dharśana and Mahāsambodhi, cf. Burgess, *Buddhist Stūpas of Amarāvatī and Jaggayyapeṭa*, Pl. XXI, Fig. 2, where the Assault of Māra is taking place immediately to the right of the Bodhighara, the Buddha being represented by a throne and Pillar of Fire.

For two other representations of fiery auras or pillars, see ibid., Pl. XXVI, Figs. 1 and 2.

FIGURE 11. Cult of the Bodhi-tree; part of an early enclosing wall (*pākāra*) from Amarāvatī, *ca.* 100 B.C. Madras Museum. India Office photograph.

This representation may not be in fact, but could be regarded as, an illustration of the Kālinga-bodhi Jātaka.

FIGURE 12. Cult of the Buddha as Supernal Sun. Amarāvatī, *ca.* 200 A.D., as before.

The pillar is represented as in Fig. 3, abbreviated. Note again the octagonal form of the lower part. The worshippers may be angelic or human.

On the lower right will be seen, as part of another composition not identified, Buddha-pada supported by a lotus like that of Fig. 7.

The paired deer right and left of the throne designate the scene as a representation of the "Final Turning of the Wheel" or "First Sermon."

PLATE III

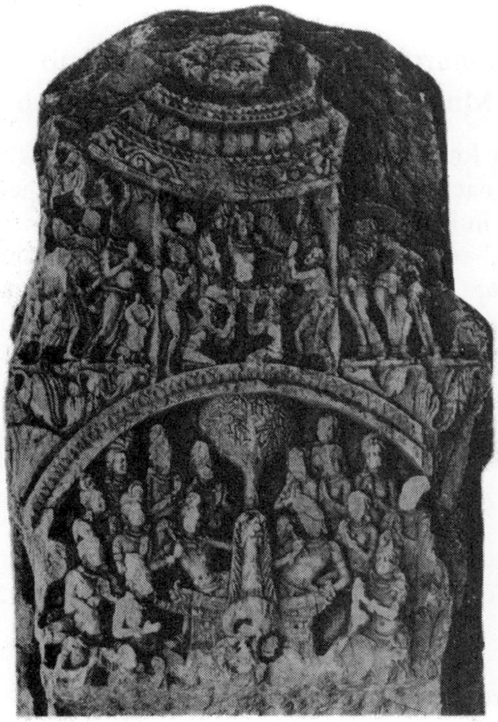

10

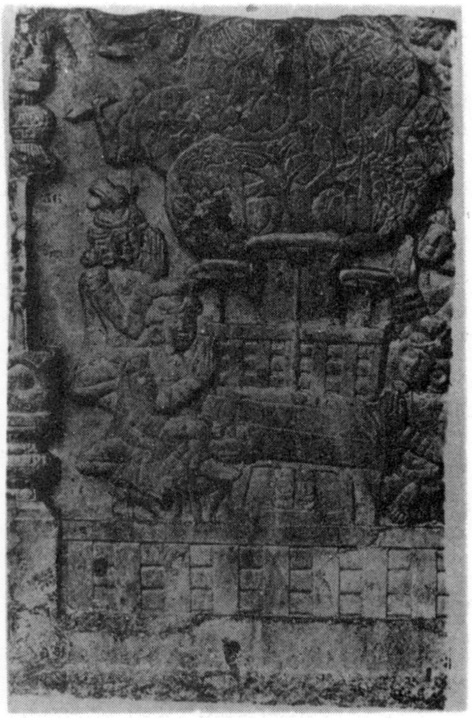

11

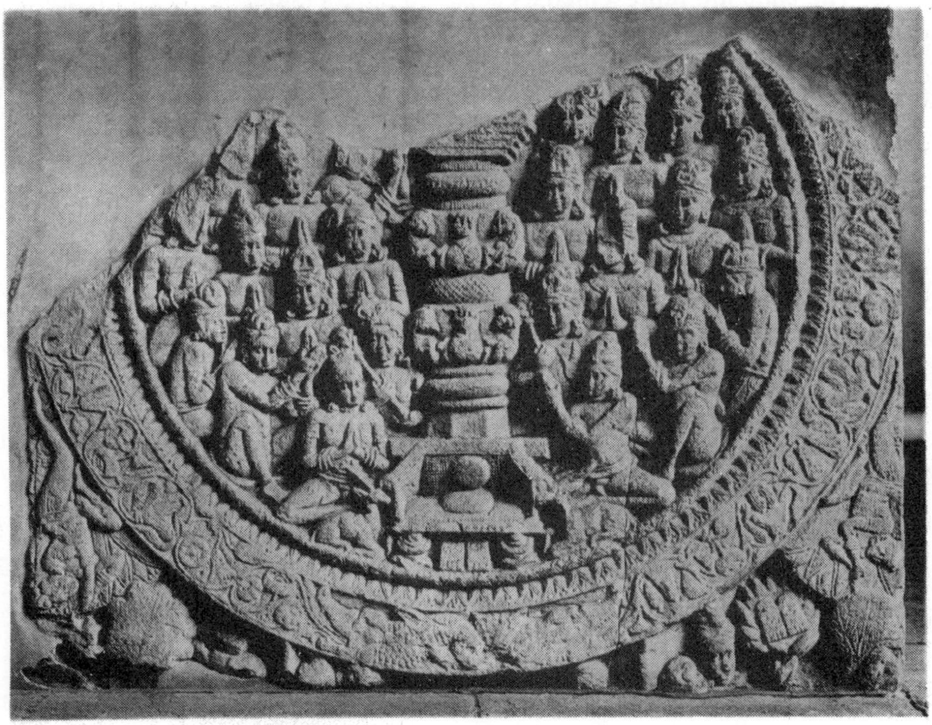

12

PLATE IV

FIGURE 13. Buddha-*pādukā*, with Dharmacakra and other symbols. Amarāvatī, *ca.* 100 B.C. Madras Museum. India Office photograph.

The Dharmacakras are as usual lotus-centred: the number of spokes is evidently intended to be sixty-four in each case. The central symbol on the heel is the same as that within the *triśūla* in Fig. 23, and which I regard as *śrīvatsa* "Notes on Indian Coins and Symbols," (*OZ*, NF IV, 1927/28, p. 183), but which Mr Johnston identifies as *vardhamāna* (*JRAS*, October, 1931, April, 1932, and July, 1933); it is the "shield" or "nāga" symbol of numismatists. The position of the feet shows that the Buddha is thought of as facing the worshipper, as in Figs. 1, 5, 7, 15, etc.

FIGURE 14. An *āyāgapaṭa*, similar to Fig. 13, but fragmentary and with additional symbols. Amarāvatī, *ca.* 200 A.D. Madras Museum. India Office photograph.

The position of the feet is reversed, and should have been as in Figs. 13, 15, etc.

FIGURE 15. Worship of the Buddha-*pādukā*. Amarāvatī, *ca.* 200 A.D. Madras Museum. India Office photograph.

The *pāda* are represented as usual on the footstool of the throne. Behind the throne must have stood a Tree or pillared Wheel.

FIGURE 16. Jaina *āyāgapaṭa*, from the Kankālī Ṭīlā, Mathurā, now J 55 in the Lucknow Museum. Photograph by the Archaeological Survey of India.

Figure of a Jina (Mahāvīra?) in the centre of a fourfold *triśūla*. The symbol occurs again in single form in the lower margin. The "shield" symbol discussed in the description of Fig. 13 occurs in the upper margin. To left a solar pillar supported by a lotus pedestal; to right an elephant pillar of similar type.

See discussion of the symbols in the literature cited under Fig. 13.

FIGURE 17. Lotus birth of the Brahmanical Trinity, Brahmā, Śiva, Viṣṇu. Thaton, Burma, about 8th century. Phayre Museum, Rangoon (?).

The stem of the lotus rise from the navel of the recumbent Nārāyaṇa. More often Brahmā (-Prajāpati) alone is thus represented as lotus-born. Cf. pp. 35-36 and Fig. B. Cf. Temple, "Notes on Antiquities from Ramannadesa," *Ind. Ant.*, 1894, Pls. XIV, XIVa; Ray, *Brahmanical Gods in Burma*, Calcutta, 1932, Pls. 4, 5; my "Stem of Jesse and Indian Parallels or Sources," *Art Bulletin*, XI, 1932; "The Stem of Jesse and Oriental Parrallels," *Parnassus*, January 1935; and my *Yakṣas*, I and II, Washington, 1928 and 1931.

PLATE IV

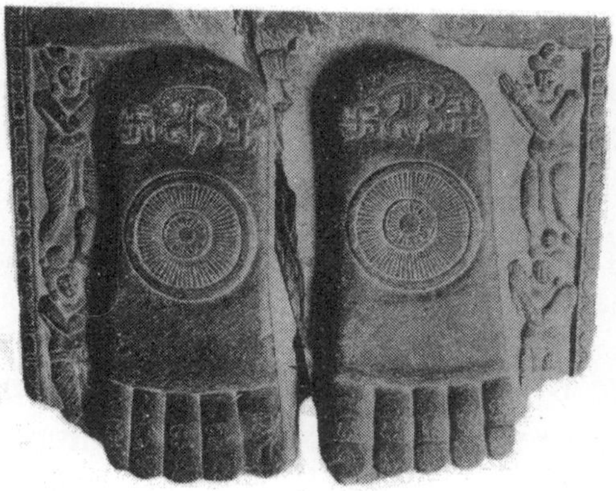

13

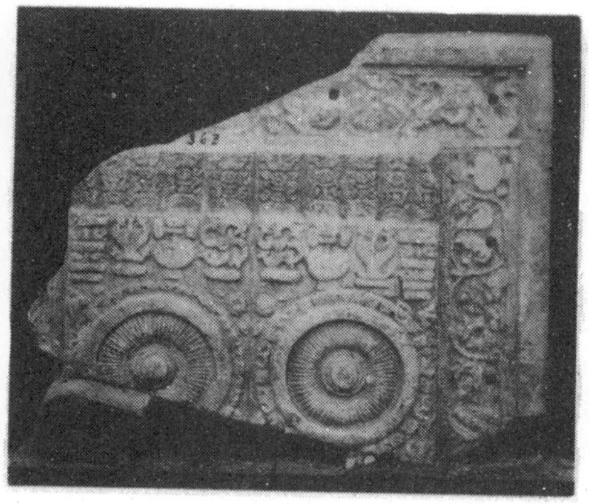

14

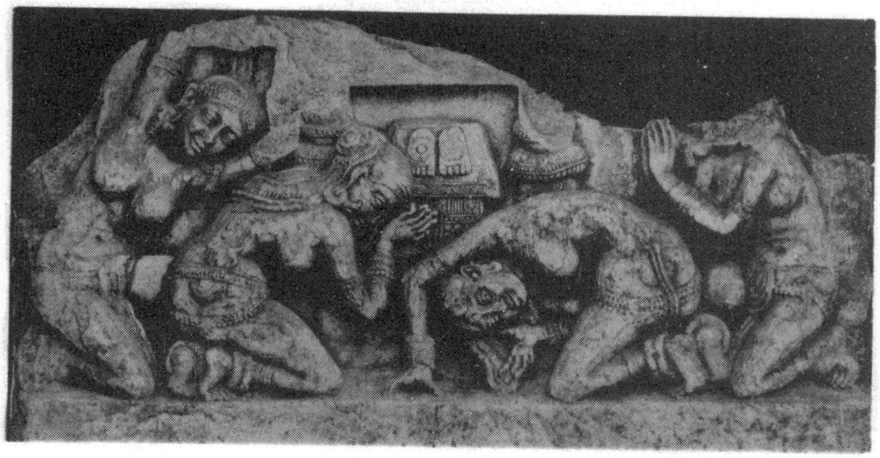

15

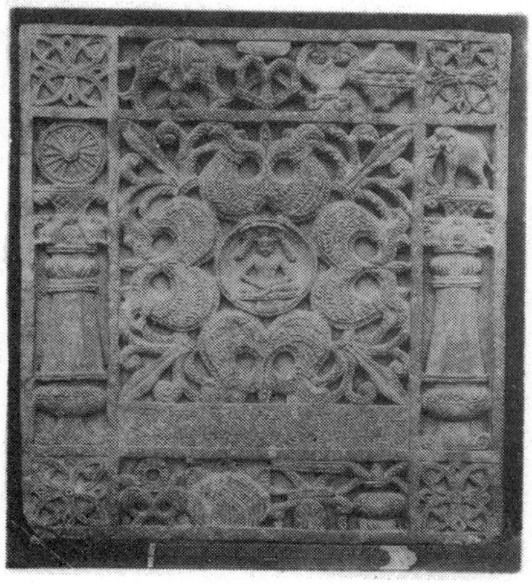

16

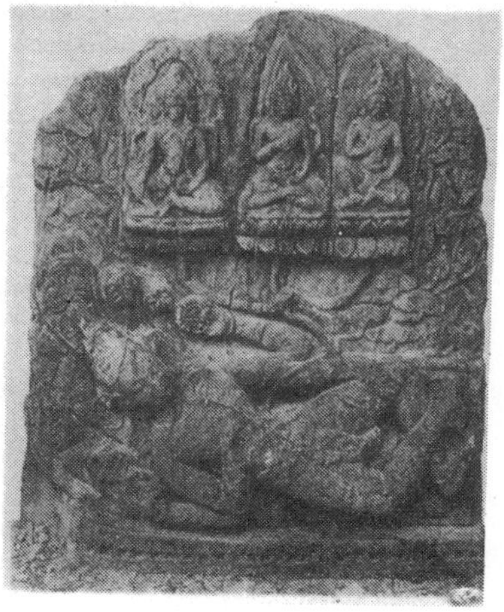

17

PLATE V

FIGURE 18. Cult of the Buddha as Dharmacakra, Principal Wheel, i.e. as Supernal Sun, cf. Figs. 2 and 3. Bharhut, *ca.* 175 B.C. Freer Gallery, Washington. Photo by same.

Above the Wheel is an umbrella of Lordship (as in Fig. 1, above the "head" of the Tree). A heavy floral garland hangs from the nave, which is of lotus form.

Figure 19. Cakravartin, surrounded by the Seven Treasures. Part of an early enclosing well (*pākāra*) from Jaggayyapeṭa, 2nd century B.C. Madras Museum. India Office photograph.

According to the *Mahāsudassana Sutta* (SBE, XI, SBB, III) and *Lakkhaṇa Suttanta* (SBB, IV) the treasures of a Cakravartin consist of a Wheel (*cakra*, explained by one commentator as representing the solar disk), an elephant, horse, light-giving jewel, queen, treasurer, and minister. In the present relief the latter is represented by a boy, evidently the Crown Prince; according to Buddhaghosa, the king's eldest son in fact officiated as *pariṇāyaka*, and the Jaggayyapeṭa relief shows that this was not "a mere putting back into the (Mahāsudassana) Sutta a later idea," as was surmised by Rhys Davids, SBE, XI, 259, note 1. That the Emperor's hand is raised to the clouds, from which falls a rain of coins, corresponds to ancient conceptions of Varuṇa and others as givers of wealth; Varuṇa or Agni as *mīḷhuṣa*; Indra's designation as Maghavat; *Ṛg Veda*, X, 19, 7, *rayyā saṁ sṛjantu naḥ*, "pour down wealth upon us"; and later passages in the *Mahābhārata* where Indra is spoken of a "raining gold" on a favorite king, and where Bhīma addresses Yudhiṣṭhira with the words " Thy hand can rain gold"; and even more striking a passage of the *Prabandhacintāmaṇi* (Tawney, p. 76), "O king! When the cloud of your hand had begun its auspicious ascent in the ten quarters of the heavens, and was raining the nectar flood of gold, with the splendor of the trembling golden bracelet flickering like lightning"; cf. also *Buddhacarita*, I, 22, "Like a range of clouds she relieved the people about her from the suffering of poverty by raining showers of gifts."

This and other representations of the Cakravartin are illustrated and discussed in my "A Royal gesture, and Some Other Motifs," in *Feestbundel K. Bataviaasch Genootschap van Kunsten en Wetenschapen.* I, 1929. T.N. Ramachandran (in *Papers published by the Rao Sahib G.V. Ramamurthi Pantulu's 70th Birthday Celebration Committee*, which I know only in an offprint) has recently connected the Cakravartin types of Jaggayyapeṭa, Amarāvatī and Goli with the *Māndhātu Jātaka*.

Figure 20. Cakravartin, similar to Fig. 18, but later style. Amarāvatī, about 200 A.D. Madras Museum. India Office photograph.

PLATE V

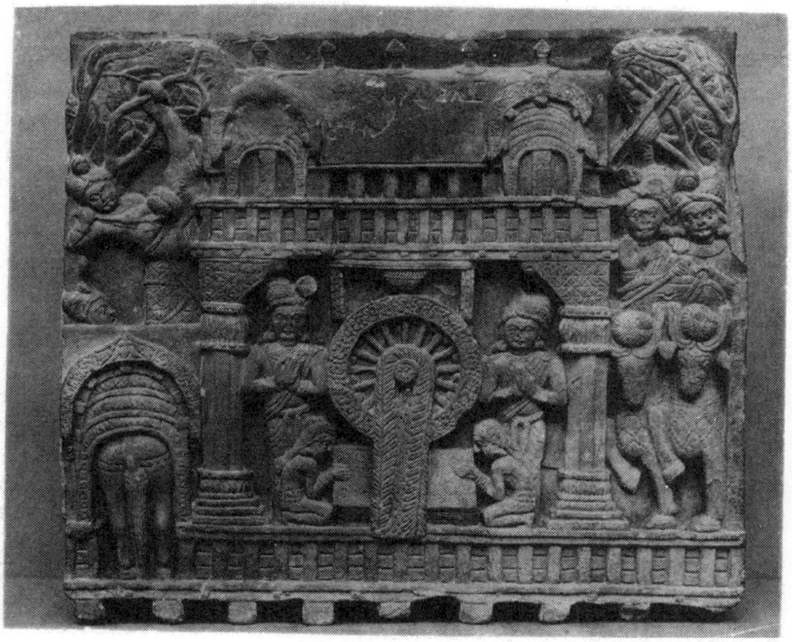

18

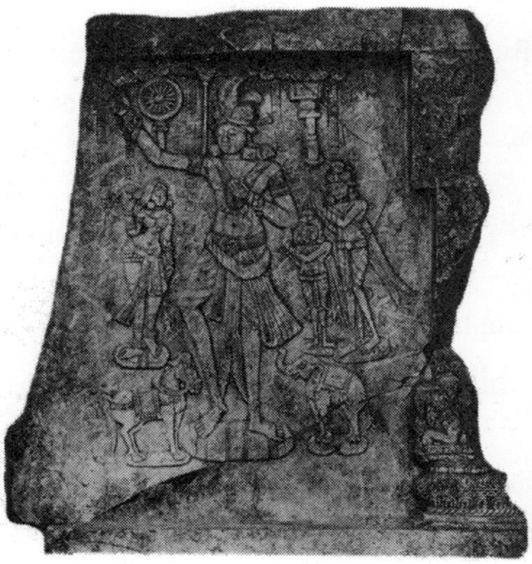

19

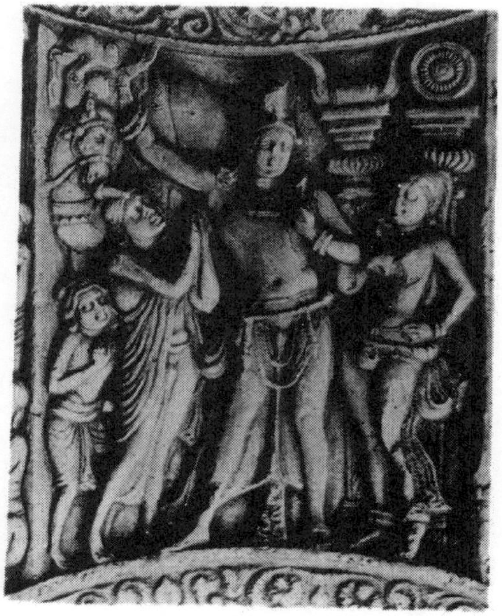

20

PLATE VI

FIGURE 21. Indus Valley seal, *ca.* 3000 B.C. Archaeological Survey of India photograph.

The cult of the deity (Yakṣa?) of the *pippala* (*Ficus religiosa*, the Bodhi-tree of Buddhism) is represented. The deity wears a three-pointed ("*triśūla*"?) symbol, cf. the Vedic conception of Agni as Vanaspati, and as latent or nascent in vegetation, etc. Cf. Marshall, *Mohenjodaro*, London (Probsthain), 1931, Pl. XII, Fig. 18, and pp. 65 f.

FIGURE 22. Indus Valley sealing, *ca.* 3000 B.C. India Office photograph.

The deity seated cross-legged as in the later iconography is three-faced, and has been identified, probably rightly, with Śiva. He has as before a three-pointed, *triśūla*-like headdress. Cf. Marshall, *Mohenjodaro*, London (Probsthain), 1931, Pl. XII, Fig. 17, and pp. 53 f.

FIGURE 23. Part of the inner face of the north *toraṇa*, Sāñcī. Early 1st century B.C. India Office photograph.

Above, the *triśūla* symbol as discussed in the text, pp. 32 f. Combined with this is the "shield" symbol discussed under Fig. 13. The supporting column is eight-sided.

Below, the *abhiṣeka* of Śrī-Lakṣmī, here perhaps regarded as Māyā-devī, the Mother of the Buddha, see text, p. 40.

Between, Śrī-Lakṣmī or Māyā-devī represented aniconically by the lotus. On the left, two *yakṣīs* with their trees.

FIGURE 24. Coping detail from Amarāvatī, *ca.* 200 A.D. Madras Museum.

In the bend of the lotus-rhizome is represented the cult of the Dharmacakra, the Buddha as Supernal Sun. Below this is a fourfold *triśūla* or *vajra*; cf. Figs. 16, 18.

FIGURE 25. *Rimbō, dharmacakra*, used in Shingon ritual. Museum of Fine Arts, Boston, No. 22.527.

Lotus centre; eight spokes of the single-*vajra* type.

FIGURE 26. *Kongō-sho, vajra*, used in Shingon ritual. Museum of Fine Arts, Boston, No. 22.509.

The "single" type, *tokkō* at each end.

FIGURE 27. *Kongō-sho, vajra*, used in Shingon ritual. Museum of Fine Arts, Boston, No. 22.510.

The usual "*triśūla*" type, *sankō* at each end.

FIGURE 28. *Katsuma-kongō, karma-vajra*, used in Shingon ritual. Museum of Fine Arts, Boston, No. 22.505.

[continued on p. 126]

PLATE VI

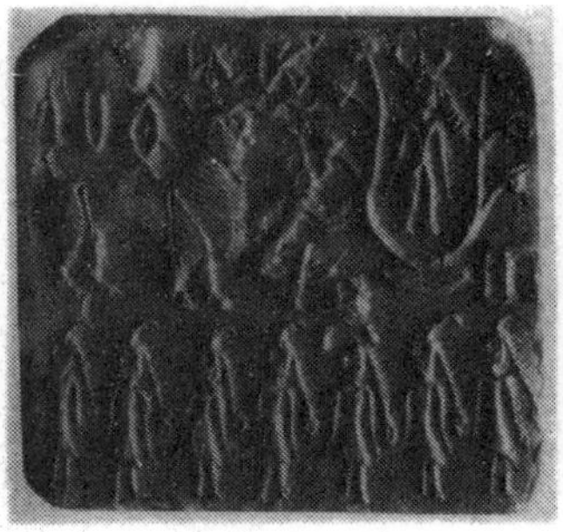

21

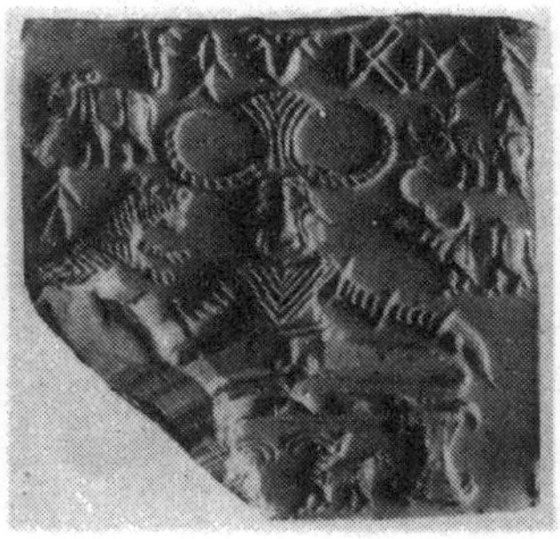

22

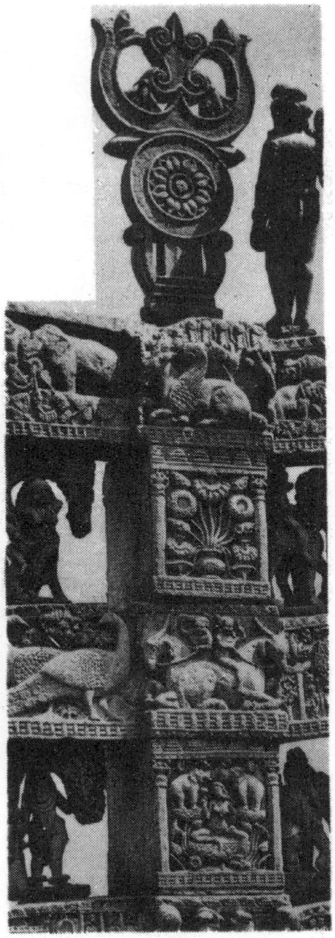

23

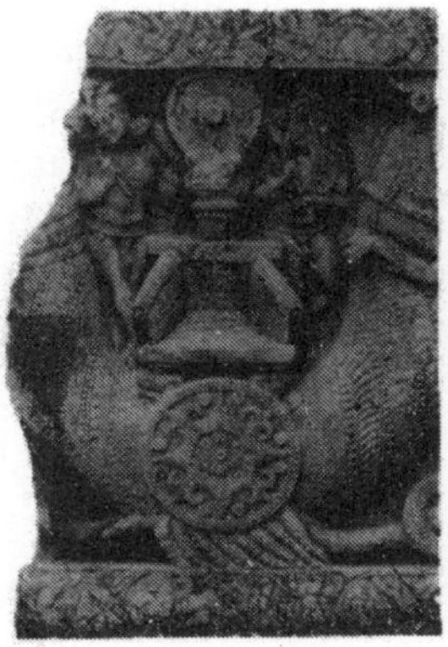

24

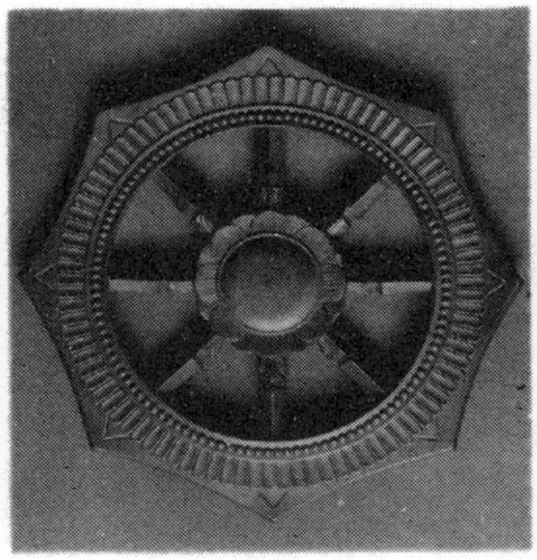

25

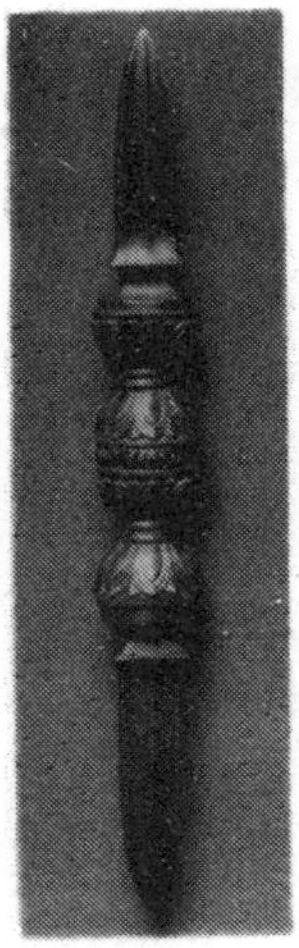

26

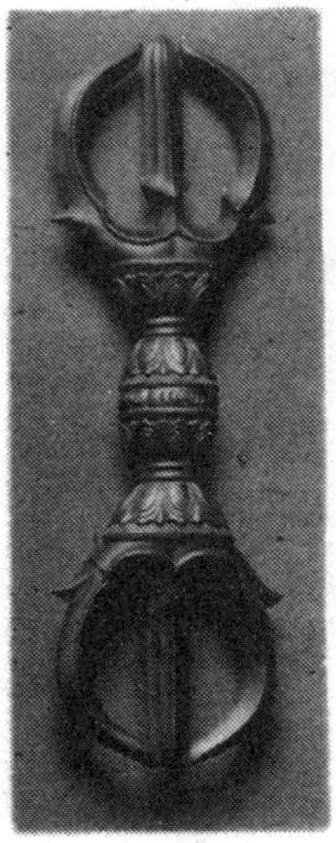

27

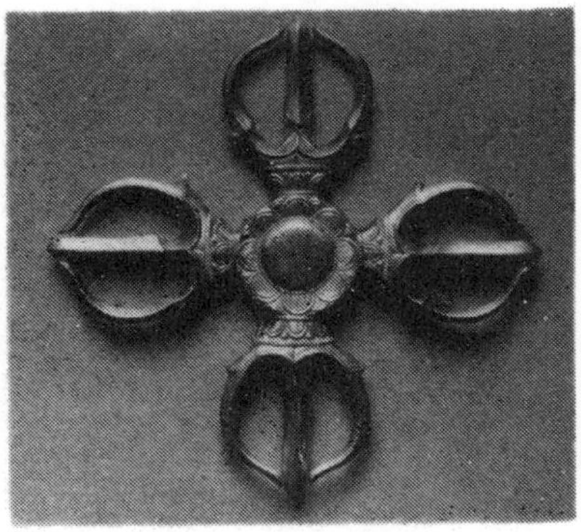

28

Cf. Ishida, *A Study on the Excavation of Buddhistic Remains at Nachi*, Tokyo Imperial Household Museum Investigation Series, No. 5, Tokyo, 1927, p. 55.

The "*vajra* in operation," tantamount to "*dharma-cakra-pravartana*." *Karma-vajra,* which is the direct equivalent of *katsuma-kongō* (*katsuma* being the regular Japanese transliteration of *karma*), occurs in *Mahābhārata*, I, 6487, where it is applied to Śūdras, "whose power is work," or "whose virtue is labor." As the designation of a symbol, *karma-vajra* is evidently equivalent to *dharma-cakra, brahma-cakra*, cf. *Śvetāśvatara Up*., VI, 1-4: ". . . it is by the all-might (*mahimā*) of the Angel that this Brahma-Wheel is whirled in the world (*loke bhrāmyate*). For it is turned (*āvṛttam*) by him—who is ever omniscient of all this (*nityam idaṁ hi sarvaṁ jñaḥ*), whose knowledge is entire (*sarvavidyaḥ*) of time, untime, and factors—it is by him that that operation (*karma*) is revolved (*vivartate*), viz. all that is regarded as solid (*pṛthvya*), phlogistical (*teja*), liquid (*āpya*), gaseous (*anila*), or spacial (*kha*), *kha* here = *ākāśa*, ether cf. Buddhist equation of *ākāśa* with *śūnya*. Having done that work (*tatkarma kṛtva*), he again desists (*vinivartya bhūyaḥ*), unifying (*sametya yogam-śaṁgamya*, Sāyaṇa), Quiddity with Quiddity (*tattvasya tattvena*, cf. the Buddhist "sameness of all *dharmas*"). . . . Thus undertaking (*ārabhya*) all these factorial operations (*guṇānvitāni karmāṇi*), and again laying them aside (*viniyojayed yaḥ*), there being a negation of active operation (*kṛta karma-nāśaḥ*) in non-being (*abhāve*), he, in that annihilation of operation (*karma-kṣaye*), remains other than the Quiddity-nature (*tattvato'nyaḥ*)."

PLATE VII

FIGURE 29. The Buddha preaching to Bodhisattvas on Mt Gṛdhrakūṭa. Kārlī, *ca.* 500 A.D. Photograph by Johnston and Hoffman, Calcutta.

See the detailed analysis in the text, pp. 71-2.

PLATE VII

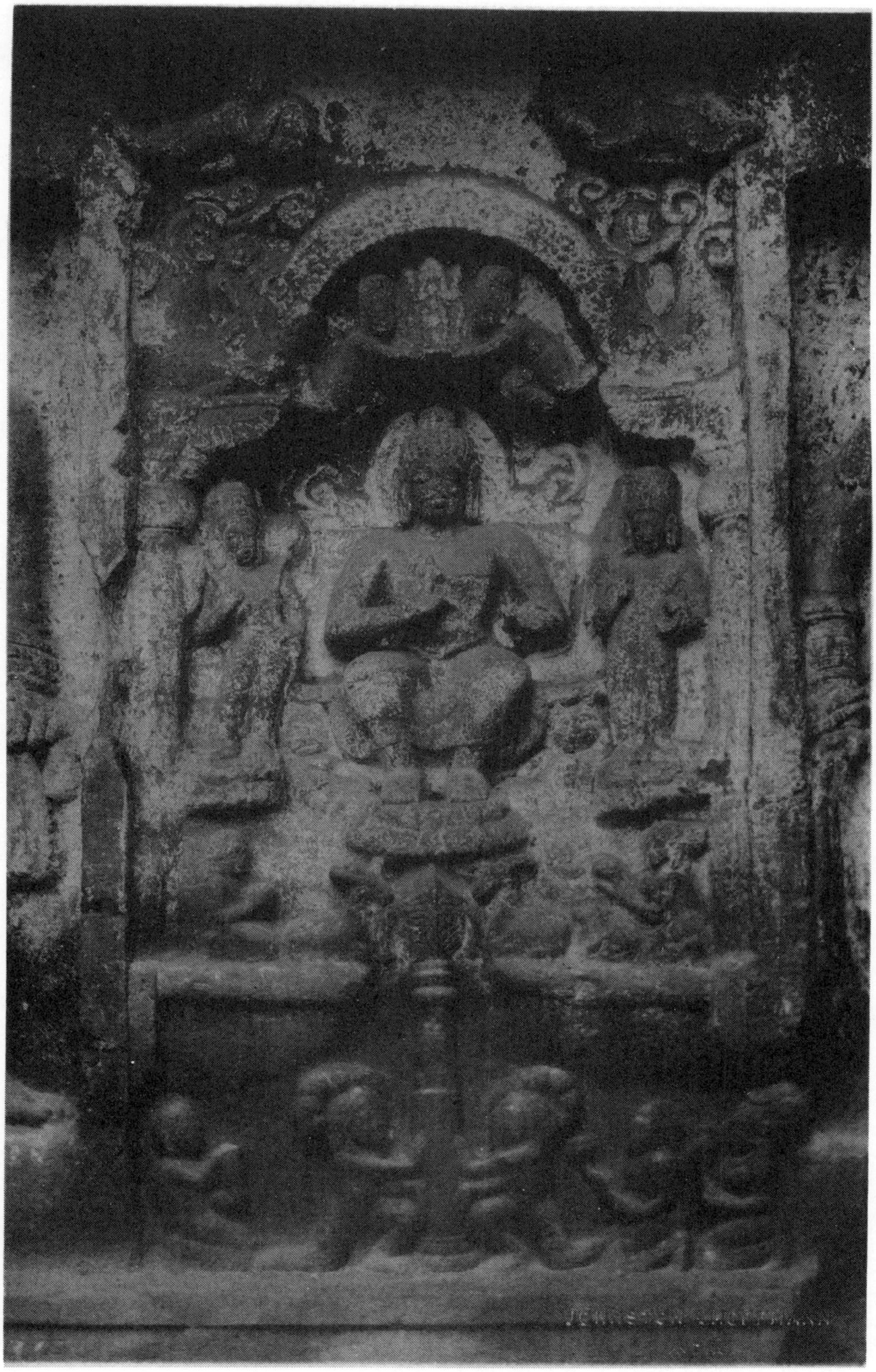

29

PLATE VIII

FIGURE 30. Hokke Mandara. Bronze, work of the monk Dōmyō, in the year Hakuhō 2, equivalent to A.D. 673. Owned by the Hasedara Monastery, Nara. From a photograph lent by Professor Langdon Warner.

In the middle panel, the Manifestation and Teaching on Mt Gṛdhrakūṭa, as described in the *Saddharma Puṇḍarīka*, Jap. *Hokke-kyo*, Chs. XI and XX. On the left, the Tathāgata, Śākya-muni, in teaching pose (cf. Fig. 29), attended by Ānanda and Rāhula and four Bodhisattvas. In the centre, the stūpa (Jap. *taho-tō*) of Prabhūtaratna ("Then arose a stūpa from the place of the earth (*pṛthivīpradeśāt*) . . . its *chatra*-spire rose up so high as to reach the Four Great Kings; therein exists the very-Self (*ātma-bhāva*) of the Tathāgata (the former Buddha Prabhūtaratna) . . . and according to his solemn vow, the stūpa is opened and shown . . . and there was seen sitting the Tathāgata Prabhūtaratna on his throne . . . and yielded to the Lord, Śākya-muni the half of the throne . . . so that both Tathāgatas were seen sitting on the throne within the great Jewel-stūpa . . . (Ch. XI) . . . the Tathāgata, Śākya-muni, and the altogether extinguished (*parinirvṛtta*) Tathāgata Prabhūtaratna, both seated on the lion-throne within the stūpa, smiled at each other, and from their opened mouths gave tongue, so that their tongues extended to the Brahmaloka, and from those two tongues there issued countless myriads of rays, and from each ray countless myriads of Bodhisattvas, of golden body, with the thirty-two particular marks of a Mahāpuruṣa, and seated on lion-thrones in lotus-calices . . . who, stationed in every quarter, preached the Law (*dharma*) . . . so that every existence in every Buddha-field heard that voice from the sky . . . (Ch. XX)").

On the right, in all respects a replica of the Buddha Śākya-muni, except as regards the costume and throne, is seated the Bodhisattva Maitreya, who is the principal speaker on behalf of the assembled Bodhisattvas, and in response to whom the Buddha utters the all-important fifteenth Chapter of the text.

It will be seen that the stūpa, which 'rises from the earth," is accordingly represented as supported by a lotus, combined with which are the four 'adamantine lions" (*kongō shishi*) mentioned in the inscription.

On the lowest level, representing the terrestrial plane (and corresponding to the lower level in Fig. 29), are placed only the dedicatory inscription and the figures of the guardian Yakṣas (*niō*).

The appearance of the "totally extinct" (*parinirvāta*) Prabhūtaratna side by side with the "still living "(*sthita*) Śākya-muni forms the theme of innumerable Chinese sculptures (cf. Sirén, *Chinese Sculpture*, Pls. 47, 55, 121, 181). The appearance of Prabhūtaratna is a resurrection of the "body," and the whole manifestation on Mt Gṛdhrakūṭa (Jap. Ryōzen Jōdo) is a "Last Judgment," at least in this sense, that those unqualified are excluded. How can such a resurrection be understood? How can one who was "totally extinguished" (in European terms, "drowned," dead and buried in the Godhead") in a former aeon now appear and be seen and heard by the still living Angels of the present aeon? Cf. resurrection of Kutsa by Indra as described in *RV* IV. 16. 10-11.

Without discussing in detail the whole problem of the condition of past and present Sādhyas, Munis, Jinas, Tīrthaṁkaras, etc., (which the Buddha refused to discuss), it may be pointed out that in all traditional formulations such beings are evidently thought of, not indeed as "individuals," but as distinct "Persons" in the same sense that the Persons of the Trinity (the "Several Angels" who are *anyonyayonita, itaretarajanmāna*, etc.) are distinct, at the same time that they are One (*ekam bhavanti, Aitareya Āraṇyaka*, II, 3, 8, "where all existence becometh of one nest," *Mahānārāyaṇa Up.*, II, 3 = *Vājasaneyī Saṁhitā*, XXXII, 8, *yatra viśvam bhavaty ekanīḍam*); and the condition of *sadasat*, tantamount to "simultaneously quick and dead in the Supernal" may be partially explained. Thus, allusion to an individual by name so and so,.and of aspect such and such, of whom it is asserted that he attained to complete extinction in a former aeon, includes the assertion that the manifestation of such a form and aspect had been amongst the primordial possibilities of existence. Now possibility in this sense is in no way bound up with time; whatever has been a possibility of manifestation remains a possibility not merely *in saecula saeculorum*, but without regard to time, as well in one aeon as another. By the same token, any such possibility will always be visible to the *jñāna-cakṣu* (for which there is no proceeding from potentiality to act) as an actuality. Or we may express this by saying that every part of the World-picture "painted by the Self on the canvas of the Self" is necessarily ever-present to the Self. Whatever has been mirrored in the *speculum eternum* (Augustine, *De Civ. Dei*, lib. a, xii, c. 29) is now and forever imaged there, and *mentes se videntium ducit in cognitionem omnium creatorum*. Inasmuch as Prabhūtaratna, who had been totally extinguished, had seen with the Eye of Wisdom, a vision that cannot change, his own image, that is his understanding of himself, must be thought of as remaining for ever within the range of his own vision, and in this sense "he" is always virtually "present." The notion is similar to that of John x, 9, "I am the door (= *loka-dvāra*); by Me if any man enter in, he shall be saved, and *shall go in and out*, and find pasture," where "find pasture" = *annam ad*, "to exist," cf. John, 1, 3 "All things that have been created were in him as life." and Matthew xii, 29, "For he is not a God of the dead but of the living: for all live unto him." This immortality of one who has been utterly extinguished and is dead and buried in the Godhead is not indeed an immortality of the ego as commonly understood; it is rather the potential being of a "name" (*nāma*) that cannot be annihilated, and of an "aspect" (*rūpa*) which must be presented whenever this "name" is recalled.

PLATE VIII

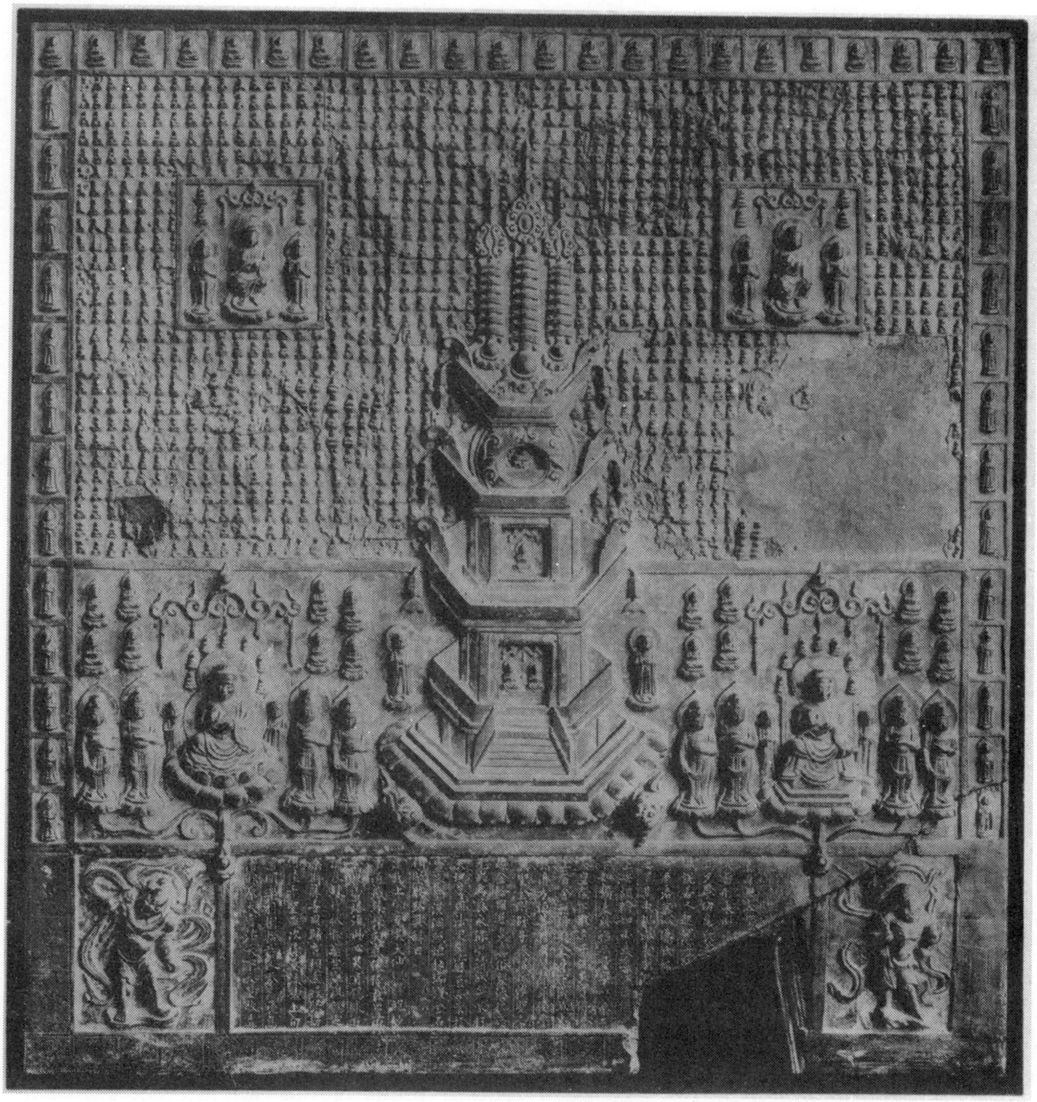

30

PLATE IX

FIGURE 31. Taizō-hō mandara, Garbha-kośa (-dhātu) maṇḍala, central portion. Japanese original in the Tōji Monastery, Kyotō. After Ōmura Seigai, *Sanbon Ryōbu Mandara*, Tokyō, I, 1913.

This Japanese original, painted in A.D. 1693, is the third copy of the Chinese original brought to Japan by Kōbō Daishi in A.D. 806, the first and second copies having been made in 1195 and 1292.

The Persons (Hypostases) are as follows:

	Hoshō Nyorai (Ratnaketu Tathāgata)	
Miroku Bosatsu (Maitreya Bodhisattva)		Fugen Basatsu (Samantabhadra Bodhisattva)
Tenkoraion Nyorai (Divyadundubhimegha-nirghoṣa Tathāgata)	Birushana Nyorai (Vairocana Tathāgata)	Kaifukeō Nyorai (Saṁkusumita-rāja Tathāgata)
Kwanjizai Bosatsu (Avalokiteśvara Bodhisattva)		Monjushiri Bosatsu (Mañjuśrī Bodhisattva)
	Muryoju Nyorai (Amitāyus Tathāgata)	

The Buddhas occupy the centre and four petals of the lotus, Bodhisattva the four remaining petals. Vairocana is the primordial (Ādi-) Buddha identified with the Supernal Sun; the four other Dhyāni Buddhas represented being those of the four quarters, the orientation in the diagram being

	East	
South		North
	West	

The exact equivalent of the *maṇḍala* as here illustrated may be seen in the Shuji (seed-letter) form in the central field of Fig. 32.

A *maṇḍala* in all respects like that of Fig. 31 is reproduced by Getty, *Gods of Nothern Buddhism* (2nd ed.), P1. XVI. A corresponding representation of Vairocana (as Ichijikinrin) in Vajra-dhātu form, No. 09.387 in the Museum of Fine Arts, Boston, is reproduced by Anesaki, *Buddhist Art* (1st ed.), Pl. XIV. Here "the fingers of the right hand clasp the forefinger of the left . . . the gesture symbolizes the unity of the cosmic and the individual souls in the final spiritual enlightenment" (*ibid*., pp. 34, 35[1]), whereas in the Garbha-dhātu form the two hands hold the Dharmacakra, implying their distinction on the plane of operation.

In the original, panels immediately above and below the central area here reproduced contain each five representations, as follows, reading from left to right:

Above, Shishigute-butsumoson (Cuṇḍā-bhagavatī, Saptakoṭi-buddha-mātṛ), Butsugen-butsuno (Buddha-locana), Issai Nyoraichi-in (Sarvatathāgata-jñāna-mudrā), Daiyūmō Bosatsu (Mahāvīra), Daianrakufukūshinjitsu (Vajrāmogha-samayasattva, Mahāsukhāmogha-vajrasattva), also smaller figures above the

[1]Cf. "Si-do-in-dzou, gestes de l'officiant dans les cérémonies mystiques des sectes Tendai et Shingon," *Annales du Musée Guimet*, VIII.

PLATE IX

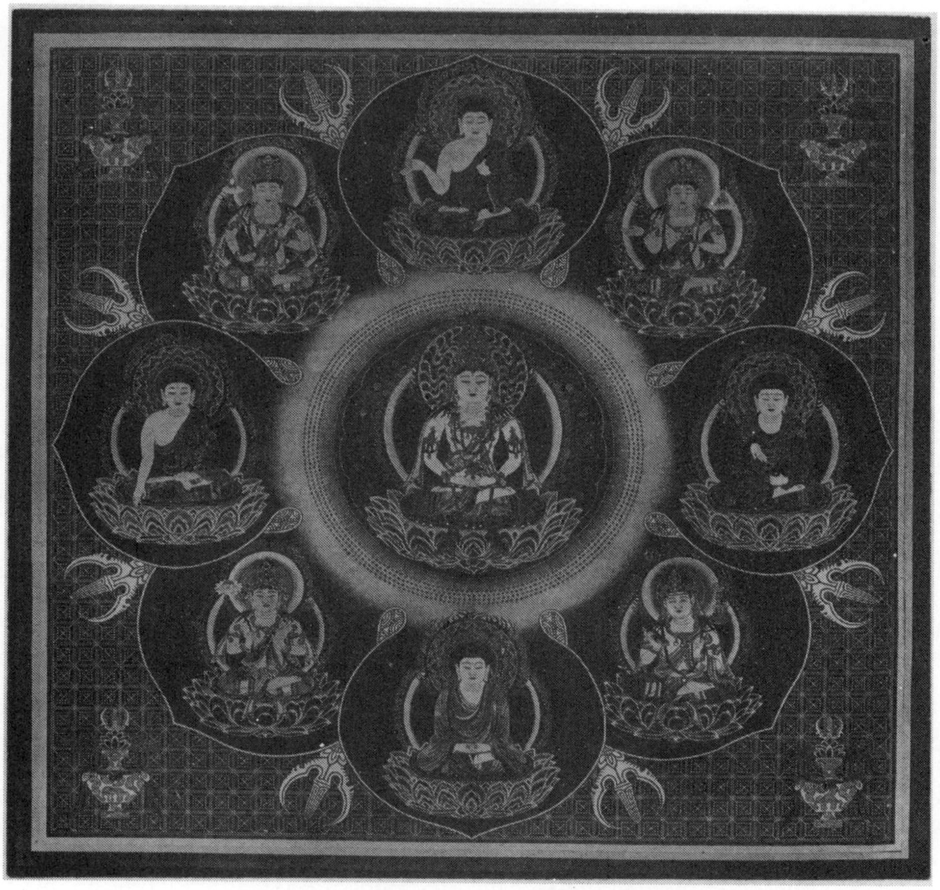

31

central symbol, viz. on the left Kaya-kasho (Gayā Kāśyapa), and on the right Urubinra-kasho (Uruvilva Kāśyapa). Below, Shosanzeson (Trailokya-vajra), Daiitokuson (Yamāntaka), Hannya-haramitsu (Prajñāpāramitā), Gōsangeson (Vajra-huṁkāra), and Fudōsan (Acalanātha).

By far the most interesting of these representations is the upper central symbol of the "Wisdom of All the Tathāgatas," corresponding to the manifested form of Prajñāpāramitā in the centre of the lower panel. Prajñāpāramitā, corresponding to Vedic Aditi and Gnostic Sophia, is also Tathāgata-garbha, "Womb of all the Buddhas," potential and maternal: for a more detailed exposition see Obermiller, E., "The Doctrine of Prajñāpāramitā, etc.", in *Acta Orientalia*, XI. This universal potentiality of the possible intellect is represented by a flaming equilateral triangle (see illustration, p. 50) resting on its base, and supported by a lotus "ground." Of the two *svastikas*, one situated at the "point" (*bindu*) within the triangle is principal, and represents the Unmoved Mover or First Cause of Motion, the second external to the triangle implies the actual motion of the worlds. As corresponding to the rising Sun, this triangle is situated in the East; it corresponds also to Manas in the Trinity Manas, Vāc, Prāṇa. The corresponding Vajra-dhātu symbol of the operative intellect is a triangle in the image of this, but with its point downwards, situated in the West, where the Sun is reflected or "sets" in the Waters, corresponding also to Vāc in the Trinity Manas, Vāc, Prāṇa.

PLATE X

Ryōbu mandara, viz., the Garbha-kośa-dhātu and Vajra-dhātu maṇḍalas represented as Shuji ("seed-letter") mandaras. "Diagrammatic representations in which Sanskrit letters are substituted for figures of the deities in the two Cycles. These letters, called *Shuji* (Sanskrit, Bīja) or seed, are regarded as efficacious symbols of the *Shingon* deities" (Anesaki, *Buddhist Art*, Pl. XVI). Japanese, late 17th century. Museum of Fine Arts, Boston, Nos. 11.7114 and 7113. The latter bears the signature "Siddha (characters) written by Kwaien in his later years," Kwaien being *alias* the Shingon monk Chōzen, who was famous for his workmanship in this kind.

FIGURE 32. Garbha-kośa-dhātu *maṇḍala*, in which the *tattvas* (Quiddities or Principles) are shown in their sensibly manifested forms. The central field corresponds to the whole area shown in Figs. 30 and 33. Vairocana is represented by the syllable (seed-letter) "*ĀḤ*:" with which may be compared a representation (Fig. 40) of Vairocana by the syllable *A* upon a lotus throne, supported by a *vajra* "stem," which rests in turn upon a lower lotus. D.C. Sircar in *Indian Culture*, 1936, p. 831 says *ĀḤ* in Fig. 32; *Tathāgata Divyadundubhimeghanirghoṣa*.

FIGURE 33. Vajra-dhātu *maṇḍala*, in which the *tattvas* (Quiddities or Principles) are shown in intellectually manifested forms. Here Vairocana is represented by the syllable (seed-letter) "VAṀ."

Compare the great density of the elements of order represented in this figure with the notion *prajñāna-ghana* in *Bṛhadāraṇyaka Up.*, IV, 5, 13, and *Māṇḍūkya Up.*, 5.

On Shingon symbolism see also Getty, *Gods of Northern Buddhism* (2nd ed.), 1928, pp. 28ff., and under *trikoṇa* and *vajra* in Index. In Anesaki, *Buddhist Art* (1st ed.), 1915, Pl. XVI, reproducing our Figs. 32, 33, the relative positions of the *mandaras* on the Plate are reversed.

PLATE X

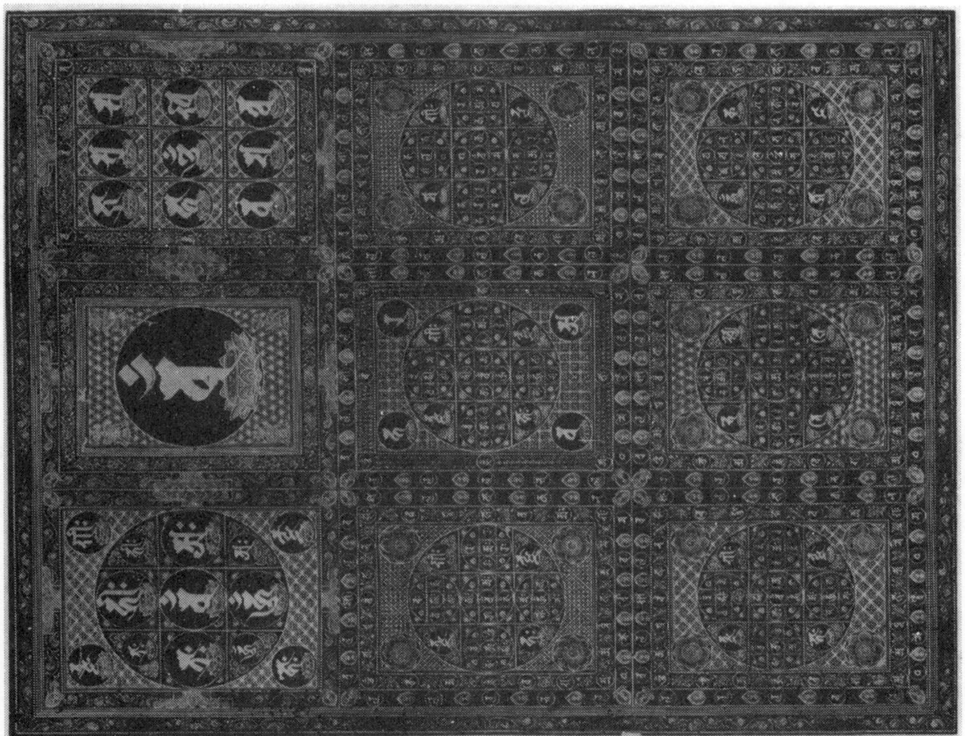

33

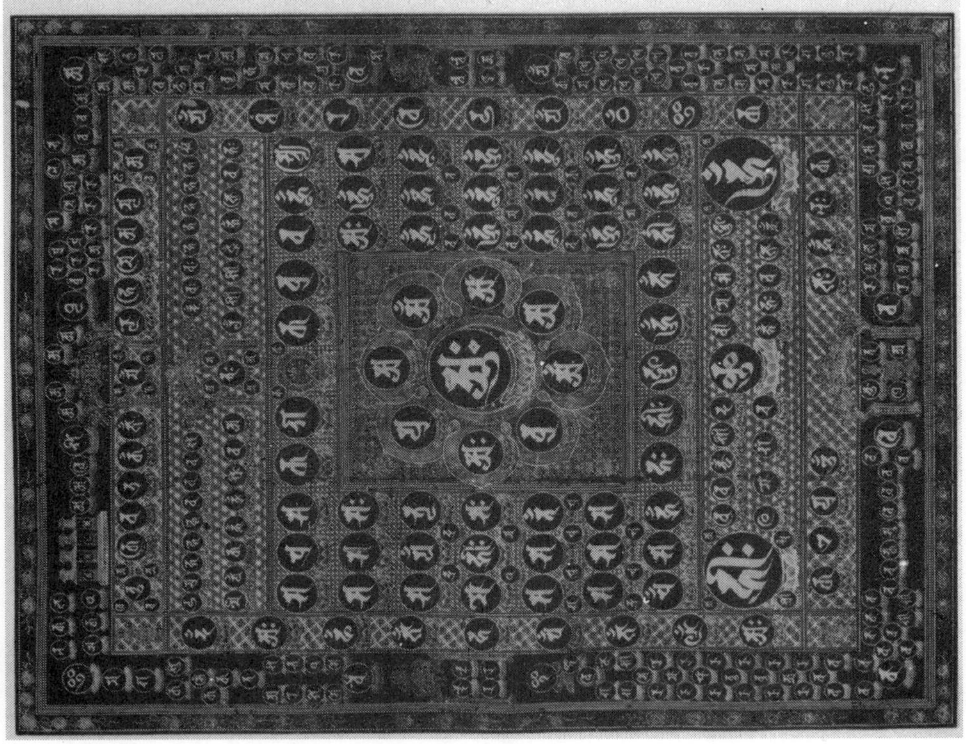

32

PLATE XI

FIGURE 34. The Buddha (Amida, Amitābha), accompanied by the Bodhisattvas, Padmapāṇi on the proper right, Mahāsthānaprāpta on the proper left. Amida Trinity of Tachibana Fujin. Japanese, early 8th century. Owned by the Hōryuji Monastery, Nara. From photographs lent by Professor Langdon Warner.

Each member of the Triad is supported by a lotus, the stems of the flowers rising from the rippled waters which form the horizontal base of the shrine.

FIGURE 35. The Waters, from which rise the stems of the lotus-thrones supporting the Trinity, as shown in Fig. 34.

PLATE XI

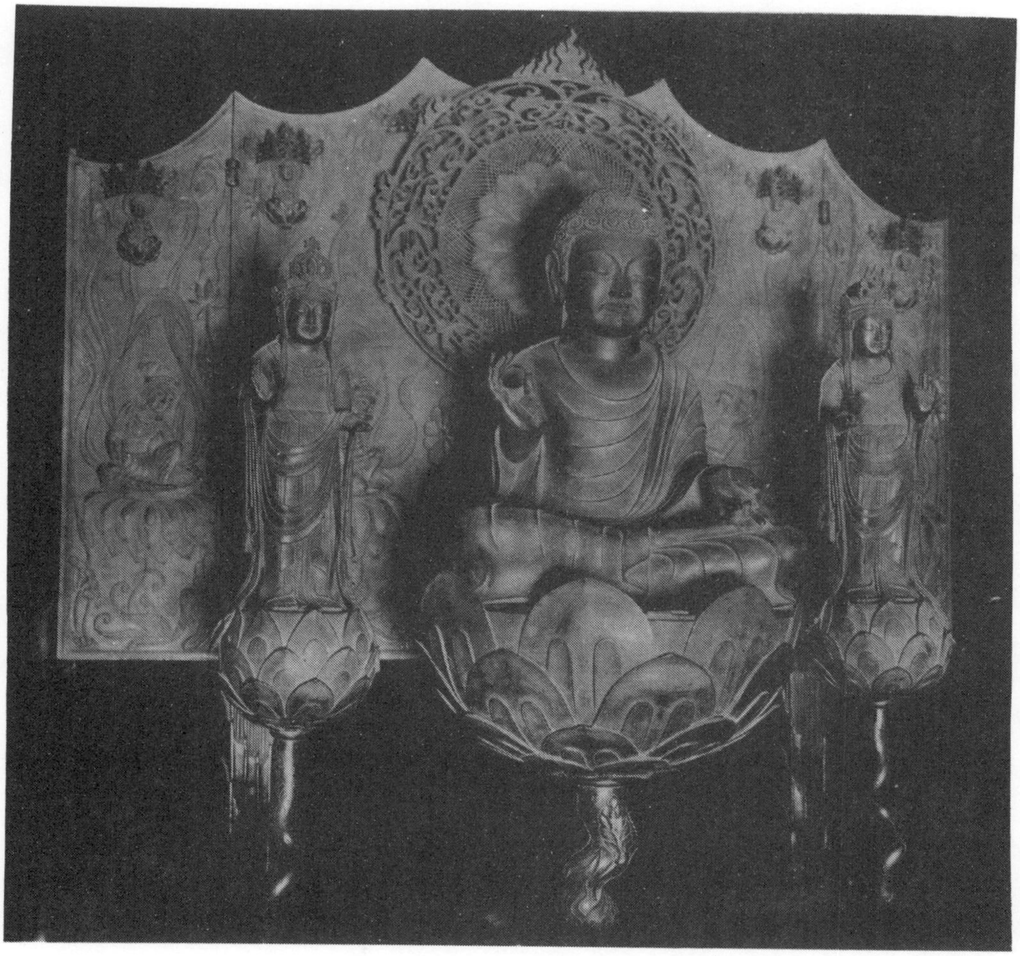

34

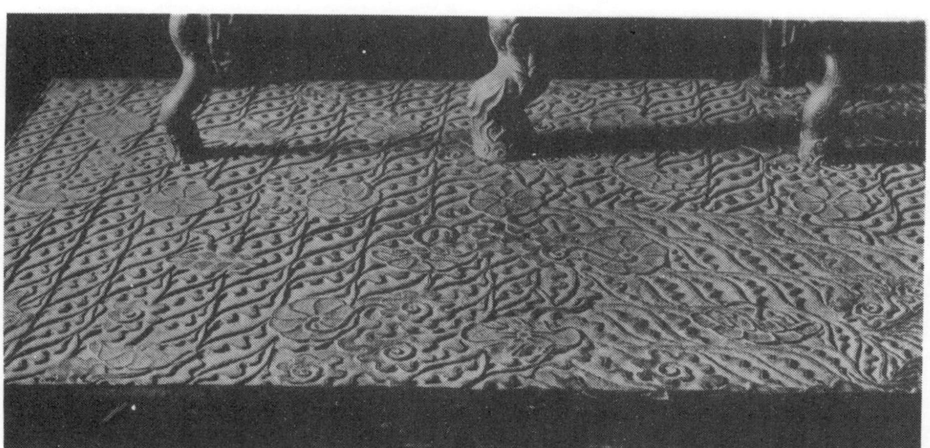

35

PLATE XII

FIGURE 36. Reredos of the Amida Trinity, Figs. 34, 35. From a photograph lent by Professor Langdon Warner.

The nimbus is represented with a central lotus, of which the supporting lotus must be regarded as a reflection in the Nether Waters.

FIGURE 37. The Buddha preaching to Bodhisattvas on Mt Gṛdhrakūṭa; or perhaps, more exactly, Amida, attended by the Bodhisattvas Padmapāṇi (?) and Maitreya. Chinese, A.D. 678. Collection of the Marquis Osokawa. After Ōmura Seigai, *Shina Bijutsushi Chosohen*, Tokyo, 1915, Pl. 777.

Double lotus-throne, the lower flower with lions, ɪorming the usual lotus- and lion-throne.

FIGURE 38. Above, the Buddha preaching to Bodhisattvas on Mt Gṛdhrakūṭa; below, the monastic manifestation on the earth-plane.

The Buddha is represented as teaching on two "levels," cf. Fig. 29. The supporting lotus and its stem forms a kind of "Jesse Tree." The feet of the Buddha at the lower level are supported by two separate lotus flowers.

A monument in the Wu Ting Village, China, A.D. 678, After Ōmura Seigai, *ut supra*, Pl. 778.

PLATE XII

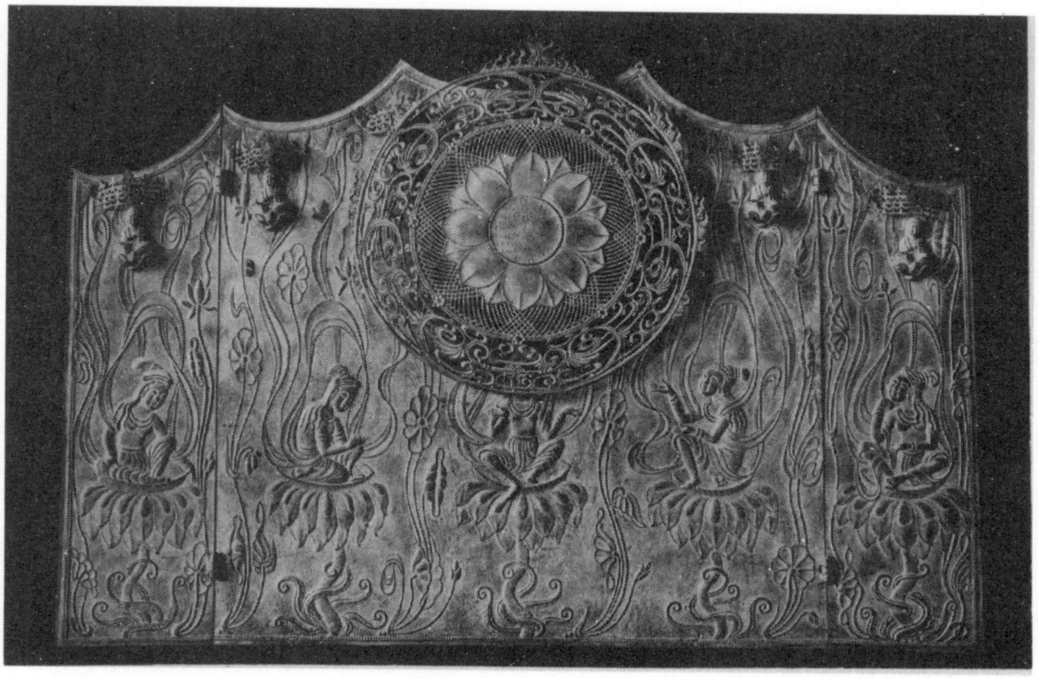

36

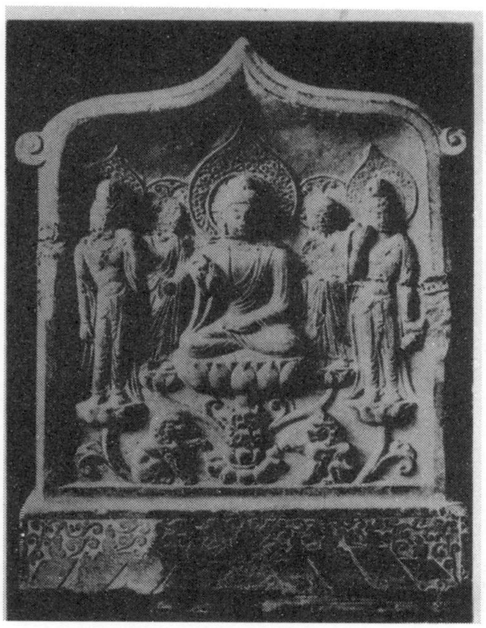

37

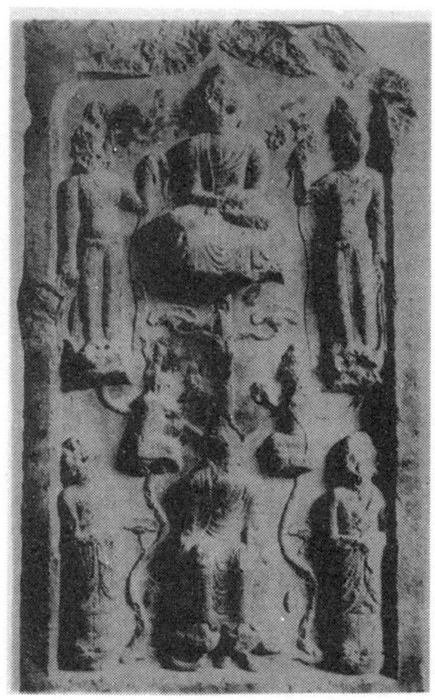

38

PLATE XIII

FIGURE 39. The Bodhisattva Mañjuśrī. Japanese, 14th century. Museum of Fine Arts, Boston, No. 17.748.

The Angel of Wisdom. He holds in his right hand the flaming sword of Understanding (with a *vajra*-handle), and in his left a lotus spray, the flower supporting a book (*Saddharma Puṇḍarīka*), upon which stands erect a flaming *vajra*, cf. Fig. H.

FIGURE 40. Garbha-dhātu form of Vairocana. Japanese, early 15th century. Museum of Fine Arts, Boston, No. 11.6296.

Vairocana is represented by the seed-letter A, supported by an encircled lotus (of the Primordial Waters), above a second lotus (of the Upper Waters), separated by an erect *vajra* (Axis of the Universe), which rests upon a third lotus (of the Nether Waters). Cf. description of Fig. 32.

PLATE XIII

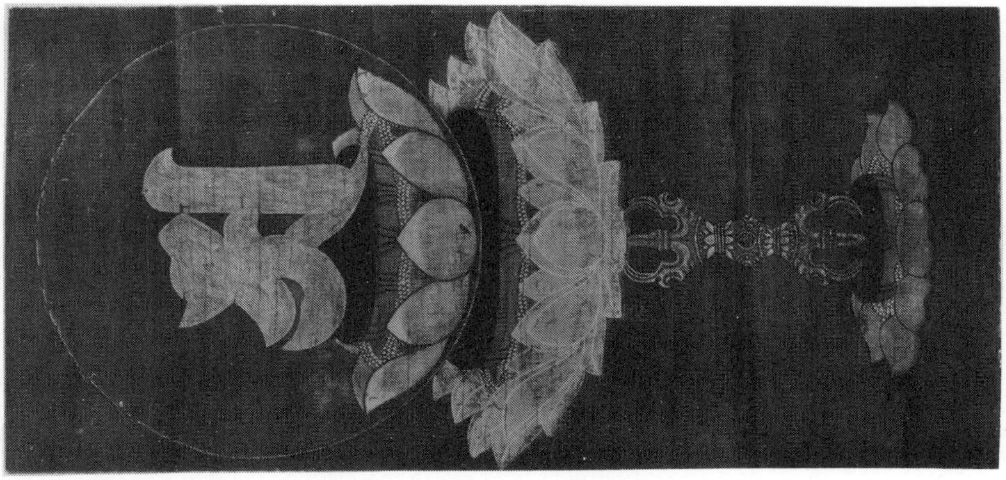

40

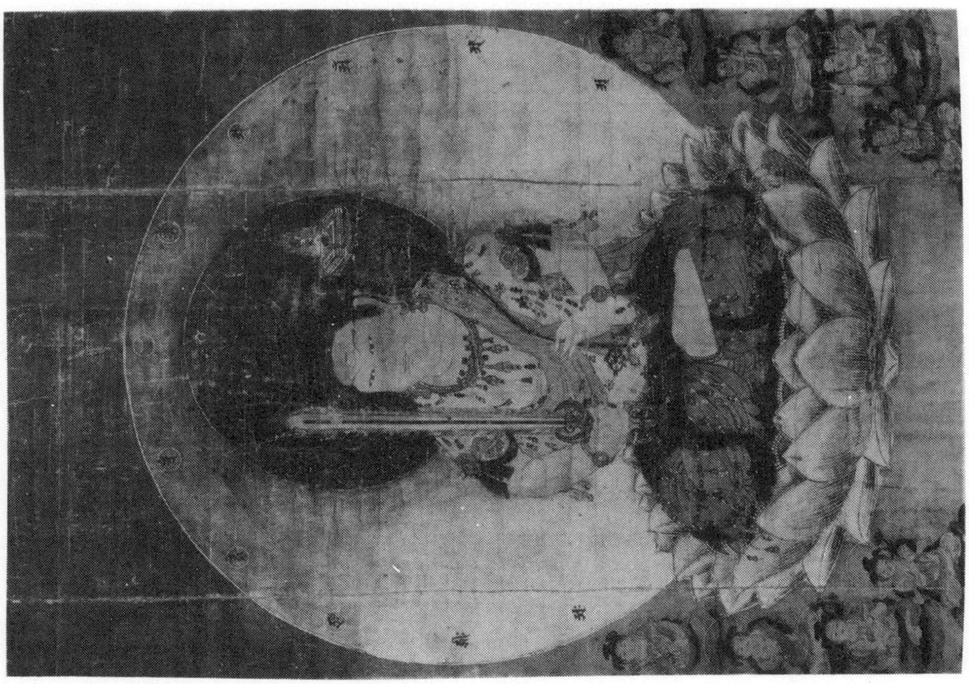

39

PLATE XIV

FIGURE 41. Front face of the pedestal of the Yakushi (Bhaiṣajyaguru Vaidūrya) Trinity. Japanese, dedicated in A.D. 597. Kondō, Yakushiji, Nara. See text, pp. 72.

FIGURE 42. Fukū-Kenjaku, Amoghapāśa, a form of Padmapāṇi (Avalokiteśvara) chiefly in Tendai usage. Japanese, probably Kamakura. Kanchi-in Temple, Kyotō. Photo by Institute of Art Research, Tokyō.

The Bodhisattva is eight-armed, the lower (normal) hands in *namaḥkāra* position, second right and left holding a rod (*daṇḍa*) and noose (*pāśa*), third right and left in *varada mudrā*, upper right holding the staff (*khakkara*, Jap. *shakujō*) with six rings. A standing Dhyāni Buddha in the crown. The central ornament of the *channavīra* is a Dharmacakra (Jap. *rimbō*) which rests immediately over the navel (cf. *Śatapatha Brāhmaṇa*, V, 7, 1, 9, and *Hiraṇyakeśin Gṛhya Sūtra*, I, 6, 24, 1, as cited in my *Yakṣas*, II, 24).The lotus-seat is supported by an eight-sided column or axis, with eight protuberances, which axis rises from a pedestal representing four earth-planes. In the Zenith hangs the Supernal Sun (Amitābha), of which the lotus-seat is the reflection, *ābhāsa*.

The form of the shaft should be compared with that of the Axis of the Universe (*vajra*) represented in Figs. 2, 3, 12, 40, 41, E.

FIGURE 43. Śiva-liṅgam. 1st or 2nd century B.C. In *pūjā*, Guḍimallam, Indra. Photograph by the Archaeological Survey of India.

Another "Axis" type. The Atlant Yakṣa may be compared with the supporting Yakṣa of Fig. 41.

Cf. Rao, *Elements of Indian Iconography*, Pt. I, Vol. II, 65-9, and my *History*, p. 68. For the Paraśurāmeśvara temple, in which, where the liṅgam is in *pūjā*, see *Indian Antiquary*, XL, 1911, 104-14, and *Mem ASI*, No. 40, p. 24, and for the dating, my note in *IHQ*, VII, 750 (830).

For other Indian examples of the Yakṣa type, see Burgess, *Stūpa of Bharhut*, Pl. XXII, Fig. 1, and Vogel, "La sculpture de Mathurā," *Ars Asiatica*, XV, Pl. XVII, Fig. b. See also above, p. 72.

PLATE XIV

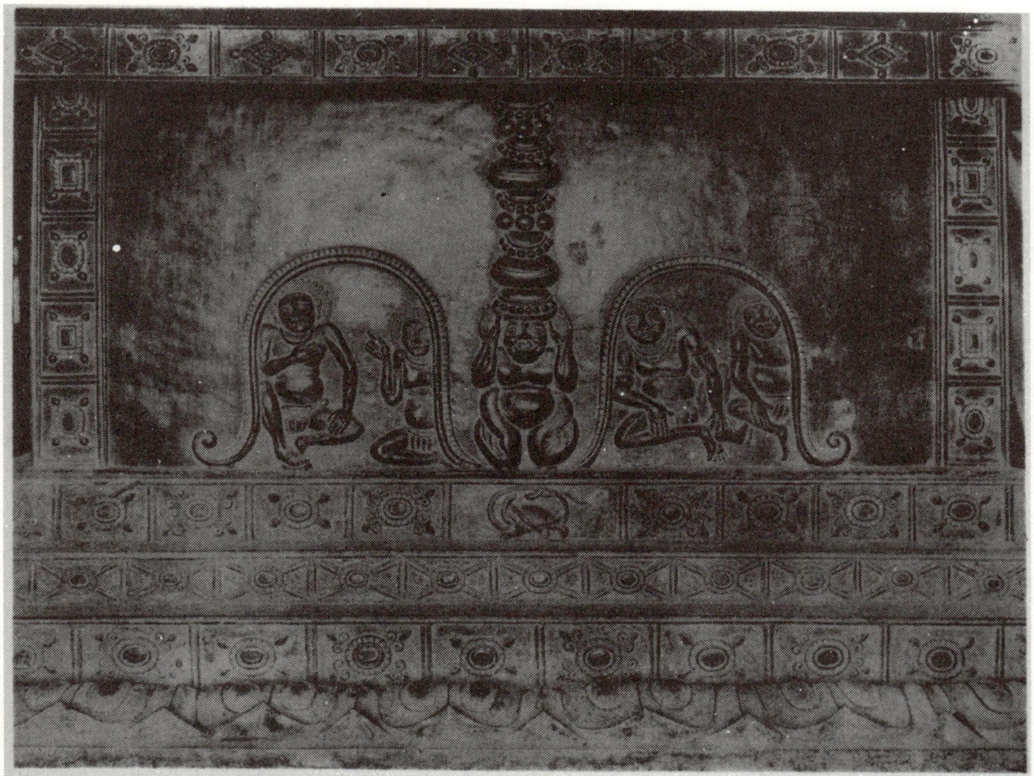

41

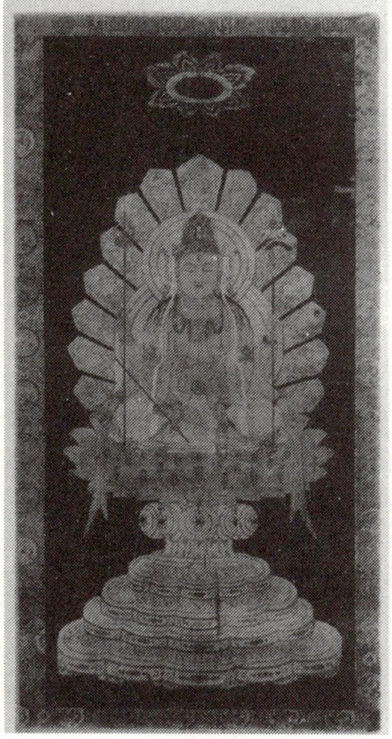

42

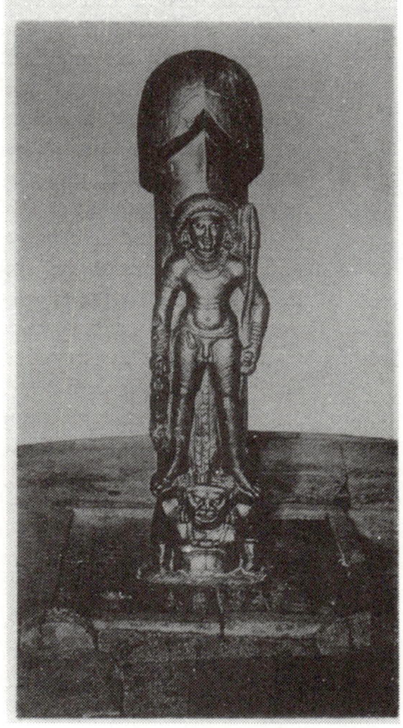

43

PLATE XV

FIGURE 44. The Bodhisattva Padmapāṇi, six-armed and supported by a lotus. From Bäzäklik, Murtuq, Turkistan, *ca*. 9th century. After Grünwedel, *Altbuddhistische Kultstätten in Chinesisch-Turkistan*, 1912, Fig. 590.

The lotus support is double. The lower stem, rising directly from the Waters, corresponds to the earthly or Nirmāṇakāya level of manifestation; its flower supporting Mt Meru, as the *skambha* or *sthauros* that pillars-apart Heaven and Earth. This sheaf-like and fasciated column is on the one hand formed like a *vajra*, and on the other corresponds in shape to such representations of Mt Meru as may be seen in Grünwedel's Figs. 243, 482. The knotted dragons or *nāgas* about the "waist" correspond to the many dragons that girdle the Meru "waist" in Grünwedel's Fig. 243, and also to the paired dragons attached to the trunk of the Tree of Life (*aśvattha*) in the well-known Indus Valley seal, Fig. 6 in my *History of Indian and Indonesian Art*. The upper lotus stem and flower, corresponding to the heavenly and Sambhogakāya level of manifestation, rest upon the plane summit of Meru. The Bodhisattva seated on the crowning flower is an aspect of the "Boundless Light" indicated by the Amitābha of the headdress. The lateral branches of the upper lotus bear unidentified nimbate figures.

This representation, like our Fig. 17, is one of those that has been compared to the Tree of Jesse formula as it appears in Christian art from the eleventh century onwards (see Kingsley Porter, "Spain or Toulouse? and other question," *Art Bulletin*, VII, 15f. ; Coomaraswamy, "The Tree of Jesse and Indian parallels or sources," ibid., XI, 217-20; Watson, *Early Iconography of the Tree of Jesse*, 1934, pp. 58-66; Coomaraswamy, "The Tree of Jesse and Oriental Parallels," *Parnassus*, VI, Jan., 1935). Without assuming any contemporary borrowing or influence, it may be safely asserted that all these are cognate forms, having an ultimately common origin and the same fundamental significance. This common significance is most apparent in the fact that the Christian *virga* (often hermeneutically assimilated to *virgo*) is identified with the Virgin, as being the ground of the divine manifestation that flowers above (St. Bernard of Clairvaux, "The Virgin Mother of God is the stem, her Son is the flower . . . O Virgin! stem of the highest, to what a summit thou liftest on high thy holiness! Even to Him that sitteth on the throne") the Indian lotus, as "earth," being in precisely the same manner the support and ground of manifestation.

As explained in our text, the lotus can be distinguished logically from the Tree of Life and Axis of the Universe in its various other aspects, at the same time that it is coincident with these and extends from base to summit of the manifested universe, with branches proceeding to right and left like those of the Cross; which branches are the supports or "nests" of individual principles, and the means of their connection with the centre, as may be seen in most examples of the Tree of Jesse, as well as in the upper half of the present figure. When there

[continued on p. 146]

PLATE XV

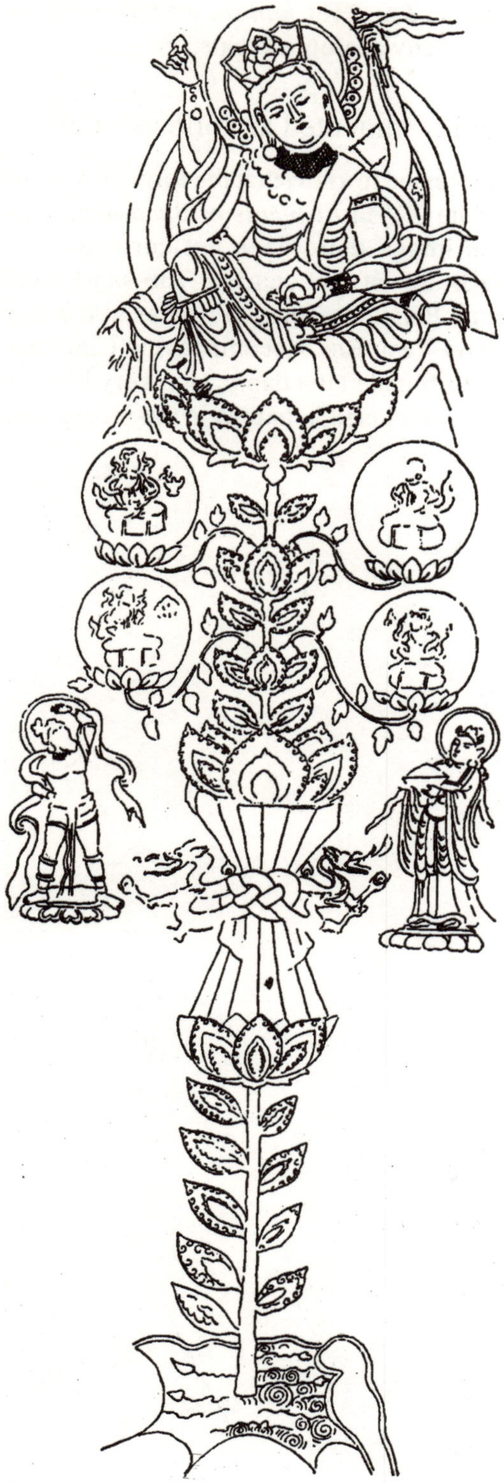

44

are doves on the branches, this corresponds exactly to *RV*, I, 164, 21, *yatra suparṇā amṛtasya bhāgam . . . abhi svaranti*, "There the Fairwings chant their share of aeviternity," X, 91, 2 where Agni "as a bird finds a home on every tree," *Bṛhadāraṇyaka Up.*, IV, 3, 2, "The *haṁsa*, the Golen Person, by the Spirit wards His lower nest," and many analogous texts.

[Mrs. Helen B. Chapin commented as follows on Fig. 44 – ed.]

"You may be interested to know that the form of Avalokiteśvara whose image is reproduced on Plate XV in *Elements of Buddhist Iconography* is Cintāmaṇi-cakra, although the image there does not correspond in every detail to the descriptions in the Buddhist dictionaries. The same hands, however, hold the *cintāmaṇi* and rest on Potalaka. The two figures at the level of the dragon kings are Śrī Mahādevī and Vasu Ṛṣi. Accompanying Cintāmaṇi-cakra in the Palace Museum roll, are four female attendants, who very likely correspond to the four figures on lotuses and enclosed in haloes in the image from Bäzäklik."